CAMBRIDGE CHECKPOINTS VCE

Fourth Edition

Chemistry Units 1 & 2

- Fully revised content matched to the study design
- Past examination questions
- Fully worked solutions

Patrick Sanders

CAMBRIDGE
UNIVERSITY PRESS

Shaftesbury Road, Cambridge CB2 8EA, United Kingdom

One Liberty Plaza, 20th Floor, New York, NY 10006, USA

477 Williamstown Road, Port Melbourne, VIC 3207, Australia

314–321, 3rd Floor, Plot 3, Splendor Forum, Jasola District Centre, New Delhi – 110025, India

103 Penang Road, #05–06/07, Visioncrest Commercial, Singapore 238467

Cambridge University Press & Assessment is a department of the University of Cambridge.

We share the University's mission to contribute to society through the pursuit of education, learning and research at the highest international levels of excellence.

www.cambridge.org

First published 2023
20 19 18 17 16 15 14 13 12 11 10 9 8 7 6 5

Cover image © Getty Images/Tetra Images
Printed in Australia by Finsbury Green

A catalogue record for this book is available from the National Library of Australia at www.nla.gov.au

ISBN 978-1-009-30832-8 Paperback

Additional resources for this publication at www.cambridge.edu.au/GO

Cambridge University Press & Assessment acknowledges the Aboriginal and Torres Strait Islander Peoples of this nation. We acknowledge the traditional custodians of the lands on which our company is located and where we conduct our business. We pay our respects to ancestors and Elders, past and present. Cambridge University Press & Assessment is committed to honouring Aboriginal and Torres Strait Islander Peoples' unique cultural and spiritual relationships to the land, waters and seas and their rich contribution to society.

Contents

Introduction vi

Data tables and periodic table vii

Unit 1: How can the diversity of materials be explained?

Chapter 1

Unit 1 Area of Study 1 – How do the chemical structures of materials explain their properties and reactions?

Multiple choice items

- Elements and the periodic table 1
- Covalent substances 4
- Reactions of metals 8
- Reactions of ionic compounds 11
- Separation and identification of the components of mixtures 14

Extended response questions

- Elements and the periodic table 15
- Covalent substances 17
- Reactions of metals 19
- Reactions of ionic compounds 21

Unit 1 Area of Study 1 test 23

Chapter 2

Unit 1 Area of Study 2 – How are materials quantified and classified?

Multiple choice items

- Quantifying atoms and compounds 31
- Families of organic compounds 34
- Polymers and society 36

Extended response questions

- Quantifying atoms and compounds 38
- Families of organic compounds 43
- Polymers and society 44

Unit 1 Area of Study 2 test 46

Chapter 3

Unit 1 Examination

Section A 52

Section B 55

Unit 2: How do chemical reactions shape the natural world?

Chapter 4

Unit 2 Area of Study 1 – How do chemicals interact with water?

Multiple choice items

- Water as a unique chemical 58
- Acid–base (proton transfer) reactions 61
- Redox (electron transfer) reactions 67

Extended response questions

- Water as a unique chemical 69
- Acid–base (proton transfer) reactions 71
- Redox (electron transfer) reactions 72

Unit 2 Area of Study 1 test 74

Chapter 5

Unit 2 Area of Study 2 – How are chemicals measured and analysed?

Multiple choice items

- Measuring solubility and concentration 81
- Analysis for acids and bases 85
- Measuring gases 87
- Analysis for salts 89

Extended response questions

- Measuring solubility and concentration 92
- Analysis for acids and bases 93
- Measuring gases 95
- Analysis for salts 96

Unit 2 Area of Study 2 test 99

Chapter 6

Unit 2 Examination

Section A 103

Section B 106

Chapter 7

Answers: Unit 1 Area of Study 1

Multiple choice items 110
Extended response questions 117
Unit 1 Area of Study 1 test 126

Answers: Unit 1 Area of Study 2

Multiple choice items 131
Extended response questions 134
Unit 1 Area of Study 2 test 142

Answers: Unit 1 Examination

Section A 146
Section B 147

Answers: Unit 2 Area of Study 1

Multiple choice items 151
Extended response questions 155
Unit 2 Area of Study 1 test 160

Answers: Unit 2 Area of Study 2

Multiple choice items 163
Extended response questions 167
Unit 2 Area of Study 2 test 173

Answers: Unit 2 Examination

Section A 175
Section B 177

Introduction

This book is a collection of hundreds of practice questions for Chemistry Unit 1 (How can the diversity of materials be explained?) and Unit 2 (How do chemical reactions shape the natural world?).

Within each area of study, the questions have been grouped under a number of major headings, for example 'Elements and the periodic Table' and 'Reactions of metals' to match the VCAA study design's sub-headings. Both multiple choice and extended response questions have been included. The book includes a small number of VCE examination questions.

At the end of each unit, an examination paper has been prepared. These are designed to allow students to complete a test on the whole of a unit. The examination papers should take approximately 90 minutes for Unit 1 and 120 minutes for Unit 2.

Questions should be attempted once the relevant theory has been completed. Answers have been included at the end of the book.

Data Table 1: The electrochemical series

	E°(in volt)
$F_2(g) + 2e^- \rightleftharpoons 2F^-(aq)$	+2.87
$H_2O_2(aq) + 2H^+(aq) + 2e^- \rightleftharpoons 2H_2O(l)$	+1.77
$Au^+(aq) + e^- \rightleftharpoons Au(s)$	+1.68
$Cl_2(g) + 2e^- \rightleftharpoons 2Cl^-(aq)$	+1.36
$O_2(g) + 4H^+(aq) + 4e^- \rightleftharpoons 2H_2O(l)$	+1.23
$Br_2(g) + 2e^- \rightleftharpoons 2Br^-(aq)$	+1.09
$Ag^+(aq) + e^- \rightleftharpoons Ag(s)$	+0.80
$Fe^{3+}(aq) + e^- \rightleftharpoons Fe^{2+}(aq)$	+0.77
$O_2(g) + 2H^+(aq) + 2e^- \rightleftharpoons H_2O_2(aq)$	+0.68
$I_2(g) + 2e^- \rightleftharpoons 2I^-(aq)$	+0.54
$4O_2(g) + 2H_2O(l) + 4e^- \rightleftharpoons 4OH^-(aq)$	+0.40
$Cu^{2+}(aq) + 2e^- \rightleftharpoons Cu(s)$	+0.34
$Sn^{4+}(aq) + 2e^- \rightleftharpoons Sn^{2+}(aq)$	+0.15
$2H^+(aq) + 2e^- \rightleftharpoons H_2(g)$	0.00
$Pb^{2+}(aq) + 2e^- \rightleftharpoons Pb(s)$	–0.13
$Sn^{2+}(aq) + 2e^- \rightleftharpoons Sn(s)$	–0.14
$Ni^{2+}(aq) + 2e^- \rightleftharpoons Ni(s)$	–0.23
$Co^{2+}(aq) + 2e^- \rightleftharpoons Co(s)$	–0.28
$Cd^{2+}(aq) + 2e^- \rightleftharpoons Cd(s)$	–0.40
$Cr^{3+}(aq) + e^- \rightleftharpoons Cr^{2+}(aq)$	–0.41
$Fe^{2+}(aq) + 2e^- \rightleftharpoons Fe(s)$	–0.44
$Cr^{3+}(aq) + 3e^- \rightleftharpoons Cr(s)$	–0.74
$Zn^{2+}(aq) + 2e^- \rightleftharpoons Zn(s)$	–0.76
$2H_2O(l) + 2e^- \rightleftharpoons H_2(g) + 2OH^-(aq)$	–0.83
$Mn^{2+}(aq) + 2e^- \rightleftharpoons Mn(s)$	–1.03
$Al^{3+}(aq) + 3e^- \rightleftharpoons Al(s)$	–1.67
$Mg^{2+}(aq) + 2e^- \rightleftharpoons Mg(s)$	–2.34
$Na^+(aq) + e^- \rightleftharpoons Na(s)$	–2.71
$Ca^{2+}(aq) + 2e^- \rightleftharpoons Ca(s)$	–2.87
$Li^+(aq) + e^- \rightleftharpoons Li(s)$	–3.0

Atomic number
Symbol
Relative Atomic Mass

Periodic Table of the Elements

1 **H** 1.0								
3 **Li** 6.94	4 **Be** 9.01							
11 **Na** 22.99	12 **Mg** 24.31							
19 **K** 39.10	20 **Ca** 40.08	21 **Sc** 44.96	22 **Ti** 47.90	23 **V** 50.94	24 **Cr** 52.00	25 **Mn** 54.94	26 **Fe** 55.85	27 **Co** 58.93
37 **Rb** 85.47	38 **Sr** 87.62	39 **Y** 88.91	40 **Zr** 91.22	41 **Nb** 92.91	42 **Mo** 95.94	43 **Tc** (98)	44 **Ru** 101.07	45 **Rh** 102.91
55 **Cs** 132.91	56 **Ba** 137.34	57 **La** 138.91	72 **Hf** 178.49	73 **Ta** 180.95	74 **W** 183.85	75 **Re** 186.21	76 **Os** 190.21	77 **Ir** 192.22
87 **Fr** (223)	88 **Ra** (226)	89 **Ac** (227)	104 **Rf** (261)	105 **Db** (262)	106 **Sg** (263)	107 **Bh** (262)	108 **Hs** (265)	109 **Mt** (266)

Lanthanides	58 **Ce** 140.12	59 **Pr** 140.91	60 **Nd** 144.24	61 **Pm** (147)	62 **Sm** 150.35	63 **Eu** 151.96
Actinides	90 **Th** 232.04	91 **Pa** (231)	92 **U** 238.03	93 **Np** (237)	94 **Pu** (242)	95 **Am** (243)

Numbers in parentheses are mass numbers of the most stable isotope of that element

								2 **He** 4.00
			5 **B** 10.81	6 **C** 12.01	7 **N** 14.01	8 **O** 16.00	9 **F** 19.00	10 **Ne** 20.18
			13 **Al** 26.98	14 **Si** 28.09	15 **P** 30.97	16 **S** 32.06	17 **Cl** 35.45	18 **Ar** 39.95
28 **Ni** 58.71	29 **Cu** 63.55	30 **Zn** 65.37	31 **Ga** 69.72	32 **Ge** 72.59	33 **As** 74.92	34 **Se** 78.96	35 **Br** 79.91	36 **Kr** 83.80
46 **Pd** 106.42	47 **Ag** 107.87	48 **Cd** 112.40	49 **In** 114.82	50 **Sn** 118.69	51 **Sb** 121.75	52 **Te** 127.60	53 **I** 126.90	54 **Xe** 131.30
78 **Pt** 195.09	79 **Au** 196.97	80 **Hg** 200.59	81 **Tl** 204.37	82 **Pb** 207.19	83 **Bi** 208.98	84 **Po** (210)	85 **At** (210)	86 **Rn** (222)
110 Ds (271)	111 Rg (272)	112 Cn (285)	113 Nh (280)	114 Fl (289)	115 Mc (280)	116 Lv (292)	117 Ts (294)	118 Og (294)

64 **Gd** 157.25	65 **Tb** 158.92	66 **Dy** 162.50	67 **Ho** 164.93	68 **Er** 167.26	69 **Tm** 168.93	70 **Yb** 173.04	71 **Lu** 174.97
96 **Cm** (247)	97 **Bk** (247)	98 **Cf** (251)	99 **Es** (254)	100 **Fm** (257)	101 **Md** (258)	102 **No** (259)	103 **Lr** (260)

Data Table 2: Physical constants

Avogadro's constant	6.023×10^{23} mol^{-1}
Gas constant	8.314 J K^{-1} mol^{-1}
Molar volume of ideal gas at SLC	24.8 L mol^{-1}
Pressure	1 atmosphere = 101 325 Pa
Ionisation constant of water, K_W	1×10^{-14}

Chapter 1

Unit 1 Area of Study 1 – How do the chemical structures of materials explain their properties and reactions?

Multiple choice items

Elements and the periodic table

Question 1

The mass number of an atom is defined as the

A. total number of neutrons and protons in an atom.
B. number of protons in an atom.
C. total mass of the neutrons and protons in the atoms.
D. number of neutrons in an atom.

Question 2

The neutral species $^{40}_{20}Ca$ would contain

A. 20 neutrons, 40 protons and 40 electrons.
B. 40 neutrons, 20 protons and 20 electrons.
C. 20 neutrons, 20 protons and 20 electrons.
D. 40 neutrons, 20 protons and 40 electrons.

Question 3

The atomic structures of three particles (X, Y, Z) are given in the table below.

Particle	No. of protons	No. of electrons	No. of neutrons
X	13	10	14
Y	12	10	13
Z	11	10	12

These particles are

A. isotopes. **B.** anions. **C.** non-metals. **D.** cations.

Question 4

An atom of copper has 29 protons and 35 neutrons. The correct symbol for this atom is

A. $^{64}_{29}Cu$ **B.** $^{35}_{29}Cu$ **C.** $^{29}_{64}Cu$ **D.** $^{64}_{35}Cu$

Question 5

The electron configuration of an atom of phosphorus is

A. $1s^22s^22p^63s^33p^3$ **B.** $1s^22s^22p^63s^23p^63d^3$
C. $1s^22s^22p^63s^23p^5$ **D.** $1s^22s^22p^63s^23p^3$

Question 6

A particle has 27 protons, 28 neutrons and 25 electrons. If the element has the symbol X, then this particle may be represented by the symbol

A. $^{55}_{27}X^{2+}$ **B.** $^{53}_{25}X^{2+}$ **C.** $^{53}_{27}X^{2-}$ **D.** $^{55}_{25}X^{2-}$

Question 7

The number of neutrons in an atom of ${}^{197}_{79}Au$ is

A. 79 **B.** 118 **C.** 197 **D.** 276

Question 8

Four particles, I, II, III and IV are described in the table below.

	Mass number	Atomic number	Number of electrons
I	127	53	54
II	127	53	53
III	129	53	53
IV	127	52	54

Which of the following pairs of particles are isotopes?

A. I and II **B.** II and III

C. I and IV **D.** II and IV

Question 9

The electron configuration of a neutral atom with its electrons in an excited state is

A. $1s^2 2s^2 2p^2$ (atomic number = 6).

B. $1s^2 2s^2 2p^3 3s^1$ (atomic number = 8).

C. $1s^2 2s^2 2p^5 3s^1$ (atomic number = 9).

D. $1s^2 2s^2 2p^5$ (atomic number = 10).

Question 10

The 3d subshell can take a maximum of

A. 2 electrons. **B.** 5 electrons.

C. 10 electrons. **D.** 14 electrons.

Question 11

An ion which has the same electron configuration as a magnesium ion and has a charge of negative two is the

A. oxide ion. **B.** sulfide ion.

C. sodium ion. **D.** aluminium ion.

Question 12

The elements chlorine (a gas), bromine (a liquid) and iodine (a solid) are placed in the same group in the periodic table because they

A. have the same chemical properties.

B. have the same number of outer-shell electrons.

C. are all non-metals.

D. show a gradation in physical properties.

Question 13

Of the following elements which one is most likely to have similar chemical properties to the element with atomic number 16?

A. phosphorus **B.** chlorine

C. argon **D.** selenium

Question 14

In going down group 1 of the periodic table, i.e. from Li to Na to K, the first ionisation energy

A. decreases and the atomic radius decreases.

B. decreases and the atomic radius increases.

C. increases and the atomic radius decreases.

D. increases and the atomic radius increases.

Question 15

The properties of the elements used to produce the modern form of the periodic table are

A. atomic number and ionisation energy.

B. atomic mass and chemical properties.

C. chemical properties and ionisation energy.

D. atomic number and electron configuration.

Question 16

The properties of the elements of the third period vary as one goes across the period from Na to Ar. Which one of the following shows how the atomic radius and first ionisation energy vary from Na to Ar?

	Atomic radius	**First ionisation energy**
A.	increases	increases
B.	increases	decreases
C.	decreases	increases
D.	decreases	decreases

Question 17

Which one of the following properties shows a general increase across the periodic table from sodium to chlorine?

A. metallic character **B.** atomic radius

C. first ionisation energy **D.** reducing strength

Question 18

Which one of the following will have the largest radius?

A. Be atom **B.** Mg atom

C. Ca atom **D.** Sr atom

Question 19

When going down group I, from lithium to caesium, which one of the following statements is correct?

A. The first ionisation energy increases.

B. The atoms are more likely to react to form 2+ cations.

C. The elements become more reactive.

D. The attraction between the nucleus and the outermost electron increases.

Question 20

Which one of the following lists contains only non-metallic elements?

A. hydrogen, helium, lithium, beryllium
B. oxygen, chlorine, sulfur, arsenic
C. lithium, sodium, magnesium, aluminium
D. iron, sulfur, carbon, phosphorus

Question 21

Which one of the following species would have the smallest radius?

A. Na^+ **B.** K^+ **C.** Cl^- **D.** F^-

Question 22

Which one of the following species will have the largest radius?

A. Na ion **B.** Na^+ ion
C. K atom **D.** K^+ ion

Question 23

The first eight ionisation energies of an element are shown in the graph below.

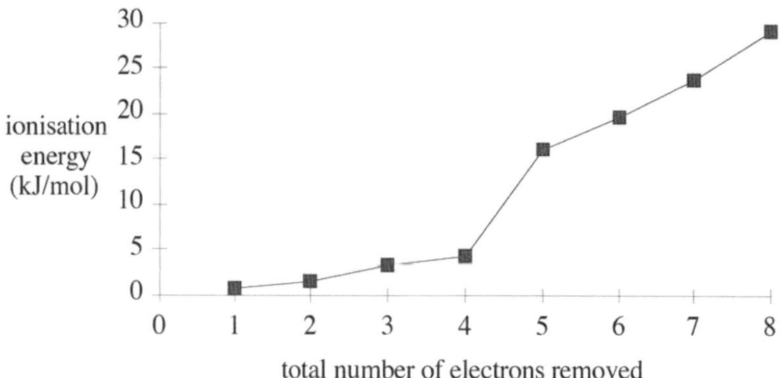

The element is most likely to be

A. carbon. **B.** oxygen. **C.** neon. **D.** silicon.

Question 24

An inert (noble) gas is most likely to have an outer-shell electron configuration of

A. d^{10} **B.** s^2p^6 **C.** $s^2p^4d^6$ **D.** $s^2p^6d^{10}$

Covalent substances

Question 25

The bonding in molecular substances is best explained as the attraction between

A. two nuclei and a pair of electrons.
B. oppositely charged ions.
C. instantaneous dipoles.
D. positive ions and a sea of electrons.

Question 26

The electron configuration of phosphorus is $1s^22s^22p^63s^23p^3$ and that of fluorine is $1s^22s^22p^5$. The formula of the compound that forms when phosphorus reacts with fluorine is expected to be

A. PF_3 **B.** P_3F **C.** P_5F **D.** PF

Question 27

Which one of the following elements does **not** form double bonds?

A. carbon **B.** oxygen **C.** nitrogen **D.** fluorine

Question 28

The number of covalent bonds formed by a nitrogen atom, which has the electron configuration $1s^22s^22p^3$, is usually

A. 1 **B.** 2 **C.** 3 **D.** 4

Question 29

The best description of covalent bonding is that it results from

A. complete transfer of one or more electrons from one atom to another.

B. sharing of electrons by two atoms.

C. a gain of electrons.

D. the formation of particles of opposite charge.

Question 30

Covalent bonding usually occurs between

A. atoms of non-metals.

B. a non-metal atom and metal atom.

C. a cation and an anion.

D. atoms of metals.

Question 31

Diamond has very high melting and boiling temperatures, whereas methane, CH_4, has very low melting and boiling temperatures. This difference is best explained because

A. there are more bonds to each carbon atom in diamond.

B. the bonds to each carbon are much stronger in diamond.

C. methane exists as small molecules and there is only weak bonding between the molecules.

D. the bonding between the molecules in diamond is strong.

Question 32

The shape of a molecule is mostly determined by the

A. size of the atoms attached to the central atom.

B. number of bonding pairs of electrons around the atom.

C. number of pairs of electrons in the valence shell.

D. difference in electronegativity between the atoms in the molecule.

Question 33

The molecular formulas of four substances are given below. For which one would the structure contain only single bonds?

A. CH_3PH_2 **B.** C_2H_3N **C.** CH_2O **D.** N_2O_3

Question 34

Of the molecules CO_2, CH_4, NH_3, H_2O, BF_3 and H_2S the two with the same shape are

A. CO_2 and H_2O **B.** H_2O and H_2S
C. CH_4, and NH_3 **D.** BF_3 and NH_3

Question 35

Which one of the following molecules has a triangular pyramid shape?

A. CH_4 **B.** NH_3 **C.** CO_2 **D.** H_2S

Question 36

Of the four molecules, C_2H_2, HCl, PCl_3 and N_2, the one with a different shape to the other three is

A. C_2H_2 **B.** HCl **C.** PCl_3 **D.** N_2

Question 37

Which of the covalent bonds shown below is the most polar?

A. C–H **B.** N–H **C.** O–H **D.** F–H

Question 38

Of the molecules CO_2, CH_4, CF_4 and PH_3 the polar molecule is

A. CO_2 **B.** CH_4 **C.** CF_4 **D.** PH_3

Question 39

Carbon dioxide is a non-polar molecule. The reason for this is that

A. carbon and oxygen have the same electronegativity.
B. bonding electrons are equally shared between carbon and oxygen atoms.
C. the covalent bonds between carbon and oxygen atoms are double bonds.
D. the carbon dioxide molecule is linear.

Question 40

Which one of the molecules below is expected to be the least polar?

A. CH_3F **B.** CH_3Cl **C.** CH_3Br **D.** CH_3I

Question 41

Which one of the molecules below is expected to have the lowest boiling temperature?

A. CH_3F **B.** CH_3Cl **C.** CH_3Br **D.** CH_3I

Question 42

Molecular substances have atoms joined together by covalent bonding and might be expected to

A. conduct electricity in the liquid state but not when solid.
B. be malleable and ductile.
C. sometimes have low melting and boiling temperatures.
D. be good thermal conductors.

Question 43

Which one of the following statements best describes molecular substances?

A. They are always compounds.

B. Molecular substances have low melting points.

C. All molecular substances are gases at room temperature.

D. Some molecular substances conduct electricity.

Question 44

The most likely order of decreasing solubility in water of the compounds listed below is

A. butan-1-ol, hydrogen fluoride, propane, oxygen.

B. hydrogen fluoride, butan-1-ol, propane, oxygen.

C. propane, oxygen, butan-1-ol, hydrogen fluoride.

D. oxygen, hydrogen fluoride, butan-1-ol, propane.

Question45

The boiling temperature of methanol, CH_3OH, is 65°C, whereas that of ethanol, CH_3CH_2OH, is 78°C. The reason for the higher boiling temperature of ethanol is an increase in the strength of the

A. dispersion forces in ethanol.

B. hydrogen bonding in ethanol.

C. dipole–dipole attractions in ethanol.

D. dispersion forces and hydrogen bonding in ethanol.

Question 46

Which one of the compounds below is expected to have the highest boiling temperature?

A. $CH_3CH_2CH_2CH_3$ **B.** $CH_3CH_2CH_2NH_2$

C. $CH_3CH_2NHCH_3$ **D.** $(CH_3)_3N$

Question 47

The structural formulas of four substances are shown below. Which one would be expected to have hydrogen bonding between its molecules?

A. $H_2C{=}O$

B. $H_3C{-}O{-}CH_3$

C. $H_3C{-}NH_2$

D. H_2CF_2

Question 48

Graphite is a good conductor of electricity and is used in electric motors. The conduction of electricity by graphite results from

A. strong bonding between carbon atoms in only two dimensions.

B. a mobile 'sea' of electrons surrounding carbon ions.

C. one electron from each carbon atom moving freely along layers.

D. the ability of sheets of carbon atoms to slide over one another.

Question 49

Diamond, graphite, carbon nanotubes and buckyballs are all forms of carbon. For these materials the number of carbon atoms each carbon atom is bonded to is

	Diamond	Graphite	Carbon nanotubes	Buckyballs
A.	3	3	3	3
B.	4	3	3	3
C.	4	3	4	4
D.	4	4	4	4

Reactions of metals

The following information refers to Questions 50 and 51.

The properties of six elements are given in the table below.

Element	Melting temperature (°C)	Boiling temperature (°C)	Electrical conductivity (MS m^{-1})	Thermal conductivity (J s^{-1} m^{-1} K^{-1})	Density (g mL^{-1})
I	1540	3000	9.6	78	7.86
II	–39	357	1.0	8.4	13.53
III	44	280	10^{-15}	—	1.82
IV	119	445	10^{-21}	0.28	2.00
V	838	1490	26	130	1.55
VI	–7	58	10^{-16}	—	3.12

Question 50

Which of the elements would be liquids at room temperature?

A. II and III
B. IV and VI
C. II and VI
D. III and IV

Question 51

The element with the greatest tensile strength is likely to be

A. I **B.** III **C.** IV **D.** V

Question 52

The bonding in metals is best explained as attraction between

A. oppositely charged ions.
B. instantaneous dipoles.
C. two nuclei and a pair of electrons.
D. positive ions in a sea of electrons.

Question 53

The most chemically reactive metals occur in groups 1 and 2 of the periodic table. The reactivity of these metals

A. increases down a group.

B. decreases down a group.

C. is approximately the same within a group.

D. is not related to the position within a group.

The following information refers to Questions 54 to 57.

Four statements about the structural features of metals are given below.

I. In metals, the particles are strongly attracted to one another.

II. The particles are tightly packed together in a metal.

III. Charged particles that are free to move are present in metals.

IV. In metals, the attractive forces between the particles are able to adjust when the particles are moved.

Question 54

Which one of the statements above is best able to explain why metals are malleable and ductile?

A. I **B.** II **C.** III **D.** IV

Question 55

Which one of the statements above is best able to explain why metals are good conductors of electricity?

A. I **B.** II **C.** III **D.** IV

Question 56

Which one of the statements above is best able to explain why most metals have high melting and boiling temperatures?

A. I **B.** II **C.** III **D.** IV

Question 57

Which one of the statements above is best able to explain why many metals have high densities?

A. I **B.** II **C.** III **D.** IV

Question 58

The chemical reactivity of a metal is often related to the historical period of its discovery. Metals with low reactivity are most likely to have been known

A. since earliest times.

B. since the discovery of chemical reduction reactions.

C. since the discovery of electrolytic processes.

D. since the discovery of nuclear reactions.

Question 59

A metal undergoes a slow reaction with dilute hydrochloric acid. It does not react with cold water but will react with steam and undergoes rapid reaction with oxygen. The metal is most likely to be

A. calcium **B.** copper **C.** silver **D.** zinc

Question 60

Small pieces of the metals calcium, iron, magnesium and zinc are added to separate test tubes containing dilute hydrochloric acid. The expected order of reactivity of the metals (from highest to lowest) is

A. iron > zinc > magnesium > calcium.

B. calcium > magnesium > zinc > iron.

C. zinc > iron > calcium > magnesium.

D. magnesium > calcium > iron > zinc.

Question 61

In which of the following lists are the metals placed in order of **decreasing** reactivity?

A. Na, Mg, Fe, Cu, Ag

B. Mg, Na, Cu, Fe, Ag

C. Fe, Na, Mg, Ag, Cu

D. Na, Mg, Fe, Ag, Cu

Question 62

Which of the following pairs of reactants is **least** likely to react spontaneously when mixed?

A. tin and dilute hydrochloric acid

B. magnesium and water when heated

C. mercury and dilute hydrochloric acid

D. sodium and oxygen

Question 63

Of the metals given below, which one is likely to be the most difficult to extract from its ores (as it is difficult to turn into its pure form)?

A. copper

B. iron

C. sodium

D. zinc

Question 64

Which of the following metals is never found in an uncombined (elemental) form on Earth?

A. copper

B. silver

C. magnesium

D. iron

Question 65

In the twenty-first century, more than sixty metals are used by human societies. By contrast, 2000 years ago only seven metals were in use. These metals were copper, gold, iron, lead, mercury, silver and tin. The best explanation for the use of metals being limited to these metals is that they

A. are malleable, ductile and most easily worked.

B. are shiny and attractive for making ornaments.

C. can be found in the uncombined state or are easily extracted from their ores

D. can easily be turned into weapons.

Reactions of ionic compounds

Question 66

Some of the properties of ionic compounds are given below.

I. Ionic compounds are usually hard and brittle.
II. Ionic compounds have high melting and boiling temperatures.
III. When solid ionic compounds do not conduct electricity.
IV. When molten or in aqueous solution ionic compounds will conduct electricity.

Which of the properties of ionic compounds above are explained by strong attractive forces between particles?

A. I and II **B.** II and III **C.** III and IV **D.** I and IV

Question 67

Ionic compounds do not conduct electricity in the solid state but are good conductors when molten. These observations are best explained by

A. There are no charged particles in the solid ionic compounds, but heating produces ions.
B. Charged particles are present but are only free to move in the melt.
C. Heating produces electrons, which can move through the melt.
D. Heating makes electrons more mobile.

Question 68

A metal, M, has the electron configuration $1s^22s^22p^63s^2$ and reacts with a non-metal, X, with the electron configuration $1s^22s^22p^5$. The formula of the ionic compound formed in this reaction is

A. MX **B.** M_2X **C.** MX_2 **D.** M_2X_5

Question 69

When a metal reacts with a non-metal to produce an ionic compound, the atoms of the metal

A. lose electrons to form positively charged cations.
B. gain electrons to form positively charged cations.
C. lose electrons to form negatively charged anions.
D. gain electrons to form negatively charged anions.

Question 70

An element X forms two ionic oxides. The formulas of the oxides are XO and XO_2. The element is most likely to be

A. carbon.
B. magnesium.
C. manganese.
D. silicon.

Question 71

An ionic compound has the empirical formula MX_2. The elements that reacted to form this compound are most likely to be

A. M = sodium and X = sulfur. **B.** M = calcium and X = fluorine.
C. M = magnesium and X = oxygen. **D.** M = aluminium and X = chlorine.

Question 72

Which one of the following is the correct formula for ammonium sulfate?

A. NH_3SO_4 **B.** $(NH_3)_2SO_4$

C. NH_4SO_4 **D.** $(NH_4)_2SO_4$

Question 73

Aluminium reacts with oxygen to form aluminium oxide. The electron configurations of the ions formed will be

	Aluminium	Oxide
A.	$1^{s2}2s^22p^63s^23p^6$	$1s_22s^22p^6$
B.	$1s^22s^22p^6$	$1s^22s^22p^6$
C.	$1s^22s^22p^63s^23p^1$	$1s^22s^22p^4$
D.	$1s^22s^22p^6$	$1s^22s^22p^63s^23p^6$

Question 74

Which one of the following is most likely to result in the formation of large crystals from a solution of copper sulfate?

A. using a very dilute solution

B. cooling the solution rapidly

C. leaving the solution uncovered

D. cooling the solution slowly

Question 75

The equation for the reaction of lead nitrate solution with potassium iodide solution is shown below with the product symbols of state omitted.

$Pb(NO_3)_2 + 2KI \rightarrow 2KNO_3 + PbI_2$

The correct ionic equation for this reaction is

A. $NO_3^-(aq) + K^+(aq) \rightarrow KNO_3(aq)$

B. $NO_3^-(aq) + K^+(aq) \rightarrow KNO_3(s)$

C. $Pb^{2+}(aq) + 2I^-(aq) \rightarrow PbI_2(s)$

D. $Pb^{2+}(aq) + 2I^-(aq) \rightarrow PbI_2(aq)$

Question 76

When strontium chloride solution is added to lithium carbonate solution, what is the correct ionic equation for the reaction?

A. $SrCl_2(aq) + Li_2CO_3(aq) \rightarrow SrCO_3(s) + 2LiCl(aq)$

B. $Li^+(aq) + Cl^-(aq) \rightarrow LiCl(s)$

C. $Sr^{2+}(aq) + CO_3^{2-}(aq) \rightarrow SrCO_3(s)$

D. $2Li^+(aq) + 2Cl^-(aq) \rightarrow 2LiCl(aq)$

Question 77

Which one of the following solutions will form a precipitate when added to a solution of potassium sulfate?

A. magnesium chloride solution **B.** sodium carbonate solution

C. lead nitrate solution **D.** copper(II) bromide solution

Question 78

The correct balanced ionic equation for the reaction between potassium hydroxide and iron(III) chloride is

A. $3KOH(aq) + FeCl_3(aq) \rightarrow 3KCl(aq) + Fe(OH)_3(s)$

B. $KOH(aq) + Fe_3Cl(aq) \rightarrow KCl(aq) + Fe_3(OH)(s)$

C. $K^+(aq) + Cl^-(aq) \rightarrow KCl(s)$

D. $3OH^-(aq) + Fe^{3+}(aq) \rightarrow Fe(OH)_3(s)$

Question 79

A student is asked to identify the cation present in two solutions, Q and R. A few drops of Q and R are added separately to the four test solutions shown in the table below.

Test solution	Solution Q	Solution R
$NaNO_3(aq)$	no change	no change
$Na_2SO_4(aq)$	no change	white precipitate
$NaCl(aq)$	no change	no change
$Na_2CO_3(aq)$	white precipitate	white precipitate

Which one of the following is a possible correct answer?

	Solution Q	Solution R
A.	Mg^{2+}	Ba^{2+}
B.	Zn^{2+}	Al^{3+}
C.	K^+	Ag^+
D.	Pb^{2+}	Ca^{2+}

Question 80

From the following choose the compound that is the least soluble in water.

A. potassium carbonate

B. zinc sulfate

C. ammonium chloride

D. copper(II) hydroxide

Question 81

Ionic compounds may be classified as soluble, partly soluble or insoluble in water. In which one of the following is the classification correct?

	Soluble	Partly soluble	Insoluble
A.	Na_2CO_3	KOH	$PbSO_4$
B.	NH_4NO_3	$Ca(OH)_2$	$MgCl_2$
C.	$MgSO_4$	$PbCl_2$	$BaCO_3$
D.	AgI	$CuCO_3$	$Zn(OH)_2$

Separation and identification of the components of mixtures

Question 82 [VCAA 2013 SA Q7]

The thin layer chromatography plate shown below has a polar stationary phase. It was developed using hexane as the solvent. Which sample has the most polar molecules?

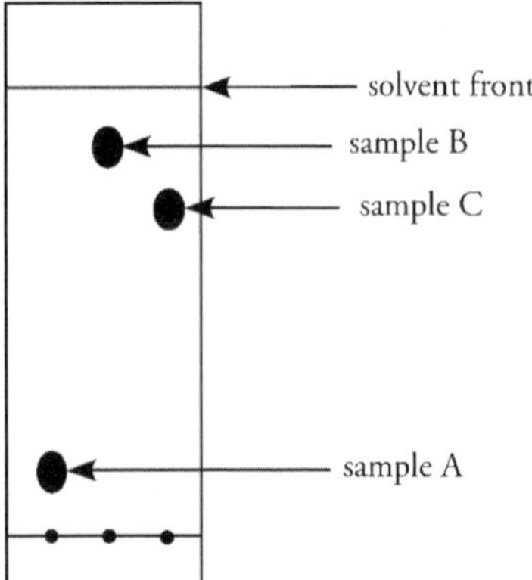

A. sample A
B. sample B
C. sample C
D. There is not enough information to determine which sample has the most polar molecules.

Question 83 [VCAA 2015 SA Q8]

Consider the following statements about a high-performance liquid chromatography (HPLC) column that uses a polar solvent and a non-polar stationary phase to analyse a solution:

Statement I –Polar molecules in the solution will be attracted to the solvent particles by dipole-dipole attraction.
Statement II – Non-polar molecules in the solution will be attracted to the stationary phase by dispersion forces.
Statement III – Polar molecules in the solution will travel through the HPLC column more rapidly than non-polar molecules.

Which of these statements are true?

A. I and II only
B. I and III only
C. II and III only
D. I, II and III

The following information refers to Questions 84 and 85.

High-performance liquid chromatography (HPLC) is a technique used to separate components of a mixture using their polarity and size. The components of the mixture are pushed through a column (tube) that contains a tightly packed substance, the stationary phase, using a high-pressured liquid, the mobile phase. Components separate based on their relative affinity (attraction to) the stationary and mobile phase. The length of time that a component takes to travel through the column is known as a retention time. Generally, if components are similar in polarity, the larger molecule will have a higher retention time.

Question 84

Which of the following would you expect to decrease the retention time of all components of a mixture?

I decreasing the pressure of the mobile phase

II increasing the temperature of the column

III using a more tightly packed column

Which of the changes would be most likely to produce chromatogram 2?

A. I only

B. II only

C. III only

D. I and II only

Question 85

If a polar mobile phase and a non-polar stationary phase are used in a particular HPLC, which of the following would have the shortest retention time?

A. a large polar molecule

B. a small non-polar molecule

C. a large non-polar molecule

D. a small polar molecule

Extended response questions

Elements and the periodic table

Question 1

A sample of element X is placed in a tube and high-energy sparks are passed through the tube. Some of the atoms in the sample now have the electron configuration $1s^22s^22p^34s^1$.

(a) What is the name and the chemical symbol of element X? (1 mark)

(b) If the electron configuration of the atoms mentioned above changed from $1s^22s^22p^34s^1$ to $1s^22s^22p^33s^1$, would the process release energy or absorb energy? Explain your reasoning. (2 marks)

(c) What is the electron configuration of the atoms of element X in their ground state? (1 mark)

(Total = 4 marks)

Question 2

Barium and calcium are in the same vertical group of the periodic table as magnesium.

(a) Explain why these three elements are in the same group. (1 mark)

(b) The electronegativity of barium (0.89) is lower than that of magnesium (1.31). Give an explanation for this difference. (2 marks)

(c) In terms of shells and subshells, give the electron configuration for a calcium atom. (1 mark)

(d) In terms of shells and subshells, describe how the electron configuration of a calcium ion, Ca^{2+}, will differ from that of a calcium atom. (1 mark)

(e) The radius of a magnesium atom is 160 pm (1.60×10^{-10} m) and the radius of a magnesium ion, Mg^{2+}, is 72 pm (0.72×10^{-10} m). Explain why the magnesium atom is significantly larger than the Mg^{2+} ion. (1 mark)

(Total = 6 marks)

Question 3

(a) In the periodic table, what type of elements are found in the s-block? (1 mark)

(b) Give the name and symbol of four of these elements. (2 marks)

(c) Identify the following elements.

(i) The element in the same group as carbon but in period 3

(ii) The element in the same period as aluminium but in group 15 (group V).

(1 + 1 = 2 marks)

(d) Identify the group and period occupied by the element selenium, Se. (1 mark)

(Total = 6 marks)

Question 4

(a) In the second period of the periodic table, identify those elements that are solids at room temperature and good conductors of heat and electricity. (3 marks)

(b) In the third period of the table, identify an element that is

(i) a solid at room temperature and a non-metal

(ii) a gas at room temperature and a non-metal. (1 + 1 = 2 marks)

(c) In the group of elements known as the 'alkali metals', identify the element that is the most reactive and the one that is the least reactive. (2 marks)

(Total = 7 marks)

Question 5

The elements of group 17 (group VII) are fluorine, chlorine, bromine and iodine. For each of the properties below, state how the property varies going down the group from F to I and give a reason for your answer.

(a) Atomic radius (2 marks)

(b) Reactivity (2 marks)

(c) Electronegativity (2 marks)

(Total = 6 marks)

Question 6

(a) In the modern periodic table, the elements are arranged in order of increasing atomic number. The relative atomic mass of the elements mostly increases in the same fashion. There are three exceptions to this general rule. For example, argon, with atomic number 18, has a relative atomic mass of 39.9, whereas potassium, with atomic number 19, has a relative atomic mass of 39.1. Explain how an element with a smaller atomic number can have a larger relative atomic mass. (2 marks)

(b) In the modern periodic table, one section consists of ten elements called the transition metals. Why does this section have ten elements? (2 marks)

(Total = 4 marks)

Covalent substances

Question 7

Draw electron dot formulas for the following substances.

(a) PH_3
(b) CF_4
(c) N_2H_4
(d) Cl_2
(e) C_2H_6
(f) NH_2OH

(Total = 6 × 1 = 6 marks)

Question 8

For each of the following molecules describe its shape and decide whether it is polar or non-polar.

	Molecule	Shape	Polar/non-polar
(a)	F_2		
(b)	CH_2O		
(c)	CCl_4		
(d)	HCN		
(e)	BF_3		

(Total = 5 × 2 = 10 marks)

Question 9

Using only the elements hydrogen, carbon, nitrogen, oxygen and fluorine, draw valence structures for the following types of molecules.

(a) A linear molecule containing four atoms (1 mark)
(b) A planar molecule containing six atoms (1 mark)
(c) A pyramidal molecule (1 mark)
(d) A tetrahedral molecule. (1 mark)

(Total = 4 marks)

Question 10

Carbon and fluorine form the molecule carbon tetrafluoride, CF_4. There is a large difference in the electronegativity of carbon and fluorine, but carbon tetrafluoride is a non-polar molecule. Explain this observation. (2 marks)

Question 11

Sulfur dioxide, SO_2, and sulfur trioxide, SO_3, are important intermediates in the industrial production of sulfuric acid.

(a) Give the electron configuration of sulfur. (1 mark)
(b) If each oxygen forms a double bond to sulfur in both SO_2 and SO_3, how many electrons are around the sulfur atom in each molecule? (2 marks)
(c) Draw valence structures for SO_2 and SO_3. (2 marks)
(d) Compounds of non-metal elements in period 2 typically have a maximum of eight electrons around the central atoms. Non-metal elements in periods 3 to 6 often form compounds in which there are more than eight electrons around the central atom. Suggest a reason for this difference. (1 mark)

(Total = 6 marks)

Question 12

Draw valence structures for the following substances.

(a) HCN (b) H_2S

(c) HNO_2 (d) CH_2O

(e) SiF_4 (f) HCO_2H

(Total = 6 × 1 = 6 marks)

Question 13

(a) Methane and water are both small molecules. However, at room temperature, methane is a gas but water is a liquid. Also, methane has very low solubility in water. Suggest reasons for these differences. (2 marks)

(b) Iodine, I_2, has low solubility in water but will dissolve in hexane, C_6H_{14}. Give a reason for this observation. (1 mark)

(Total = 3 marks)

Question 14

Methyl chloride, methyl bromide and methyl iodide are polar molecules with approximately the same dipole. The boiling temperatures of three halomethanes are given below.

Compound	**Boiling temperature (°C)**
Methyl chloride, CH_3Cl	–24.2
Methyl bromide, CH_3Br	3.6
Methyl iodide, CH_3I	42.4

(a) Calculate the number of electrons in each molecule. (3 marks)

(b) Give an explanation for the variation in the boiling temperatures of the three compounds. (2 marks)

(Total = 5 marks)

Question 15

The table below contains the boiling temperatures and relative masses of three compounds, propane, C_3H_8, dimethyl ether, CH_3OCH_3, and ethanol, CH_3CH_2OH.

Compound	**Boiling temperature (°C)**	**Relative mass**
Propane	–42	44.1
Dimethyl ether	–23	46.1
Ethanol	+78	46.1

(a) Draw the structural formulas of the three compounds. (3 marks)

(b) How are dimethyl ether and ethanol related? (1 mark)

(c) How many electrons are present in a molecule of each compound? (1 mark)

(d) How would you expect the size of the dispersion forces to vary between the three compounds? (2 marks)

(e) Why is the boiling temperature of dimethyl ether higher than that of propane but lower than that of ethanol? (3 marks)

(Total = 10 marks)

Question 16

Methane, CH_4, and ammonia, NH_3, are both gases at room temperature. It might be expected that they would have similar boiling temperatures.

(a) Suggest a reason why this might be the case. (1 mark)

(b) The boiling temperatures of the two compounds are as follows:
methane = –161°C and ammonia = –33°C.
Explain why the boiling temperatures of the two compounds are so different. (3 marks)

(Total = 4 marks)

Question 17

(a) Diamond and graphite are allotropes of carbon. Explain the meaning of the term 'allotrope'. (1 mark)

(b) Briefly describe the chemical bonding and structure in each of diamond and graphite. (2 marks)

(c) Explain how the chemical bonding in each substance accounts for the properties listed below.
(i) Diamond is much harder than graphite.
(ii) Graphite is a good conductor of electricity but diamond is not.
(iii) Diamond has a higher density than graphite.
(iv) Both allotropes have high melting points but the melting point of graphite is slightly higher. (4 marks)

(ci) Explain how the properties of each substance accounts for the **uses** listed below.
Diamonds are used for:
(i) cutting and drilling tools to drill, e.g. rock.
(ii) jewellery.
(iii) tools used in some surgical operations.
Graphite is used:
(iv) in 'grey lead' pencils.
(v) as containers for high temperature work.
(vi) in powder form as a dry lubricant.
(vii) as electrodes.
(viii) in making ink.
(ix) in reactors to slow down nuclear reactions. (9 marks)

(Total = 16 marks)

Reactions of metals

Question 18

Potassium (K) has an atomic number of 19. It is a solid at room temperature and is easily cut with a knife. Chromium (Cr) has an atomic number of 24, is also a solid at room temperature but is a hard substance.

(a) Give the electron configurations of potassium and chromium. (2 marks)

(b) Describe the bonding expected in potassium and chromium. (2 marks)

(c) Give two more properties that potassium and chromium have in common. (2 marks)

(Total = 6 marks)

Question 19

Explain each of the following statements.

(a) Aluminium is not a suitable structural metal to use when building a bridge. (1 mark)

(b) Silver is not used to make so called 'silver' coins such as 20 cent pieces. (1 mark)

(c) Recycling aluminium is more economical than producing it from bauxite. (1 mark)

(d) After Iron Age battles, it was difficult to maintain an iron sword in a shiny and sharp condition. (1 mark)

(e) Artificial joints in the human body are constructed from titanium. (1 mark)

(Total = 5 marks)

Question 20

(a) Use a diagram to show the structure of a typical metal at the atomic level. (3 marks)

(b) By using the structure from part (a) explain the following properties of metals:

(i) electrical conductivity (2 marks)

(ii) malleability and ductility (2 marks)

(iii) metallic bonding (2 marks)

(Total = 9 marks)

Question 21

Write balanced formula equations for the following reactions.

(a) The reaction of chromium with oxygen to form chromium(III) oxide. (2 marks)

(b) The reaction of lead with chlorine (Cl_2) to form lead(IV) chloride. (2 marks)

(c) The reaction of potassium with water. (2 marks)

(d) The reaction of aluminium with steam. (2 marks)

(e) The reaction of iron with dilute hydrochloric acid to form iron(III) chloride. (2 marks)

(f) The reaction of aluminium with sulfuric acid to form aluminium sulfate. (2 marks)

(Total = 12 marks)

Question 22

Explain the following:

(a) Iron objects in the desert or deep parts of the ocean do not rust. (2 marks)

(b) Although aluminium reacts with atmospheric oxygen it is used as a building material in e.g. window frames. (2 marks)

(c) Sodium reacts rapidly with oxygen but is stored in oil rather than deoxygenated water. (2 marks)

(d) Gold does not react with water or atmospheric gases but is often alloyed with other metals before being used to make jewellery. (2 marks)

(Total = 8 marks)

Question 23

The melting temperature of lead is 327°C and that of tin is 232°C. For many years a mixture of 60% tin and 40% lead was used by electricians to join metals together, especially in electrical circuits. Why was this material used in this way? (Total = 3 marks)

Question 24

Iron is a metal widely used in the building industry.

(a) State two advantages and two disadvantages of iron as a building material. (4 marks)

(b) Iron is often modified or coated so that its properties are more suited to its use. State two ways in which iron can be modified or coated and in what way this alters its properties. (4 marks)

(Total = 8 marks)

Reactions of ionic compounds

Question 25

The melting temperature of sodium fluoride, NaF, is 992°C, while that of magnesium oxide, MgO, is 2800°C.

(a) Write the formulas of the ions present in

(i) sodium fluoride

(ii) magnesium oxide. (2 marks)

(b) Write the electron configuration for the ions in part (a). (1 mark)

(c) Suggest a reason why the melting temperature of magnesium oxide is so much higher than that of sodium fluoride. (2 marks)

(Total = 5 marks)

Question 26

Give the correct formulas for the following compounds.

(a)	Chromium(III) oxide	(b)	Potassium nitrate
(c)	Magnesium carbonate	(d)	Mercury(II) chloride
(e)	Aluminium hydroxide	(f)	Lithium phosphate
(g)	Sodium hydrogen carbonate	(h)	Calcium fluoride
(i)	Barium nitride	(j)	Iron(II) sulfate

(Total = 10 × ½ = 5 marks)

Question 27

For the following formulas give the correct name.

(a)	LiBr	(b)	$Al_2(SO_4)_3$	(c)	PbS	(d)	$CrBr_3$
(e)	$Zn(NO_3)_2$	(f)	K_2O	(g)	$Ni(OH)_2$	(h)	$Cu_3(PO_4)_2$
(i)	$FeCl_3$	(j)	AgI	(k)	$SnCO_3$	(l)	Sc_2O_3

(Total = 12 × ½ = 6 marks)

Question 28

For each of the following compounds, determine the oxidation state (charge) of the cation.

(a)	TiO_2	(b)	$V(OH)_2$	(c)	AuI	(d)	$Co(NO_3)_3$
(e)	$InCl_3$	(f)	$PdBr_2$	(g)	$Ga_2(SO_4)_3$	(h)	$SrCO_3$

(Total = 8 × 1 = 8 marks)

Question 29

Magnesium chloride, $MgCl_2$, conducts electricity when in an aqueous solution or when molten but does not conduct when it is solid. Use your knowledge of ionic bonding to explain these observations. (Total = 3 marks)

Question 30

When the following pairs of elements react together an ionic compound is formed. In each case give the balanced formula of the product and the electron configurations of the ions formed.

	Elements	Formula	Configurations
(a)	Lithium and phosphorus		
(b)	Sodium and sulfur		
(c)	Potassium and oxygen		
(d)	Calcium and fluorine		
(e)	Aluminium and chlorine		
(f)	Magnesium and nitrogen		

(Total = 6 × 2 = 12 marks)

Question 31

The melting temperatures of the group I fluorides are given in the table below along with the ionic radii of the cations.

Compound	Melting temperature (°C)	Radius of cation (pm)
NaF	992	99
KF	857	136
RbF	775	148
CsF	683	169

Suggest a reason for the variation in the melting temperatures of the fluorides. (2 marks)

Question 32

For each of the pairs of soluble salts listed below:

(a) State whether they would react in aqueous solution to form an insoluble precipitate. (5 marks)

(b) If an insoluble precipitate is formed, write a balanced equation for the reaction. (4 marks)

(c) For each of your answers in part (b), state the spectator ions and write a balanced ionic equation. (4 marks)

Pair		Reaction (yes/no)
1	sodium nitrate and barium chloride	
2	silver nitrate and potassium iodide	
3	lead nitrate and magnesium chloride	
4	sodium carbonate and copper chloride	
5	potassium hydroxide and aluminium sulfate	

(Total = 13 marks)

Question 33

A student wishes to identify the anion and cation present in a colourless solution of an ionic salt. The student pours some of the solution into each of five different test tubes (A, B, C, D and E) and then adds another solution to test tubes A, B, C and D. Test tube E is retained as reference. The results are given in the table below.

Test tube	Solution added	Observations
A	Barium nitrate solution	No change
B	Silver nitrate solution	White solid forms
C	Sodium sulfate solution	No change
D	Sodium carbonate solution	White solid forms

From these results, deduce the identity of the ionic salt (or salts) dissolved in the given solution. (Total = 4 marks)

Unit 1 Area of Study 1 test

Section A

Elements and the periodic table

Question 1

A very dangerous radioactive isotope of strontium produced during nuclear explosions is ${}^{90}_{38}Sr$. When this isotope decays, a stable isotope of zirconium, ${}^{90}_{40}Zr$, is eventually formed. Compared with the isotope of Sr, the isotope of Zr has

A. two more protons and two less neutrons.

B. two more neutrons and two less protons.

C. one more proton and one more neutron.

D. two more protons and the same number of neutrons.

Question 2

Which one of the following species has a different number of electrons from the other three?

A. ${}_{12}Mg^{2+}$ **B.** ${}_{16}S^{2-}$ **C.** ${}_{21}Sc^{3+}$ **D.** ${}_{19}K^{+}$

Question 3

Which one of the following species has the largest number of neutrons?

A. ${}^{55}_{25}Mn$ **B.** ${}^{58}_{26}Fe$ **C.** ${}^{58}_{27}Co$ **D.** ${}^{59}_{28}Ni$

Question 4

The metal calcium forms the Ca^{2+} ion. The electron configuration of this ion is

A. $1s^22s^22p^6$

B. $1s^22s^22p^63s^23p^64s^2$

C. $1s^22s^22p^63s^23p^63d^2$

D. $1s^22s^22p^63s^23p^6$

The following information refers to Questions 5 and 6.

The graphs below show the first six ionisation energies for four *different* elements.

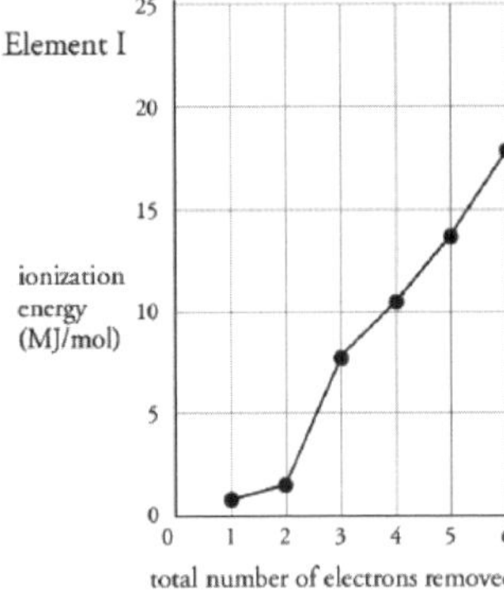

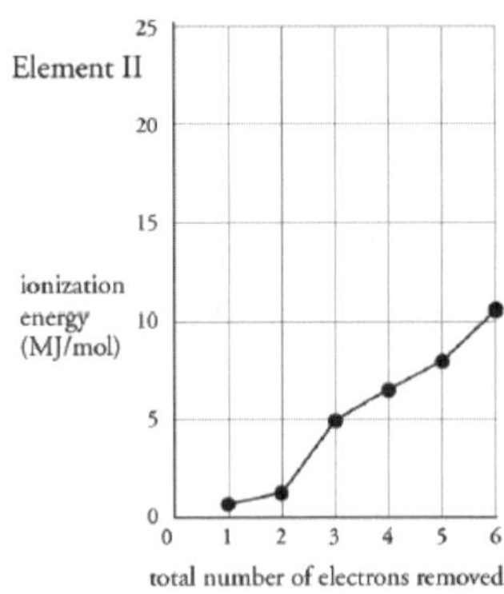

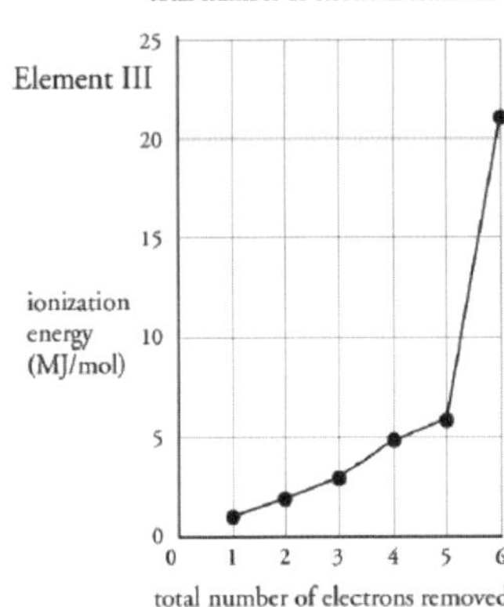

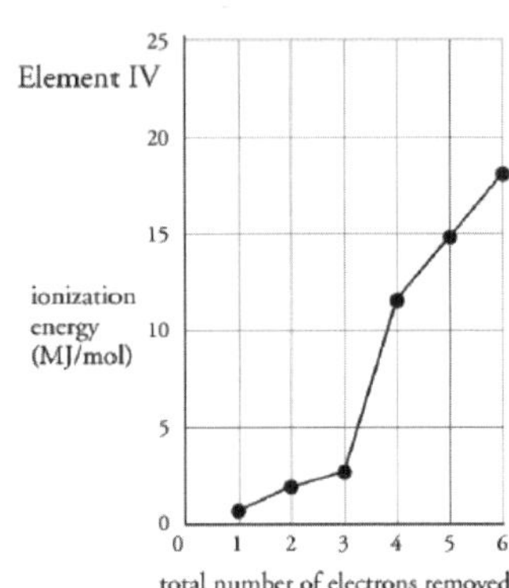

Question 5

Which of these elements is from group 3 of the periodic table?

A. element I **B.** element II

C. element III **D.** element IV

Question 6

Which two elements are in the same group in the periodic table?

A. I and II

B. I and IV

C. II and III

D. III and IV

Question 7

Which one of the following transitions could **not** contribute to the emission spectrum of an excited magnesium atom?

A. An electron in a 4s orbital moves to a 3p orbital.

B. An electron in a 3s orbital moves to a 4p orbital.

C. An electron in a 5p orbital moves to a 4s orbital.

D. An electron in a 5d orbital moves to a 3p orbital.

Question 8

Lithium and fluorine are both in period 2. It is expected that fluorine would have the

A. smaller radius and lower electronegativity.
B. smaller radius and higher electronegativity.
C. larger radius and lower electronegativity.
D. larger radius and higher electronegativity.

Question 9

Which of the following species has the largest radius?

A. K^+ **B.** Cl^- **C.** S^{2-} **D.** Ca^{2+}

Question 10

Amounts of substance in chemistry are measured in moles. The mole is a measure of the

A. concentration of particles.
B. density of particles.
C. volume of particles.
D. number of particles.

Covalent substances

Question 11

Which of the following pairs of elements is most likely to combine by forming covalent bonds?

A. potassium and fluorine
B. carbon and chlorine
C. iron and oxygen
D. lithium and bromine

Question 12

Which one of the following valence structures is incorrect?

A. O=P–O–P=O (each P with a single bond down)

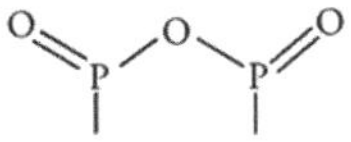

B. H–S–H (S with two lines above)

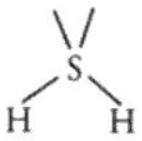

C. $H_2N=NH_2$ (H, H / N=N \ H, H)

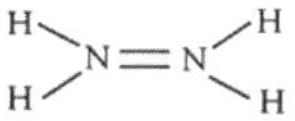

D. H—C≡C—H

Question 13

A covalent bond will only be polar if

A. one of the atoms is bonded to oxygen.
B. it is a double or triple bond.
C. one of the atoms has non-bonding electrons.
D. the atoms sharing electrons have different electronegativities.

Question 14

Methanol has the chemical formula CH_3OH. The strongest bonding **between** the methanol molecules will be

A. covalent.
B. dipole-dipole attraction.
C. hydrogen bonding.
D. dispersion forces.

Question 15

The strength of dispersion forces between molecules of a substance will increase the greater the

A. temperature of the substance.
B. unsaturation of the molecules.
C. polarity of the molecules.
D. number of electrons per molecule.

Question 16

In which of the following substances does carbon form four single bonds?

A. diamond
B. CH_2O
C. graphite
D. HCN

Reactions of metals and ionic compounds

Question 17

A characteristic of metals is that they

A. bond by sharing electrons with non-metal atoms.
B. have high electronegativities.
C. have delocalised electrons.
D. form metal-metal bonds by electron transfer between atoms.

Question 18

The element vanadium forms an oxide with the formula V_2O_5. The charge on the vanadium ion in this compound is

A. +5. **B.** –5. **C.** +2. **D.** –2

Question 19

Which of the following electron configurations is **least** likely to be that of a metallic element?

A. $1s^22s^22p^63s^23p^5$ **B.** $1s^22s^22p^63s^23p^6\,3d^94s^2$
C. $1s^22s^22p^63s^23p^64s^2$ **D.** $1s^22s^22p^63s^1$

Question 20

The properties of a pure metal, such as iron, can be modified. Which one of the following is **least** likely to modify the properties of a metal?

A. careful heating and cooling of a substance
B. hammering and working the cold metal
C. passing an electric current through the metal
D. mixing it with another metal, heating the mixture and then allowing it to cool

Question 21

The bonding in ionic compounds is best explained as the attraction between

A. positive ions and a sea of electrons.
B. oppositely charged ions.
C. instantaneous dipoles.
D. two nuclei and a pair of electrons.

Question 22

Which one of the following lists contains only correct formulas?

A. $Li(NO_3)_2$, $MgBr_2$, Al_2O_3, $PbSO_4$
B. $Ca(NO_3)_2$, $Zn_3(PO_4)_2$, $FeCl_3$, AgO
C. $BaSO_4$, K_2O, $AlCl_3$, $(NH_4)_3PO_4$
D. SnS, $Cr_2(SO_4)_3$, $CuBr_3$, $NaCO_3$

Question 23

Ionic salts at room temperature are

A. liquids with positively and negatively charged ions free to move.
B. solids in which the positively and negatively charged ions are grouped together in pairs.
C. liquids in which the positively and negatively charged ions are randomly arranged.
D. solids with alternate positively and negatively charged ions fixed in place in a giant lattice.

Question 24

Although many metals can be produced by reacting their compounds with another chemical, a small number of metals can only be produced by electrolysis. Which one of the lists below contains metals that can only be produced in this way?

A. iron, calcium, aluminium
B. tin, titanium, zinc
C. lead, nickel, copper
D. aluminium, sodium, magnesium

Question 25

Hard water contains a higher than acceptable concentration of dissolved calcium and magnesium ions. Which of the equations below does **not** represent a method of removing these ions from water?

A. $Mg^{2+}(aq) + 2OH^-(aq) \rightarrow Mg(OH)_2(s)$
B. $H_2O(l) + CO_2(aq) + CaCO_3(s) \rightarrow Ca(HCO_3)_2(aq)$
C. $Ca^{2+}(aq) + CO_3^{2-}(aq) \rightarrow CaCO_3(s)$
D. $Ca(HCO_3)_2(aq) \rightarrow H_2O(l) + CO_2(aq) + CaCO_3(s)$

Question 26

When lead nitrate solution and magnesium sulfate solution are mixed a white precipitate of lead sulfate forms. After mixing the solutions the strongest attractive forces are between

A. lead ions and sulfate ions.
B. lead ions and magnesium ions.
C. lead ions and nitrate ions.
D. magnesium ions and sulfate ions.

Section B

Elements and the periodic table

Question 1

Explain what is meant by each of the following terms:

(a) Atomic number (2 marks)
(b) Mass number (2 marks)
(c) Isotopes (2 marks)
(Total = 6 marks)

Question 2

The atomic number of iron is 26.

(a) Using the s, p, d notation, give the electron configuration of an iron atom in its ground state. (1 mark)
(b) Explain why iron is classified as a transition metal. (1 mark)
(c) In many compounds, iron is often present as a 3+ cation. Give the electron configuration of Fe^{3+}. (1 mark)
(Total = 3 marks)

Question 3

Explain what is meant by each of the following terms:

(a) Electronegativity (2 marks)
(b) Core charge (2 marks)
(c) First ionisation energy (2 marks)
(Total = 6 marks)

Question 4

(a) Write the correct chemical symbols for the following elements by using the periodic table.

(i) The element that forms a –1 ion with the electron configuration $1s^22s^22p^6$. (1 mark)

(ii) The element from the second period that has the smallest atomic radius. (1 mark)

(iii) The element from group 17 that has the largest electronegativity. (1 mark)

(iv) The element from the first transition series that has 7 electrons in the 3d subshell. (1 mark)

(v) The element whose excited state has the electron configuration $1s^22s^22p^53s^23p^43d^1$. (1 mark)

(b) Across the third period, from sodium to chlorine the electronegativity of the elements increases. Give an explanation for this observation. (2 marks)

(Total = 7 marks)

Covalent substances

Question 5

(a) Draw an electron dot diagram for methyl sulfide, CH_3SH. (1 mark)

(b) How many bonding pairs of electrons are present? (1 mark)

(c) How many non-bonding electron pairs are present? (1 mark)

(d) Draw the structural formula of methyl sulfide. (1 mark)

(e) Is the methyl sulfide molecule polar or non-polar? (1 mark)

(f) Is methyl sulfide more or less polar than methanol? (1 mark)

(g) Give a reason for your answer to part (f). (1 mark)

(Total = 7 marks)

Question 6

Draw valence structures for each of the following molecules.

(a) Nitrogen, N_2

(b) Ethyne, C_2H_2

(c) Arsenic trifluoride, AsF_3

(d) Silicon tetrachloride, $SiCl_4$

(e) Hydrogen fluoride, HF

For each species: (i) name their shape and (ii) state whether they are polar or non-polar.

(Total = 5 × 2 = 10 marks)

Question 7

Although ethane, C_2H_6 and hydrazine, NH_2NH_2, molecules have a similar mass, ethane has a much lower boiling point (–88.6°C) than hydrazine (114°C).

(a) (i) Calculate the number of electrons in each molecule.

(ii) Calculate the molar mass of each molecule. (2 marks)

(b) Describe the intermolecular bonding in both compounds. (3 marks)

(c) Explain the difference in boiling points. (3 marks)

(Total = 8 marks)

Reactions of metals and ionic compounds

Question 8

Explain the following.

(a) The melting temperature of calcium oxide is higher than that of potassium fluoride. (2 marks)

(b) The melting temperature of potassium fluoride is slightly lower than the melting temperature of lithium fluoride. (2 marks)

(Total = 4 marks)

Question 9

What is the most likely formula for the ionic compound formed between

(a) an element X in group 2 and an element Y in group 16. (1 mark)

(b) an element R in group 1 and an element Q in group 15. (1 mark)

(c) an element M in group 3 and an element G in group 17. (1 mark)

(Total = 3 marks)

Question 10

Use the model of metallic bonding to explain the following observations.

(a) Builders often attach a lead weight to a piece of string to make the string hang vertically. (2 marks)

(b) Copper is used to make electrical wires. (2 marks)

(c) Some saucepans have a thick base made from copper. (2 marks)

(d) Tungsten wire is used as the filament in some electric light globes. (2 marks)

(e) Jewellery is often made from silver or gold. (2 marks)

(Total = 10 marks)

Question 11

Write balanced formula equations for the following reactions.

(a) Magnesium reacting with steam (2 marks)

(b) Calcium reacting with dilute hydrochloric acid (2 marks)

(c) Sodium reacting with oxygen. (2 marks)

(Total = 6 marks)

Question 12

Give the correct name for the following formulas.

(a) Cr_2O_3

(b) K_2SO_4

(c) CuCl

(d) $BaCO_3$ (Total = 4 marks)

Chapter 2

Unit 1 Area of Study 2 – How are materials quantified and classified?

Multiple choice items

Quantifying atoms and compounds

Question 1

If an atom of ^{12}C was assigned a value of 24 units on the relative mass scale, then

A. all relative isotopic masses would be doubled.

B. all relative isotopic masses would be halved.

C. the relative mass of ^{12}C would be the same as that of ^{24}Mg.

D. there would be no change in the relative isotopic masses since all masses are relative.

Question 2

If the mass of an atom of ^{12}C is taken as 12 units exactly, then the relative atomic mass of an element is defined as the

A. mass of one atom of the element relative to an atom of ^{12}C.

B. weighted mean of the relative masses of the isotopes of the element on the ^{12}C scale.

C. mass of one mole of the element in grams.

D. average mass of one mole of the isotopes of the element in grams.

Question 3

Naturally occurring iridium has a relative atomic mass of 192.2 and consists of two isotopes, $^{191}_{77}Ir$ and $^{193}_{77}Ir$. The percentage of the lighter isotope is

A. 80%

B. 60%

C. 40%

D. 20%

Question 4

One mole is defined as

A. the number of atoms in 12 g of carbon-12.

B. 12 g of naturally occurring carbon.

C. the number of atoms in 1.0 g of hydrogen.

D. the mass of 6.02×10^{23} atoms of carbon-12.

Question 5

The molar mass of a substance is the

A. sum of the relative atomic masses of the elements in the formula of the substance.

B. ratio of the mass of one mole of the substance to 12 g of carbon-12.

C. mass of one mole of the substance.

D. mass of one molecule of the substance relative to the mass of one atom of ^{12}C taken as 12 exactly.

Question 6

The number of mole of oxygen atoms in 40.0 g of iron(III) sulfate, $Fe_2(SO_4)_3$, (formula mass = 400 g mol^{-1}) is closest to

A. 0.400
B. 0.700
C. 1.20
D. 120

Question 7

A student weighs a sample of aluminium nitrate, $Al(NO_3)_3$, and then finds that he has taken 0.15 mol of the compound. The mass of nitrogen present in this sample is closest to

A. 96 g.**B.** 32 g. **C.** 6.3 g. **D.** 2.1 g.

Question 8

An element forms an oxide with the formula X_2O_5. If the formula mass of the oxide is approximately 182 g mol^{-1}, then the relative atomic mass of the element is closest to

A. 166. **B.** 102. **C.** 51. **D.** 30.

Question 9

The formula mass of chromium(III) oxide, Cr_2O_3, in g mol^{-1} is

A. 188. **B.** 68. **C.** 73. **D.** 152.

Question 10

A student weighs 2.20 g of lithium sulfate, Li_2SO_4. The number of mole of compound present in 2.20 g is

A. 50.0.**B.** 25.0. **C.** 0.0400. **D.** 0.0200.

Question 11

The mass of oxygen, in grams, that reacts with manganese to form 5.00 g of manganese(III) oxide, Mn_2O_3, is closest to

A. 0.510. **B.** 1.52. **C.** 2.54. **D.** 48.0.

Question 12

Iodine will react with fluorine to form a compound with the formula IF_5. The percentage by mass of fluorine in this compound is approximately

A. 42.81. **B.** 57.19. **C.** 13.02. **D.** 83.35.

Question 13

Which one of the following compounds contains the greatest percentage of carbon?

A. $C_2H_4O_2$ **B.** CH_5N **C.** $C_3H_8O_3$ **D.** CH_4O

Question 14

A compound of sodium, chlorine and oxygen contains 18.78% sodium and 28.98% chlorine. What mass of oxygen is present in 6.40 g of the compound?

A. 1.20 g **B.** 1.85 g **C.** 3.06 g **D.** 3.34 g

Question 15

A compound of sodium, sulfur and oxygen was analysed. 5.65 g of the compound contained 1.72 g of oxygen and 1.64 g of sodium. The percentage of sulfur in the compound is closest to

A. 59.5.**B.** 40.5. **C.** 30.4. **D.** 29.0.

Question 16

The mass of 1.50 mol of propanoic acid, CH_3CH_2COOH, is

A. 111 g. **B.** 0.0203 g. **C.** 49.3 g. **D.** 74.0 g.

Question 17

The number of hydrogen atoms present in 4.0 g of methane, CH_4, is

A. 1.5×10^{23} atoms. **B.** 6.0×10^{23} atoms.

C. 2.4×10^{24} atoms. **D.** 9.6×10^{24} atoms.

Question 18

Ethane, C_2H_6, is one of the compounds found in natural gas. Which one of the following statements about ethane is **not** correct?

A. 0.1 mole of C_2H_6 contains 4.8×10^{23} atoms.

B. 3.0 g of ethane contains 2.4 g of carbon.

C. 1.0 g of ethane contains 4.0×10^{22} atoms of carbon.

D. 1 molecule of ethane has a mass of 30 g.

Question 19

A compound of carbon and hydrogen contains 80% carbon. The empirical formula of the compound is most likely to be

A. C_4H. **B.** C_3H. **C.** CH_3. **D.** CH_4.

Question 20

A student adds 3.561 g of tin to 5.076 g of iodine and allows the reaction to proceed until all of the iodine has been consumed. The student finds that at the end of the reaction 2.374 g of tin remains. From these results the empirical formula of tin iodide is

A. Sn_3I_4 **B.** SnI_2 **C.** SnI_4 **D.** Sn_4I

Question 21

Lactic acid has the molecular formula $C_3H_6O_3$. The percentage of carbon in lactic acid is

A. 2.5 **B.** 25 **C.** 36 **D.** 40

Question 22

Which one of the following compounds contains the greatest percentage of carbon?

A. C_2H_5F

B. C_3H_7N

C. C_3H_8O

D. C_4H_9Cl

Question 23

Four compounds of carbon, hydrogen and oxygen have the molecular formulae CH_4O, $C_2H_4O_2$, $C_3H_8O_3$ and $C_4H_8O_3$. When placed in order of increasing percentage of oxygen the order is (smallest first)

A. $CH_4O < C_2H_4O_2 < C_3H_8O_3 < C_4H_8O_3$.
B. $C_4H_8O_3 < C_3H_8O_3 < C_2H_4O_2 < CH_4O$.
C. $C_4H_8O_3 < CH_4O < C_3H_8O_3 < C_2H_4O_2$.
D. $C_2H_4O_2 < C_3H_8O_3 < CH_4O < C_4H_8O_3$.

Families of organic compounds

Question 24

The structural formulas of four functional groups are represented by I, II, III and IV below.

I: $>C{=}C<$ II: $-C{\equiv}C-$

III: $\diagdown O{-}H$ IV: $-C({=}O){-}O{-}H$

The correct names for these functional groups are

	I	II	III	IV
A.	alkane	alkene	alcohol	hydroxy
B.	alkyne	alkene	hydroxy	carboxy
C.	alkene	alkyne	alcohol	hydroxy
D.	alkene	alkyne	hydroxy	carboxy

Question 25

Which one of the following formulas is that of a saturated hydrocarbon?

A. CH_3OH **B.** C_2H_2 **C.** C_3H_8 **D.** C_4H_8

Question 26

The formulas of four substances are given below. For which one would the structure contain a carbon-carbon double bond?

A. CH_2O **B.** C_3H_6 **C.** C_2H_2 **D.** C_4H_{10}

Question 27

The general formula of alkenes is

A. C_nH_n **B.** C_nH_{2n} **C.** C_nH_{2n-2} **D.** C_nH_{2n-4}

Question 28

Which one of the following is most likely to be the formula of an alkyne?

A. C_5H_8 **B.** C_5H_{10} **C.** C_6H_{12} **D.** C_6H_{14}

Question 29

The correct names for the structural formulas

$$\underset{\underset{CH_3}{|}}{CH_3C}\overset{\overset{OH}{|}}{H}CHCH_2CH_3 \quad \text{and} \quad CH_3CH_2\overset{\overset{COOH}{|}}{C}HCH_2CH_3 \text{ are}$$

A. 4-methyl-3-hydroxy-hexane and hexanoic acid respectively.

B. 2-methylpentan-3-ol and 2-ethylpropanoic acid respectively.

C. 4-methylpentan-3-ol and hexanoic acid respectively.

D. 2-methylpentan-3-ol and 2-ethylbutanoic acid respectively.

Question 30

Isomers are best described as

A. particles that have the same atomic number but different mass numbers.

B. compounds whose chemical formulas differ by $-CH_2-$.

C. particles that have the same number of electrons but different atomic numbers.

D. compounds that have the same chemical formulas but different structures.

Question 31

The formula below is that of pentane.

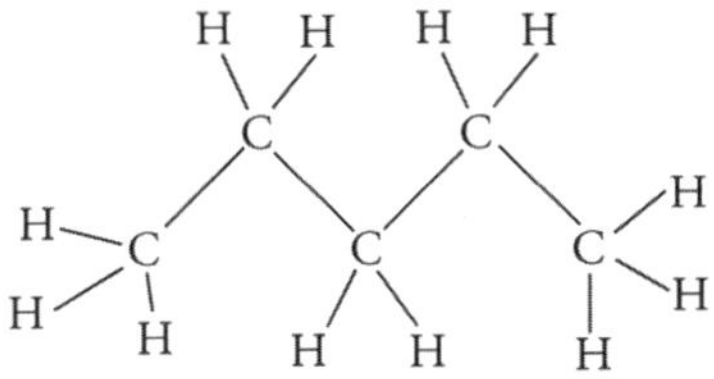

It is best described as

A. an empirical formula **B.** a molecular formula

C. a structural formula **D.** a semi-structural formula

Question 32

The members of a homologous series have similar

A. physical properties and the formula of one differs from the next member by $-CH_2-$.

B. chemical and physical properties but different structural formulas.

C. chemical properties and the formula of one differs from the next member by $-CH_2-$.

D. formulas but different chemical and physical properties.

Question 33

The molecules butene and butane both have the same

A. number of carbon atoms. **B.** number of isomers.

C. boiling point **D.** chemical reactivity

Question 34
An organic compound has the systematic name 2,3-dimethylbutane. Which one of the statements about this compound is ***incorrect***?

A. It is an alkane.
B. Each molecule contains six carbon atoms.
C. The molecule is symmetrical.
D. The molecules contain a double bond.

Question 35
The number of carbon atoms in 2,4-dimethyloctan-1-ol is

A. 7 **B.** 8 **C.** 9 **D.** 10

Question 36
When 1 mole of a hydrocarbon is burnt in oxygen equal amounts (in mole) of CO_2 and H_2O are formed. The formula of the hydrocarbon is most likely to be

A. C_5H_6 **B.** C_5H_8 **C.** C_5H_{10} **D.** C_5H_{12}

Polymers and society

Question 37
Part of a polymer chain is shown below.

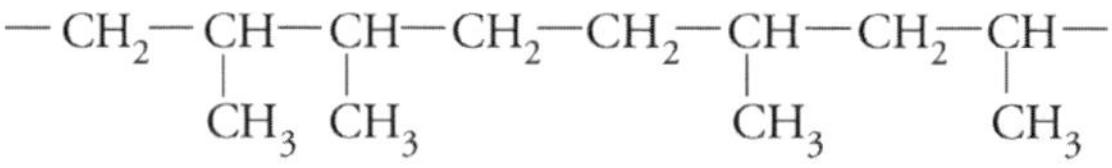

```
—CH2—CH—CH—CH2—CH2—CH—CH2—CH—
     |   |            |       |
    CH3 CH3          CH3     CH3
```

The monomer from which this polymer could be made has the structure

A.
```
CH2=CH—CH=CH2
    |   |
   CH3 CH3
```

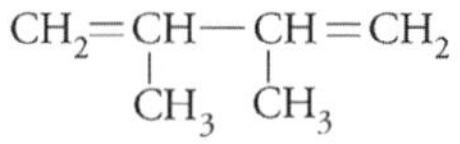

B.
```
CH=CH
|   |
CH3 CH3
```

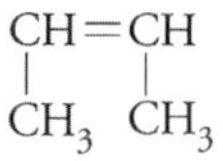

C. $CH_2{=}CH_2$

D.
```
CH=CH2
|
CH3
```

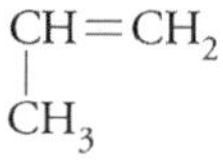

Question 38
Propene will undergo addition 36olymerized36on to make polypropene. Which one of the diagrams below could **not** represent the structure of polypropene?

A.
```
 CH3 H  CH3 H  CH3 H
  |  |   |  |   |  |
—C—C—C—C—C—C—
  |  |   |  |   |  |
  H  H   H  H   H  H
```

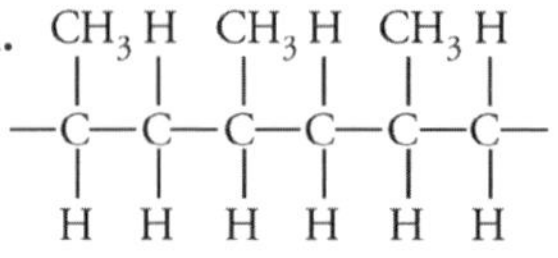

B.
```
 CH3 H  CH3 H  CH3 H
  |  |   |  |   |  |
—C—C—C—C—C—C—
  |  |   |  |   |  |
  H CH3  H CH3  H CH3
```

C.
```
 CH3 H  H  H  H  H
  |  |  |  |  |  |
—C—C—C—C—C—C—
  |  |  |  |  |  |
  H  H  H CH3 CH3 H
```

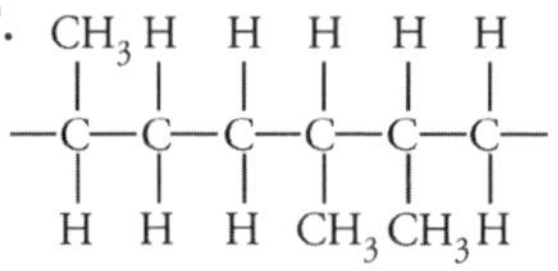

D.
```
 CH3 H  H  H CH3 H
  |  |  |  |  |  |
—C—C—C—C—C—C—
  |  |  |  |  |  |
  H  H CH3 H  H  H
```

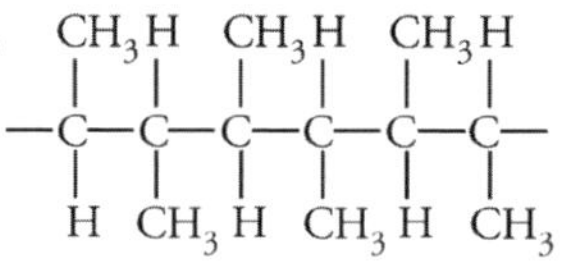

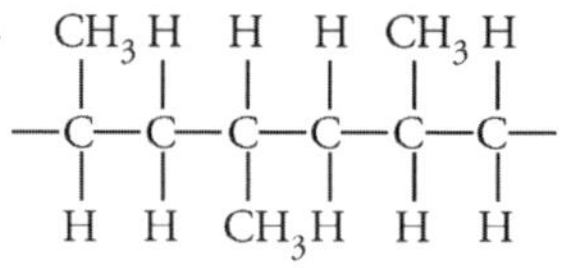

Question 39

The same monomer is used to make two different materials as shown below.

Material 1: the chains are longer and relatively unbranched.

Material 2: the chains are shorter and there are many branches.

Which one of the statements below is correct?

A. The average molar mass of the polymers in material 2 will be greater than that of the polymers in material 1.

B. The degree of crystallinity of material 2 will be greater than that of material 1.

C. The density of material 2 will be less than that of material 1.

D. The melting temperature of material 2 will be greater than that of material 1.

Question 40

When compared to thermosetting polymers it is expected that thermoplastic polymers will be

A. more difficult to melt.

B. softer and easier to mold.

C. harder and be more resistant to impact.

D. difficult to recycle.

Question 41

A major constituent of 'white' glue is polyvinyl acetate (PVA). This glue is often used to glue wooden surfaces. A section of a PVA molecule is shown below.

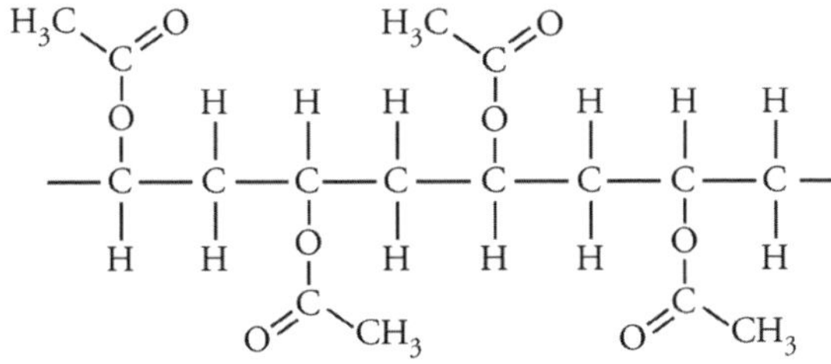

When a 'white' glue sets

A. the water evaporates, leaving a large number of tangled polymer chains bonded to each other and to the wood surfaces.

B. covalent bonds form between the polymer chains and between the polymer chains and the wood surfaces.

C. water promotes extensive cross linking between the linear polymer chains.

D. there is hydrogen bonding between the linear polymer chains and between chains and the wood surfaces.

Question 42

Polyethene can exist in two forms, high density polyethene (HDPE) and low density polyethene (LDPE). Which one of the following statements regarding the properties of these polymers is **least** likely to be correct?

A. HDPE has more branching in its molecules than LDPE.
B. HDPE is harder than LDPE.
C. HDPE has a higher melting point than LDPE.
D. HDPE is less flexible than LDPE.

Question 43

When the degree of 38olymerized38on is increased, the chain length of the polymer molecules also increases. When this occurs

A. the average molar mass of the polymer chains is unchanged.
B. there is an increase in the strength and toughness of the material.
C. the melting temperature of the polymer decreases.
D. there is an increase in the cross linking between the polymer chains.

Question 44

A polymer material that has a high degree of crystallinity is likely to be

A. a material with a low melting temperature.
B. a hard thermally stable material.
C. a polymer with short chains.
D. a material where there are many side branches to the polymer chains.

Extended response questions

Quantifying atoms and compounds

Question 1

Naturally occurring gallium, an element in the fourth period, consists of a mixture of two isotopes. The relevant information on the isotopes is given in the table below.

Isotope	Relative isotopic mass	% abundance
^{69}Ga	68.9256	60.108
^{71}Ga	70.9247	39.892

(a) How many neutrons are present in the nucleus of the heavier gallium isotope? (1 mark)

(b) What is the mass, in grams, of one atom of ^{69}Ga? (1 mark)

(c) The graph on the following page shows part of the mass spectrum of naturally occurring gallium.

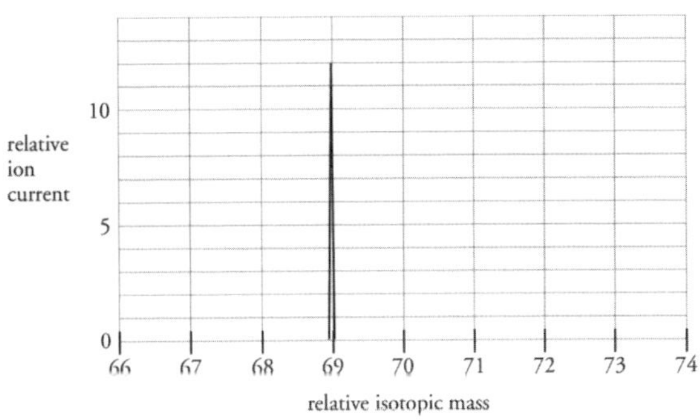

What height and position would you expect to see for the other peak in the mass spectrum of gallium? Sketch the second peak on the graph above. (2 marks)

(d) Calculate the relative atomic mass of gallium. (2 marks)

(Total = 6 marks)

Question 2

The element rubidium has two naturally occurring isotopes, ^{85}Rb and ^{87}Rb. The percentage abundance of the lighter isotope is 72.17% and its accurate relative isotopic mass is 84.912. If the relative atomic mass of rubidium is 85.468 calculate a value for the relative isotopic mass of the ^{87}Rb isotope. (3 marks)

Question 3

Naturally occurring bromine consists of two isotopes, $^{79}_{35}Br$ and $^{81}_{35}Br$. However, the mass spectrum of bromine molecules, Br_2, shows three peaks at relative masses 158, 160 and 162. Give an explanation for this observation. (Total = 3 marks)

Question 4

Give concise explanations for the following statements.

(a) Potassium has a relative atomic mass of 39.1 and argon has a relative atomic mass of 39.9 but argon is placed before potassium in the periodic table. (2 marks)

(b) For many elements the relative atomic mass is not a whole number. (2 marks)

(c) The only naturally occurring atoms of the element europium, Eu, are $^{151}_{63}Eu$ and $^{153}_{63}Eu$, but the relative atomic mass of europium is 152. (2 marks)

(Total = 6 marks)

Question 5

Naturally occurring lead consists of four isotopes, $^{204}_{82}Pb$, $^{206}_{82}Pb$, $^{207}_{82}Pb$, $^{208}_{82}Pb$.

The relative isotopic masses and relative abundances of the four isotopes are given in the table below.

Isotope	Relative isotopic mass	% Abundance
$^{204}_{82}Pb$	203.973	1.4
$^{206}_{82}Pb$	205.975	24.1
$^{207}_{82}Pb$	206.976	22.1
$^{208}_{82}Pb$	207.977	52.4

(a) In each atom of the $^{207}_{82}Pb$ isotope, how many protons and neutrons are present? (1 mark)

(b) What is meant by the expression 'relative atomic mass'? (1 mark)

(c) Use the data in the table to draw a graph showing how the mass spectrum of lead would appear. (3 marks)

(d) Calculate a value for the relative atomic mass of lead. (3 marks)

(Total = 8 marks)

Question 6

In the nineteenth century, scientists calculated the relative atomic mass of an element by measuring the mass of oxygen that reacted with a known mass of the element. With this method the scientists had to make an assumption about the formula of the oxide. Before 1869 scientists had calculated that the element indium, In, had a relative atomic mass of 75. This value of the relative atomic mass was incorrect since the scientists had assumed an incorrect formula for the oxide. In a typical experiment 5.00 g of indium was converted into 6.06 g of indium oxide.

(a) Deduce the formula the scientists had assumed for indium oxide. (3 marks)

(b) Later scientists assumed that the formula of indium oxide was In_2O_3. What value did they calculate for the relative mass of indium? (3 marks)

(Total = 6 marks)

Question 7

Bornite is an ore of copper and has the formula Cu_2FeS_4.

(a) Calculate the relative formula mass of bornite. (1 mark)

(b) What is the percentage composition of bornite? (3 marks)

(c) What mass of copper could be obtained from 1.0 kg of bornite? (2 marks)

(Total = 6 marks)

Question 8

All plants need a source of nitrogen in order to grow. Urea, $CO(NH_2)_2$, ammonium sulfate, $(NH_4)_2SO_4$, and ammonium nitrate, NH_4NO_3 have all been used as nitrogen fertilisers.

(a) For each compound calculate the percentage of nitrogen present. (3 marks)

(b) How many moles of nitrogen are present in 100 g of ammonium nitrate? (2 marks)

(c) What mass of nitrogen could be obtained from 500 g of ammonium sulfate? (2 marks)

(Total = 7 marks)

Question 9

One of the components of natural gas is propane, C_3H_8. For an 11.0 g sample of propane calculate:

(a) the molar mass of propane. (1 mark)

(b) the number of mole of molecules present. (1 mark)

(c) the number of molecules present. (1 mark)

(d) the number of moles of hydrogen atoms present. (1 mark)

(e) the total number of atoms present. (1 mark)

(Total = 5 marks)

Question 10

Explain what is meant by:

(a) relative molecular mass (2 marks)

(b) molar mass (2 marks)

(Total = 4 marks)

Question 11

A sample of ethane, C_2H_6, contains 1.2×10^{23} atoms of carbon.

(a) How many mole of carbon are present? (1 mark)
(b) What mass of carbon does this represent? (1 mark)
(c) How many molecules of ethane are present? (1 mark)
(d) How many atoms of hydrogen are combined with this number of carbon atoms? (1 mark)
(e) What is the total mass of ethane? (2 marks)

(Total = 6 marks)

Question 12

Sodium carbonate, Na_2CO_3, is a base often used in acid-base reactions. For a 0.250 mol sample of sodium carbonate calculate the following:

(a) the relative formula mass (1 mark)
(b) the mass of sodium carbonate in this sample. (1 mark)
(c) the number of mole of sodium present. (1 mark)
(d) the mass of oxygen atoms present in this sample. (2 marks)

(Total = 5 marks)

Question 13

A 15.00 g sample of an oxide of nitrogen is heated and decomposes to nitrogen and oxygen. All of the oxygen is removed, and 3.89 g of nitrogen remains.

(a) What mass of oxygen was also formed when the sample decomposed? (1 mark)
(b) Calculate the number of mole of nitrogen and the number of mole of oxygen that were combined in the compound. (2 marks)
(c) Deduce the empirical formula of this oxide of nitrogen. (2 marks)

(Total = 5 marks)

Question 14

A compound contains 0.15 mole of carbon combined with 0.40 g of hydrogen and 9×10^{22} atoms of oxygen. What is the empirical formula of the compound?

(3 marks)

Question 15

The following method was used to determine the empirical formula of magnesium oxide. A crucible and lid were weighed, then a small piece of magnesium ribbon was added and the crucible and lid reweighed. The crucible and lid were then strongly heated. Occasionally the lid was raised for a few moments and then lowered again. Heating was continued until no more reaction occurred. After cooling the crucible, lid and contents were then weighed again.

Results:
Mass of crucible and lid = 15.67g
Mass of crucible, lid and magnesium = 15.86 g
Mass of crucible, lid and magnesium oxide = 15.96 g

(a) Why was the lid raised for a few moments? (1 mark)
(b) Use the above results to calculate the empirical formula of magnesium oxide. (3 marks)
(c) The accepted empirical formula of magnesium oxide is MgO. Suggest two reasons why it differs from the answer calculated in part (b). (2 marks)

(Total = 6 marks)

Question 16

A student determines the formula of zinc iodide by the following method. The student weighs a conical flask adds a small amount of zinc and weighs the flask again. A similar amount of iodine was then added, and the flask weighed for a third time. Approximately 5 mL of water and a few drops of ethanoic acid were added to the flask. The flask was warmed slightly until the colour of iodine had completely disappeared. Some zinc remained unreacted. The liquid was decanted from the remaining zinc. The remaining zinc was washed and then dried.

Results:	Mass of flask	= 24.62 g
	Mass of flask and zinc	= 26.58 g
	Mass of flask, zinc and iodine mass of flask	= 28.66 g
	Remaining zinc	= 26.04 g

(a) Why was the remaining zinc washed? (1 mark)

(b) Use the above results to calculate the empirical formula of zinc iodide. (3 marks)

(Total = 4 marks)

Question 17

A hydrocarbon (a compound that contains only carbon and hydrogen atoms) contains 0.48 g of carbon chemically combined with 0.12 g of hydrogen.

(a) Calculate the number of mole of hydrogen and the number of mole of carbon in this compound. (2 marks)

(b) What is the empirical formula of the compound? (2 marks)

(c) If the molar mass of the compound is 30.0 g mol^{-1}, deduce the molecular formula of the compound. (2 marks)

(Total = 6 marks)

Question 18

A compound of carbon, hydrogen, nitrogen and oxygen has the following percentage composition:

% carbon = 50.00; % hydrogen = 8.33; % nitrogen = 19.44

(a) Calculate the percentage of oxygen in the compound. (1 mark)

(b) Deduce the empirical formula of the compound. (3 marks)

21.6 g is found to represent 0.15 mol of the compound.

(c) Calculate the molar mass of the compound. (1 mark)

(d) Deduce the molecular formula of the compound. (2 marks)

(Total = 7 marks)

Question 19

A compound of carbon and hydrogen is burnt in air to give carbon dioxide, CO_2, and water. In a typical experiment 1.00 g of the compound gave 3.14 g of carbon dioxide on combustion.

(a) How many mole of carbon dioxide were produced? (1 mark)

(b) How many mole of carbon are present in the carbon dioxide and thus in the original compound? (1 mark)

(c) What mass of carbon is present in 1.00 g of the compound? (1 mark)

(d) What mass of hydrogen is present in 1.00 g of the compound? (1 mark)

(e) Deduce the empirical formula of the compound. (2 marks)

(f) If 0.25 mole of the compound weighs 14.0 g, what is the molecular formula of the compound? (2 marks)

(Total = 8 marks)

Families of organic compounds

Question 20

(a) Draw the semi-structural formulas for three of the alkene isomers with the molecular formula C_5H_{10}. (3 marks)

(b) Name each isomer. (3 marks)

(c) For one of the isomers write a balanced equation for its combustion in air. (2 marks)

(Total = 8 marks)

Question 21

Give the correct names for the following semi-structural formulas.

(a) $CH_3CH(CH_3)CH_2CH_2CH_3$

(b) $CH_3CH(CH_3)CH{=}CH_2$

(c) $CH_3CH(CH_3)CH_2C{\equiv}CCH_2CH_3$

(d) $CH_3CH(OH)CH(CH_3)CH_2CH_3$

(e) $(CH_3)_3CCH_2COOH$ (Total = 5 × 1 = 5 marks)

Question 22

For the following names give the correct semi-structural formulas.

(a) 2,3-dimethylheptane

(b) 2-methylhept-3-ene

(c) 2-methylhex-3-yne

(d) 2,3 dimethylbutan-2-ol

(e) 2-methylpropanoic acid (Total = 5 × 1 = 5 marks)

Question 23

For each of the semi-structural formulas shown below, write the semi-structural formula of an isomer.

(a) $CH_3CH_2CH_2OH$

(b) $CH_3CH_2CH_2COOH$

(c) $(CH_3)_2C{=}CHCH_3$

(d) $CH_3(CH_2)_3CH_3$

(e) $HC{\equiv}CCH_2CH_3$ (Total = 5 × 1 = 5 marks)

Question 24

Give the correct names for the following organic molecules.

(a)

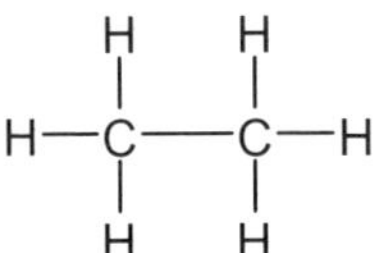

(b)

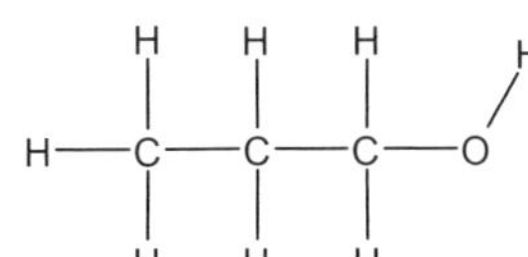

(c)

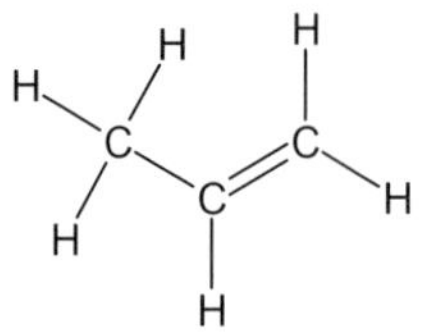

(d)

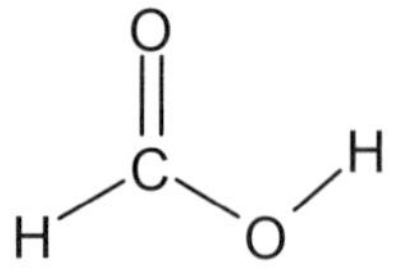

(Total = 5 × 1 = 5 marks)

Question 25

A scientist isolates two hydrocarbons from two different reactions. He labels them compound 'A' and compound 'B'. He finds that both compounds will undergo addition reactions with hydrogen, H_2, as shown below.

'A' + H_2 → 2-methylpropane
'B' + H_2 → butane

The two compounds will also undergo addition reactions with hydrogen bromide, HBr. The scientist finds that a mixture of two isomers is formed when compound A is reacted in this way. However, when compound B reacts with HBr only one product is formed. The new compounds are labelled 'C', 'D' and 'E'. C, D and E are all found to have the same molecular formula, C_4H_9Br.

'A' + HBr → C_4H_9Br (compound C)
'A' + HBr → C_4H_9Br (compound D)
'B' + HBr → C_4H_9Br (compound E)

(a) From the information given above, deduce the molecular formulas of compounds 'A' and 'B'. (2 marks)
(b) What type of hydrocarbon are compounds 'A' and 'B'? (1 mark)
(c) Use the result of the hydrogenation reaction to deduce the structural formula of compound 'A'. (1 mark)
(d) What are the structural formulas of the compounds 'C' and 'D'? (2 marks)
(e) The result of the hydrogenation of compound 'B' would suggest that 'B' can have one of two structures. What these two structures? (2 marks)
(f) Only one product ('E') is formed when HBr is added to compound 'B'. Use this result to deduce the correct structures of compounds 'B' and 'E'. (2 marks)

(Total = 10 marks)

Polymers and society

Question 26

The following molecules have all been used as monomers to prepare useful polymers.

(a) $CH_2{=}CH(C_6H_5)$
(b) $CF_2{=}CF_2$

In each case draw a section of the polymer that would result when the monomer is polymerised. Use three monomer units in each of your answers.

(Total = 2 × 2 = 4 marks)

Question 27

Part of the structures of three polymers are shown below.

(a)

$$\begin{array}{ccccccccccccc} & \mathrm{H} & & \mathrm{H} & & \mathrm{H} & & \mathrm{H} & & \mathrm{H} & & \mathrm{H} & \\ & | & & | & & | & & | & & | & & | & \\ - & \mathrm{C} & - & \mathrm{C} & - & \mathrm{C} & - & \mathrm{C} & - & \mathrm{C} & - & \mathrm{C} & - \\ & | & & | & & | & & | & & | & & | & \\ & \mathrm{H} & & \mathrm{CN} & & \mathrm{H} & & \mathrm{CN} & & \mathrm{H} & & \mathrm{CN} & \end{array}$$

(2 marks)

(b)

$$\begin{array}{ccccccccccccc} & \mathrm{CH_3} & & \mathrm{H} & & \mathrm{CH_3} & & \mathrm{H} & & \mathrm{CH_3} & & \mathrm{H} & \\ & | & & | & & | & & | & & | & & | & \\ - & \mathrm{C} & - & \mathrm{C} & - & \mathrm{C} & - & \mathrm{C} & - & \mathrm{C} & - & \mathrm{C} & - \\ & | & & | & & | & & | & & | & & | & \\ & \mathrm{H} & & \mathrm{CH_3} & & \mathrm{H} & & \mathrm{CH_3} & & \mathrm{H} & & \mathrm{CH_3} & \end{array}$$

(2 marks)

Draw the structural formula of the monomer used to make each of the polymers.

(Total = 4 marks)

Question 28

The diagrams below represent three different types of polymers.

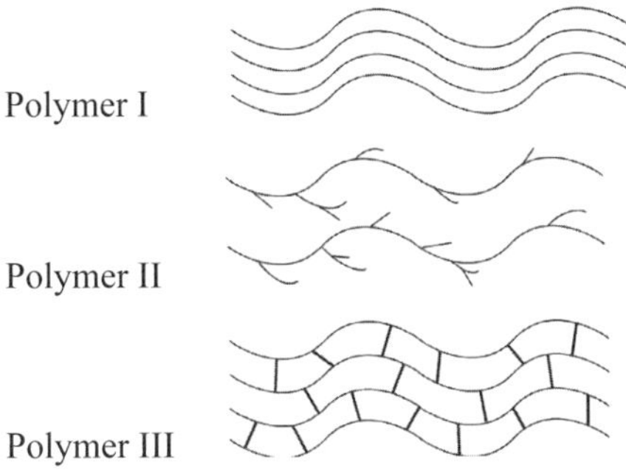

(a) Identify the diagram that best represents
   (i) a cross-linked polymer.
   (ii) high density polyethene.
   (iii) low density polyethene. (3 marks)

(b) Suggest a use for each polymer and describe the properties that make it suitable for the use. (6 marks)

(Total = 9 marks)

Question 29

The twentieth century has been described as 'the polymer age' because of the large-scale use of polymers. Describe two advantages and two disadvantages associated with the use of polymers.

(Total = 4 marks)

Unit 1 Area of Study 2 test

Section A

Quantifying atoms and compounds

Question 1

The mass of potassium, in grams, in 0.25 mol of potassium chloride, KCl is closest to

A. 9.78 **B.** 18.65 **C.** 39.1 **D.** 156.4

Question 2

Which one of the following contains the smallest mass of hydrogen?

A. 20 g of methane, CH_4
B. 36 g of water, H_2O
C. 10 g of hydrogen, H_2
D. 40 g of butane, C_4H_{10}

Question 3

The number of mole of sodium atoms in 16.4 g of sodium phosphate, Na_3PO_4 (molar mass = 164 g mol^{-1}), is closest to

A. 0.10 **B.** 0.30 **C.** 10 **D.** 30

Question 4

An oxide of chlorine contains 38.8% chlorine. The empirical formula of the compound is

A. ClO. **B.** ClO_3. **C.** ClO_4. **D.** Cl_2O_7.

Question 5

When 8.8 g of an oxide of nitrogen are decomposed 3.2 g of oxygen are formed. The empirical formula of the oxide is most likely to be

A. N_2O. **B.** N_3O. **C.** N_4O_2. **D.** NO_2.

Question 6

Naturally occurring thallium has a relative atomic mass of 204.4 and consists of two isotopes, ${}^{203}_{81}Tl$ and ${}^{205}_{81}Tl$. The percentage of the lighter isotope is

A. 30% **B.** 40% **C.** 60% **D.** 70%

Question 7

Which one of the following has the smallest number of atoms?

A. 0.10 mol of hydrogen, H_2
B. 6.0×10^{22} molecules of ethyne, C_2H_2
C. 1.0 g of water, H_2O
D. 5.0×10^{-2} mol of butane, C_4H_{10}

Question 8

A compound of tin and chlorine has the formula $SnCl_4$ and contains 45.53% tin. The mass of chlorine, in grams, in 6.25 g of the compound is

A. 1.25. **B.** 2.85. **C.** 3.40. **D.** 5.00.

Question 9

Avogadro's constant is best defined as

A. the number of atoms in exactly 12 g of carbon.

B. the number of atoms in exactly 12 g of carbon-12.

C. one mole of carbon-12.

D. the mass of carbon-12 that contains one mole of atoms.

Families of organic compounds and polymers in society

Question 10

Which one of the following empirical formulas is most likely to be that of a carboxylic acid?

A. C_2H_4 **B.** C_2H_4Cl **C.** C_2H_4O **D.** C_2H_5O

Question 11

The number of carboxylic acids that are isomeric with pentanoic acid is/are

A. 1 **B.** 2 **C.** 3 **D.** 4

Question 12

The correct names for the semi-structural formulas $CH_3CH(CH_3)CH_2CH_3$ and $CH_3CH{=}CHCH_2CH_3$ are, respectively

A. 2–methylbutane and 3–pentene.

B. 2–methylbutane and 2–pentene.

C. 3–methylbutane and 3–pentene.

D. 3–methylbutane and 2–methylbutene.

Question 13

Polyvinyl alcohol is a polymer used to make coatings and in papermaking. A section of a polyvinyl alcohol molecule is shown below.

```
   OH  H   H   H   OH  H   H   H
   |   |   |   |   |   |   |   |
 — C — C — C — C — C — C — C — C —
   |   |   |   |   |   |   |   |
   H   H   OH  H   H   H   OH  H
```

Which one of the following statements about polyvinyl alcohol is incorrect?

A. Polyvinyl alcohol is a linear polymer made by addition polymerisation.

B. This polymer will be water soluble.

C. The monomer has the same empirical formula as the polymer.

D. A condensation reaction is used to make this polymer.

Question 14

Polyethene is a thermoplastic polymer. When polyethene is heated, which one of the following statements is **incorrect**?

A. Some intermolecular dispersion forces are overcome.

B. The polymer softens.

C. The -C-C- bonds in the polymer 'backbone' are overcome.

D. The tensile strength of the polymer decreases.

Question 15

Which one of the following is most likely to be made from a cross-linked polymer?

A. cling film **B.** a calculator case

C. supermarket carry bag **D.** a rope

Question 16

An elastomer is a rubbery material that can recover to its original shape after being stretched. An elastomer is most likely to be

A. a polymer which has a few covalent bonds between the chains.

B. an atactic polymer.

C. a polymer made from more than one monomer.

D. a polymer with little branching of its chains.

Question 17

The structure of part of a polymer is shown below.

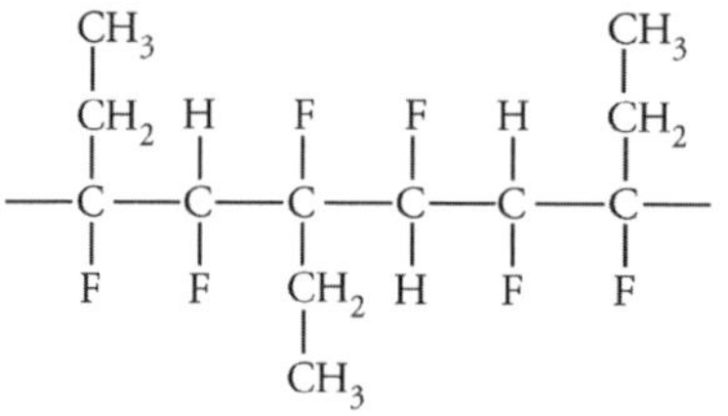

```
  CH3                        CH3
  |                          |
  CH2  H   F    F   H        CH2
  |    |   |    |   |        |
—-C----C---C----C---C--------C—-
  |    |   |    |   |        |
  F    F   CH2  H   F        F
           |
           CH3
```

Which one of the following statements about this polymer is correct?

A. Hydrogen bonding contributes to the attractive forces between the polymer chains.

B. The monomer used to make this polymer has the empirical formula C_2H_3F.

C. The structure of the monomer used to make this polymer is

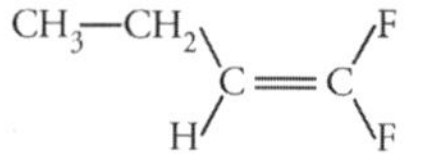

```
CH3—CH2       F
       \     /
        C = C
       /     \
      H       F
```

D. More than one monomer was used to make this polymer.

Question 18

The extensive production of non-biodegradable plastics has produced a problem in accumulation of waste plastic. With respect to atmospheric pollution, which one of the following would be the **least** satisfactory method of addressing this problem?

A. Incinerate the plastic.

B. Expose the plastic to sunlight.

C. Increase production of biodegradable plastics.

D. Utilise biomass rather than petrochemicals.

Question 19

Which one of the following is **not** an advantage of using a polymer?

A. Polymers are lightweight and easily molded.

B. Polymers are good thermal and electrical insulators.

C. Polymers burn easily.

D. Polymers are corrosion resistant and chemically inert.

Section B

Quantifying atoms and compounds

Question 1

A diagram of a mass spectrometer is shown below. Three of the regions have been labelled A, B and C. A sample of dichloromethane, CH_2Cl_2, is injected into the injection port.

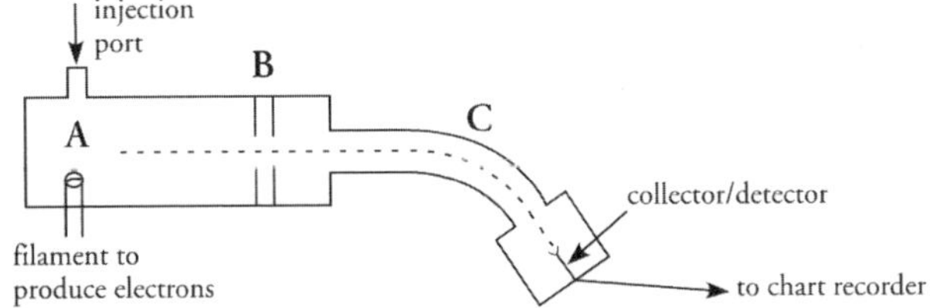

(a) Describe what happens to the particles at each of the regions A, B and C. (3 marks)

Part of the mass spectrum of dichloromethane, CH_2Cl_2, is shown in the diagram below. The most common atoms found in dichloromethane are ^{12}C, ^{1}H and two isotopes of chlorine, ^{35}Cl and ^{37}Cl.

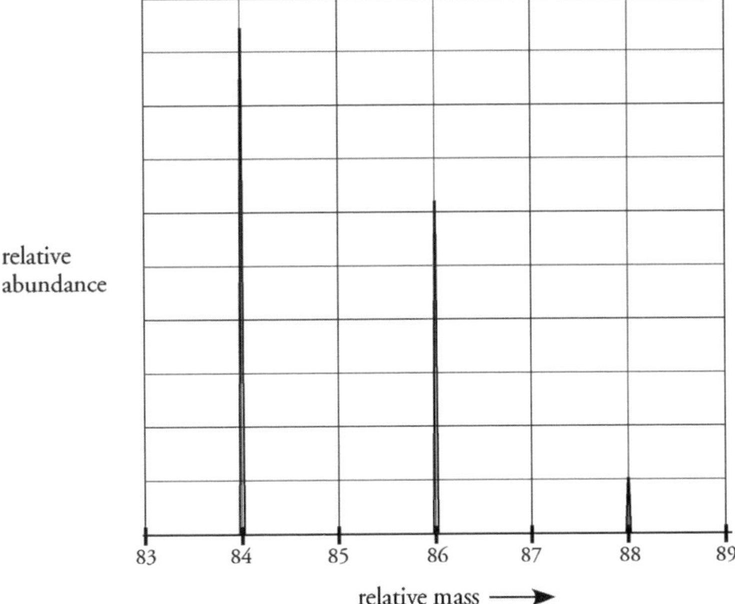

(b) If the line at 84 mass units is caused by the ion $^{12}C(^{1}H)_2(^{35}Cl)_2^{+}$, suggest possible formulas for the ions with mass units of 86 and 88. (2 marks)

(c) If the percentage abundance of ^{35}Cl is 75.53% and that of ^{37}Cl is 24.47%, explain why the peaks in the spectrum are different heights. (2 marks)

(Total = 7 marks)

Question 2

A scientist determines a value for Avogadro's constant by the following method. Using a Geiger counter the scientist measures the number of particles emitted by a sample of radium in one second and obtains a value of 6.2×10^{10}. Each particle is converted into an atom of helium. The helium is collected and after 10 days the mass of helium is 3.68×10^{-7} g. Use the scientist's results to calculate a value for Avogadro's constant. (Total = 4 marks)

Question 3

(a) Determine the relative formula mass of the mineral malachite, $Cu_2CO_3(OH)_2$ (1 mark)

(b) What is the percentage composition of copper (Cu) in malachite? (2 marks)

(c) What mass of copper could be obtained from 500 kg of malachite? (3 marks)

(Total = 6 marks)

Question 4

A student determines the formula of copper oxide by the following method. 0.256 g of copper oxide was dissolved in 50 mL of dilute sulfuric acid. Small amounts of zinc were added until the blue colour of copper sulfate completely disappeared and all of the copper had been formed. The copper solid was collected washed and dried. The mass of copper was 0.203 g. Use these results to determine the empirical formula of copper oxide. (Total = 3 marks)

Families of organic compounds and polymers in society

Question 5

Give the correct names for the following semi-structural formulas.

(a) $CH_3CH_2CH(CH_3)CH_2CH_2CH_3$

(b) $CH_3C(CH_3)_2CH{=}CH_2$

(c) CH_3OH

(d) $CH_3CH(CH_3)CH_2CH_2CH_2OH$

(e) CH_3COOH (Total = 5 × 1 = 5 marks)

Question 6

Give the correct names for the following organic molecules.

(a)

```
     H    H    H    H
     |    |    |    |
 H — C —  C —  C —  C — H
     |    |    |    |
     H    H    H    H
```

(b)

```
           H
        H  |  H
         \ | /
      H    C    H       H
      |    |    |      /
  H — C —  C —  C — O
      |    |    |
      H    H    H
```

(c)

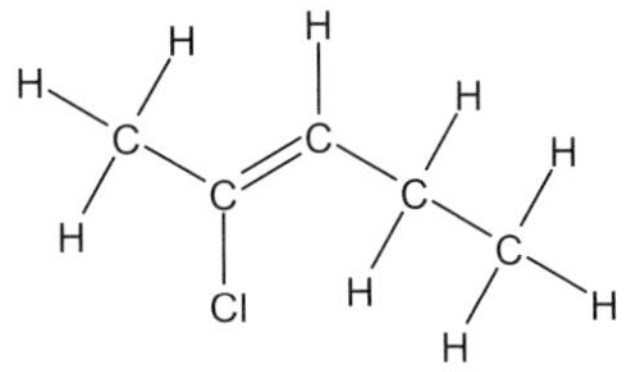

(d)

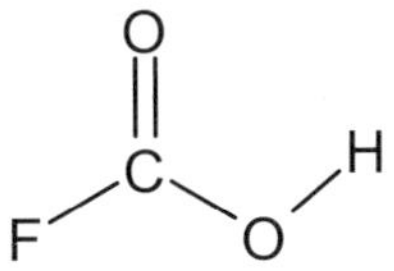

(Total = 4 × 1 = 4 marks)

Question 7

For the following names give the correct semi-structural formula.

(a) 2,2-dimethylpentane
(b) ethene
(c) 2-methylhex-3-yne
(d) 2,3-dichlorobutan-2-ol
(e) pentanoic acid

(Total = 5 × 1 = 5 marks)

Question 8

The following molecules have all been used as monomers to prepare useful polymers.

$CH_2{=}CCl_2$

In each case, draw a section of the polymer that would result when the monomer is polymerised. Use three monomer units of each in your answer. (2 marks)

Question 9

Part of the structure of a polymer is shown below.

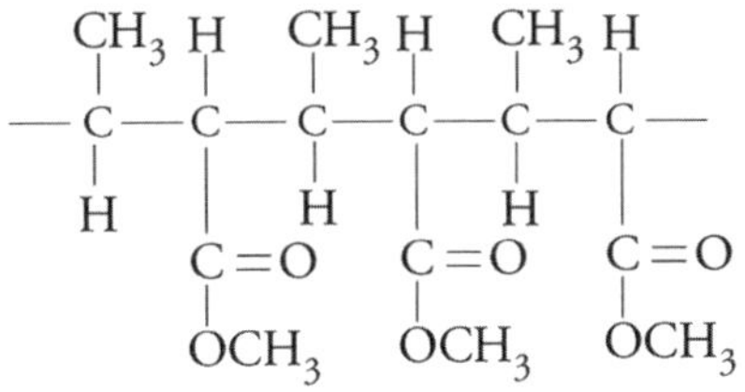

Draw the monomer used to make the polymer. (2 marks)

Question 10

A sample of low density polyethene (LDPE) has an average molar mass of 80 000 g mol^{-1} and a sample of high density polyethene (HDPE) has an average molar mass of 400 000 g mol^{-1}.

(a) Why is the molar mass of a polymer given as an average? (1 mark)

(b) When HDPE and LDPE are compared, how are the following properties likely to vary?

(i) melting temperatures
(ii) hardness
(iii) amount of branching
(iv) average chain length

(5 marks)

(Total = 6 marks)

Chapter 3

Unit 1 Examination

Section A

Question 1

Which one of the following elements has the lowest electronegativity?

A. lithium
B. oxygen
C. boron
D. carbon

Question 2

The number of neutrons and electrons in the ion $^{79}Se^{2-}$ is

A. 34 neutrons, 36 electrons.
B. 45 neutrons, 47 electrons.
C. 45 neutrons, 36 electrons.
D. 45 neutrons 34 electrons.

Question 3

Which one of the following electron configurations is that of a transition metal?

A. $1s^22s^22p^63s^23p^6$
B. $1s^22s^22p^63s^23p^63d^{10}4s^24p^5$
C. $1s^22s^22p^63s^23p^2$
D. $1s^22s^22p^63s^23p^63d^74s^2$

Question 4

Which of the following has the greatest mass?

A. 60 g of zinc
B. 6.0 moles of copper
C. 4.0×10^{22} molecules of oxygen
D. 2.4×10^{23} atoms of mercury

Question 5

Which pair of elements can react together to form an ionic compound?

A. carbon and silicon
B. calcium and iodine
C. sodium and potassium
D. hydrogen and bromine

Question 6

Which one of the following molecules does **not** contain a double bond?

A. oxygen, O_2
B. ethene, C_2H_4
C. hydrogen cyanide, HCN
D. sulfur dioxide, SO_2

Question 7

Which of the following molecules is polar?

A. $CHCl_3$. **B.** CF_4. **C.** Br_2. **D.** CO_2.

Question 8

The group 17 elements show a change in physical state at room temperature from fluorine (gas) to bromine (liquid) to iodine (solid). This is explained by increasing strength of the

A. covalent bonds within molecules.
B. covalent bonds between molecules.
C. dispersion forces within molecules.
D. dispersion forces between molecules.

Question 9

For which one of the following molecular formulae is only one isomer possible?

A. C_4H_8 **B.** CH_2Cl_2 **C.** C_3H_7OH **D.** $C_2H_4O_2$

Question 10

Which of the following compounds has the least hydrogen atoms per molecule?

A. butene **B.** butane
C. 2-methylbutane **D.** pentene

Question 11

Which of the following is the empirical formula of ethanoic acid?

A. CH_3COOH **B.** $C_2H_4O_2$
C. CH_2O **D.** $CH_3-C(=O)-O-H$

Question 12

Naturally occurring rhenium consists of two isotopes, ^{185}Re and ^{187}Re, with relative isotopic masses 184.95 and 186.96 respectively. If the relative atomic mass of rhenium is 186.21, then the percentage of the heavier isotope is closest to

A. 80% **B.** 60% **C.** 40% **D.** 20%

Question 13

From which ore would it be most difficult to extract the metal (because it contains the most reactive metal)?

A. Fe_3O_4 **B.** ZnS **C.** $CuFeS_2$ **D.** Al_2O_3

Question 14

Which of the following is a structural isomer of ethanoic acid?

A. CH_3CH_2OH
B. $CH(OH)CH(OH)$
C. CH_3CH_2COOH
D. CH_2CH_2

Question 15

Which one of the following is **not** expected to increase the strength of a polymer?

A. increasing the degree of crystallinity
B. increasing the percentage of cross links
C. increasing the amount of branching
D. increasing the average chain length

Question 16

The bonding and structures of the four materials iron, graphite, fullerene C_{60} and potassium bromide are

	Iron	**Graphite**	**C_{60}**	**Potassium bromide**
A.	metallic giant structure	covalent giant structure	covalent molecular	ionic giant structure
B.	covalent giant structure	metallic giant structure	metallic molecular	covalent molecular
C.	metallic molecular	covalent molecular	covalent giant structure	metallic giant structure
D.	metallic giant structure	metallic giant structure	covalent molecular	ionic molecular

Question 17

In which one of the following lists are the metals in the correct order of reactivity (from lowest to highest)?

A. copper < silver < iron < magnesium
B. iron < nickel < sodium < zinc
C. gold < zinc < iron < sodium
D. mercury < copper < zinc < sodium

Question 18

When the properties of diamond and graphite are compared it is found that graphite

A. is harder and has a higher density.
B. is a poorer conductor of heat and electricity.
C. is better for cutting rocks.
D. is softer and has a higher melting temperature.

Question 19

A scientist adds 2.540 g of iodine to 2.298 g of indium and heats the mixture in a solvent until all of the iodine has reacted. The remaining indium is washed, dried and weighed. 1.532 g of indium remains. The empirical formula of indium iodide is

A. InI **B.** In_3I_2 **C.** In_2I_3 **D.** InI_3

Question 20

Which one of the following methods would be least suitable for use in preventing the corrosion of iron?

A. painting
B. plating with an unreactive metal
C. formation of a surface layer of an oxide of iron
D. sacrificial oxidation of another metal in contact with the iron; e.g. magnesium

Section B

Question 1

The relative atomic mass of sodium is 23.0 and its melting temperature is 98°C. However, chlorine, which has a higher relative atomic mass (35.5), melts at –101°C.

(a) Describe the nature of the bonding in solid sodium and solid chlorine. (2 marks)

(b) In terms of the bonding described in part (a), give an explanation for the difference in the two melting temperatures. (2 marks)

When sodium and chlorine are mixed, a reaction occurs and sodium chloride is formed. The melting temperature of sodium chloride is 801°C.

(c) Use an electron transfer diagram to explain the formation of sodium chloride from sodium and chlorine atoms. (2 marks)

(d) Describe the nature of the bonding in solid sodium chloride and account for the high melting temperature of this compound. (2 marks)

(Total = 8 marks)

Question 2

Choose an element or elements from period 2 of the periodic table to answer the following questions.

(a) Write the formula of an ionic compound. (1 mark)

(b) (i) Write the formula of a covalent molecular compound. (1 mark)

(ii) Draw the valence structure of the molecule in part (b)(i) and state whether the molecule is polar or non-polar. (2 marks)

(c) (i) Name an element which exists as a monatomic gas and an element which exists as a diatomic gas.

(ii) Explain why one gas is monatomic and the other diatomic.

(2 + 2 = 4 marks)

(d) (i) Name the element in period two with the least number of electrons.

(ii) Name the element with the smallest atomic radius.

(iii) Explain why your answers are the same or why they differ.

(1 + 1 + 2 = 4 marks)

(Total = 12 marks)

Question 3

But-1-ene, butane and 1-propanol have the molar masses and boiling temperatures given in the table below.

		Molar mass (g mol^{-1})	Boiling temperature (°C)
But-1-ene	C_4H_8	56	–6.3
Butane	C_4H_{10}	58	–0.5
1-propanol	C_3H_7OH	60	97.2

(a) Explain the similar boiling points of but-1-ene and butane. (2 marks)

(b) Explain why the boiling points of butane and 1-propanol which might have been expected to be similar are very different. (2 marks)

(c) Explain why 1-propanol is soluble in water but but-1-ene and butane are not. (2 marks)

(Total = 6 marks)

Question 4

2.167 g of a compound of carbon, hydrogen and oxygen is completely burnt in oxygen. 4.761 g of carbon dioxide and 2.605 g of water are formed.

(a) Calculate the percentage composition of the compound. (3 marks)

(b) Calculate the empirical formula of the compound. (2 marks)

(c) The molecular formula of this compound must be the same as its empirical formula. Suggest a reason for this. (1 mark)

(d) To which homologous series does the compound belong? (1 mark)

(e) Draw the structural formulas for two isomers with this formula. (2 marks)

(Total = 9 marks)

Question 5

Calculate the percentage composition of each element within iron(III) sulfate. (3 marks)

Question 6

Naturally occurring magnesium consists of three isotopes, ^{24}Mg, ^{25}Mg and ^{26}Mg, with relative isotopic masses of 23.985, 24.986 and 25.983, respectively. If the relative atomic mass of magnesium is 24.305 and the percentage abundance of the ^{25}Mg isotope is 10.00%, calculate the percentage abundances of the other two isotopes. (4 marks)

Question 7

Four substances, I, II, III and IV, have the properties given in the table below. Identify them as either covalent network, ionic, metallic or covalent molecular materials.

I	Hard, high melting point, brittle, crystalline, only conducts electricity when in solution or molten.
II	Solid which sublimes, non-conductor of electricity, insoluble in water.
III	Hard, high melting point, crystalline, non-conductor, insoluble in water, does not melt.
IV	Fairly hard, high melting point, malleable, solid conducts electricity, insoluble in water.

(4 marks)

Question 8

Propene, $CH_3CH{=}CH_2$ can be used to produce polypropene and vinyl alcohol, $CH_2{=}CHOH$ can be converted into polyvinyl alcohol.

(a) Draw a small section of each polymer (use three monomers in each polymer). (2 marks)

(b) The melting temperatures of the two polymers are 176°C for polypropene and 230°C for polyvinyl alcohol. If the average chain length is approximately the same for the two polymers suggest a reason for the difference in melting temperatures. (2 marks)

(Total = 4 marks)

Question 9

Draw the structural formulas of the below molecules.

(a) 2,2,3-trimethylheptane

(b) 2-methylbutan-2-ol

(c) 2-chloro-3-methylbutanoic acid

(Total = 1 + 1 + 1 = 3 marks)

Question 10

Give the correct names for the following semi-structural formulas.

(a) H_3C \ CH / CH_2—CH_2 \ CH—CH_3
with the first CH bonded to CH_3 below, and the second CH bonded to H_3C—CH_2 below

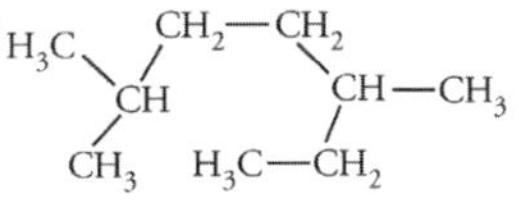

(b) CH_3CH_2 \ CH—CH$=$C / CH_3 \ CH_2
with CH bonded to CH_3 below, and CH_2 bonded to H_3C—CH_2 below

(c) CH_3CH_2 above CH_2—C≡C—CH, with CH bonded to CH_3 above and CH_2—CH_3 below

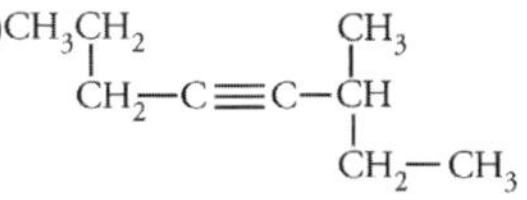

(d) CH_3CH_2—C—CH_3, with C bonded to CH_2—CH_3 above and COOH below

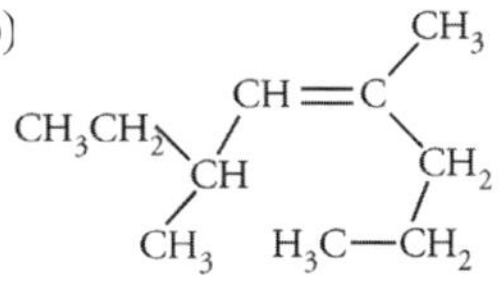

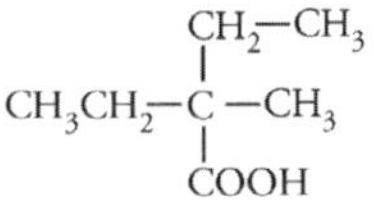

(Total = 1 + 1 + 1 + 1 = 4 marks)

Chapter 4

Unit 2 Area of Study 1 – How do chemicals interact with water?

Multiple choice items

Water as a unique chemical

The following information refers to Questions 1 and 2.

The boiling temperatures of the group 14 and group 16 hydrides are shown in the graph below.

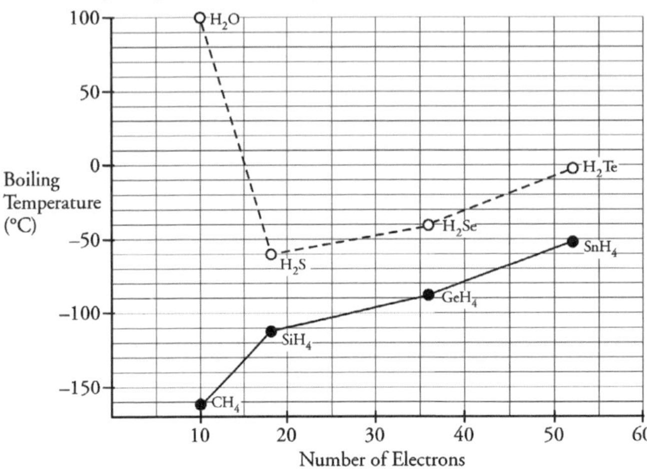

Question 1

Which one of the following statements best explains the anomalous boiling temperature of water?

A. The dispersion forces between water molecules are greater than for the other substances.

B. The hydrogen bonds between the water molecules are stronger than the intermolecular forces in the other substances.

C. There are hydrogen bonds between the water molecules but only dispersion forces between the molecules of the other substances.

D. The dipole-dipole bonding in the other substances is not as strong as the hydrogen bonding between the water molecules.

Question 2

Which one of the following statements best explains the difference in boiling temperatures of GeH_4 and H_2Se?

A. The hydrogen bonding is stronger in H_2Se than in GeH_4.

B. The dispersion forces are stronger in H_2Se than in GeH_4.

C. The dispersion forces are similar in H_2Se and GeH_4 but the hydrogen bonding is greater in H_2Se.

D. The dispersion forces are similar in H_2Se and GeH_4 but there are dipole-dipole attractions between molecules of H_2Se.

Question 3
Which one of the following compounds is expected to have the lowest melting temperature?

A. H_2O **B.** H_2S **C.** H_2Se **D.** H_2Te

Question 4
The water molecule has

A. polar bonds and is a polar molecule.
B. polar bonds but is a non-polar molecule.
C. non-polar bonds and is a non-polar molecule.
D. non-polar bonds but is a polar molecule.

Question 5
The types of chemical bonding present in ice are

A. covalent, ion-dipole and dispersion forces.
B. covalent, hydrogen bonding and dispersion forces.
C. covalent, ion-dipole and hydrogen bonding.
D. ion-dipole, hydrogen bonding and dispersion forces.

Question 6
When ice melts the chemical bonding which is partially overcome is

A. dispersion forces and hydrogen bonding.
B. hydrogen bonding only.
C. dispersion forces and covalent bonding.
D. dispersion forces only.

Question 7
Methane, CH_4, ammonia, NH_3, water, H_2O, and hydrogen fluoride, HF, have similar relative masses but the boiling point of methane is much lower than that of the other compounds. Which one of the following contributing reasons for this is **incorrect**?

A. Only ammonia, water and hydrogen fluoride have hydrogen bonding between molecules.
B. Only methane is a non-polar molecule.
C. Only methane has intermolecular dispersion forces.
D. The electronegativity of carbon is less than that of nitrogen, oxygen and fluorine.

Question 8
Which one of the statements below about the properties of water is **incorrect**?

A. Water has its greatest density at 4°C.
B. The freezing and boiling points of water decrease when solutes are dissolved in it.
C. The boiling point of water varies according to the air pressure.
D. Substances which absorb water from the atmosphere are said to be hygroscopic.

Question 9
The density of water at 0°C formed from melting ice is

A. the same as that of ice at 0°C.
B. lower than that of ice at 0°C.
C. higher than that of ice at 0°C.
D. may be higher or lower than that of ice at 0°C.

Question 10

Water is vital for plants and animals to live. Which one of the following properties of water is the **least** important for the processes that occur in plants and animals?

A. Water is a colourless and odourless compound.

B. Many substances will dissolve in water.

C. The heat of vaporisation of water is high compared with substances of similar molecular size.

D. Water can be a reactant in many chemical reactions.

Question 11

The boiling temperatures of the hydrides of the elements of group 15 (group V) are shown in the graph below.

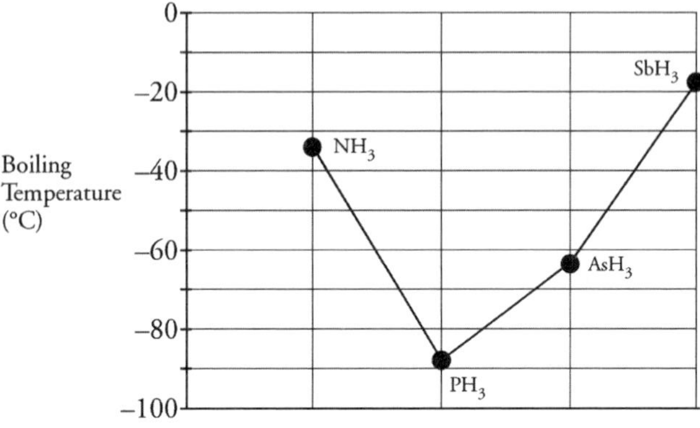

When compared to the other hydrides from this group ammonia, NH_3, has a much higher boiling temperature than expected. Which one of the following statements best explains this observation?

A. Although the substances have similar formulae, ammonia is the only molecule with eight electrons in the outer shell.

B. There is hydrogen bonding between ammonia molecules but not between molecules of the other substances.

C. Ammonia is the only molecule that is pyramidal.

D. All four molecules are polar but there are greater dispersion forces between the ammonia molecules.

Question 12

When water is compared with other substances whose molecules are about the same size as water molecules it is found that water has a higher latent heat of vaporisation. This can be explained by water molecules having

A. stronger covalent bonds within the molecules.

B. stronger dispersion forces between the molecules.

C. two non-bonding electron pairs per molecule.

D. hydrogen bonding between the molecules.

Question 13

When water at its boiling point changes into steam, energy is

A. absorbed and the temperature remains constant.
B. released and the temperature remains constant.
C. absorbed and the temperature increases.
D. released and the temperature decreases.

Question 14

The specific heat capacity of ethanol is 2.44 J g^{-1} °C^{-1} and that of water is 4.18 J g^{-1} °C^{-1}. If 100 g of ethanol and 100 g of water at the same temperature and under the same conditions are each given the same amount of heat energy the temperature of

A. both liquids will increase by the same amount.
B. ethanol will be higher.
C. water will be higher.
D. both liquids will decrease by the same amount.

Question 15

Ice at –10°C is placed in a beaker and is slowly heated. When the temperature reaches 0°C the ice starts to melt. The temperature remains constant at 0°C until all of the ice has melted. Which one of the following statements is correct?

A. The ice has a higher density than the water and floats.
B. All of the heat energy is used to increase the kinetic energy of the molecules.
C. The covalent bonds within the molecules are being broken.
D. The heat energy breaks some of the hydrogen bonds between the molecules.

Acid–base (proton transfer) reactions

The following information applies to Questions 16 to 18.

The equation for the reaction of hydrogen cyanide with water is

$HCN(aq) + H_2O(l) \rightleftharpoons H_3O^+(aq) + CN^-(aq)$

Question 16

The proton donors is/are

A. HCN and H_3O^+ **B.** H_2O and CN^-
C. HCN only **D.** CN^- only

Question 17

An acid-base conjugate pair is

A. HCN/H_3O^+ **B.** H_2O/CN^-
C. HCN/CN^- **D.** H_3O^+/CN^-

Question 18

The reversible arrow '$\rightleftharpoons$' indicates that

A. there are equal concentrations of reactant and product particles.

B. not all the HCN molecules are ionised to CN^-.

C. all the HCN molecules are ionised to CN^-.

D. HCN is acting as an acid and as a base.

Question 19

In which one of the following lists are all the substances acidic?

A. baking powder, laundry detergent, oven cleaner

B. coffee, deionised water, oil

C. sea water, wine, indigestion tablets

D. vinegar, lemon juice, soda water

Question 20

Four properties of materials are given below.

I. change the colour of indicators

II. low pH

III. sour taste

IV. 'soapy' feeling on skin

Which of the above are typical properties of an acid?

A. I, II and III **B.** I, II and IV

C. II, III and IV **D.** I, III and IV

Question 21

In a neutral aqueous solution of sodium chloride, the chemical species present are

A. Na^+ ions, Cl^- ions and H_2O molecules only.

B. Na^+ ions, Cl^- ions, H_2O molecules and equal concentrations of H_3O^+ ions and OH^- ions.

C. Na^+ ions, Cl^- ions, H_2O molecules and a greater concentration of H_3O^+ ions than OH^- ions.

D. Na^+ ions, Cl^- ions, H_2O molecules and a smaller concentration of H_3O^+ ions than OH^- ions.

Question 22

Which one of the following lists places the scientists in correct chronological order for their work on acids and bases?

A. Lavoisier, Davy, Arrhenius, Brønsted and Lowry

B. Brønsted and Lowry, Arrhenius, Davy, Lavoisier

C. Lavoisier, Arrhenius, Davy, Brønsted and Lowry

D. Davy, Lavoisier, Arrhenius, Brønsted and Lowry

Question 23

When sulfur dioxide, SO_2, and sulfur trioxide, SO_3, dissolve in water

A. both gases form sulfurous acid, H_2SO_3.

B. sulfur dioxide forms sulfuric acid and sulfur trioxide forms sulfurous acid.

C. both gases form sulfuric acid, H_2SO_4.

D. sulfur dioxide forms sulfurous acid and sulfur trioxide forms sulfuric acid.

Question 24

Which of the following chemical species is amphiprotic?

A. H_3O^+ **B.** H_2SO_4 **C.** $H_2PO_4^-$ **D.** PO_4^{3-}

Question 25

Which of the following is a polyprotic acid?

A. CH_3COOH **B.** NH_3

C. $Al(OH)_3$ **D.** H_3BO_3

Question 26

Aqueous solutions of phosphoric acid contain the following species:

I H_3PO_4 II $H_2PO_4^-$ III HPO_4^{2-} IV PO_4^{3-}

Which of these species are amphiprotic?

A. I, II and III

B. I and II

C. IV

D. II and III

Question 27

Four reactions involving water are given below.

I. $HNO_2(aq) + H_2O(l) \rightleftharpoons H_3O^+(aq) + NO_2^-(aq)$

II. $HF(aq) + H_2O(l) \rightleftharpoons H_3O^+(aq) + F^-(aq)$

III. $PH_3(aq) + H_2O(l) \rightleftharpoons PH_4^+(aq) + OH^-(aq)$

IV. $2H_2O(l) + 2NaH(s) \rightarrow 2NaOH(aq) + H_2(g)$

In which of the above reactions does water act as an acid?

A. I and II **B.** III

C. III and IV **D.** IV

Question 28

Balanced equations for four reactions are shown below.

I. $H_2(g) + Cl_2(g) \rightarrow 2HCl(g)$

II. $NH_3(g) + HCl(g) \rightarrow NH_4Cl(s)$

III. $2H_2O_2(aq) \rightarrow 2H_2O(l) + O_2(g)$

IV. $2HCO_3^-(aq) \rightarrow CO_3^{2-}(aq) + HC_2O_3(aq)$

Which of the above reactions are Brønsted–Lowry acid-base reactions?

A. II **B.** II and IV

C. I, III and IV **D.** III

Question 29

Below are four reactions involving acids. Which one contains a species acting as a diprotic acid?

A. $H_2PO_4^-(aq) + 2OH^-(aq) \rightarrow PO_4^{3-}(aq) + 2H_2O(l)$

B. $2HCl(aq) + Ba(OH)_2(aq) \rightarrow BaCl_2(aq) + 2H_2O(l)$

C. $2HCOOH(aq) + Mg(OH)_2(s) \rightarrow Mg(HCOO)_2(aq) + 2H_2O(l)$

D. $H_3PO_4(aq) + 3KOH(aq) \rightarrow K_3PO_4(aq) + 3H_2O(l)$

Question 30

Below are four statements about indicators.

I. Indicators are acids or their conjugate bases.

II. Indicators change colour at various pH values.

III. All indicators are red at low pH.

IV. Indicators may be a mixture of several compounds.

Which of the above statements are correct?

A. I, II and III **B.** I, II and IV

C. II, III and IV **D.** I, III and IV

Question 31

What is the pH at 25°C of a 0.050 M solution of a strong triprotic acid?

A. 0.050 **B.** 0.15 **C.** 0.82 **D.** 1.3

Question 32

The pH of an exactly 0.0001 M barium hydroxide solution at 25°C is

A. 10.3. **B.** 10.0 **C.** 4.00 **D.** 3.70

Question 33

A sample of rainwater has a pH of 6.2. The concentrations of hydronium ions, H_3O^+, and hydroxide ions, OH^-, in mol L^{-1} are respectively,

A. $10^{-6.2}$ and 0. **B.** 6.2 and 7.8.

C. $10^{-6.2}$ and $10^{-7.8}$. **D.** $10^{-7.8}$ and $10^{-6.2}$.

Question 34

The colours and pH ranges for a number of indicators are shown in the diagram below. The numbers indicate the pH range over which the indicator changes colour; for example, congo red changes from blue to red when the pH changes from 3.0 to 5.0.

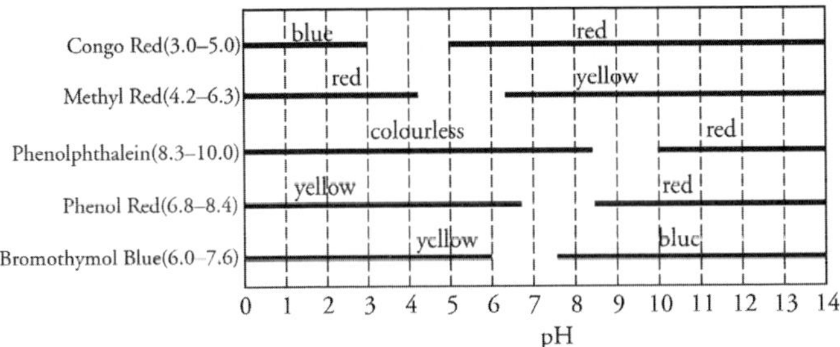

Equal volumes of two indicators are mixed together. Which combination of indicators would be orange at pH 6.5?

A. congo red and phenol red
B. methyl red and phenol red
C. methyl red and phenolphthalein
D. congo red and bromothymol blue

Question 35

The pH of some common substances is given in the diagram below.

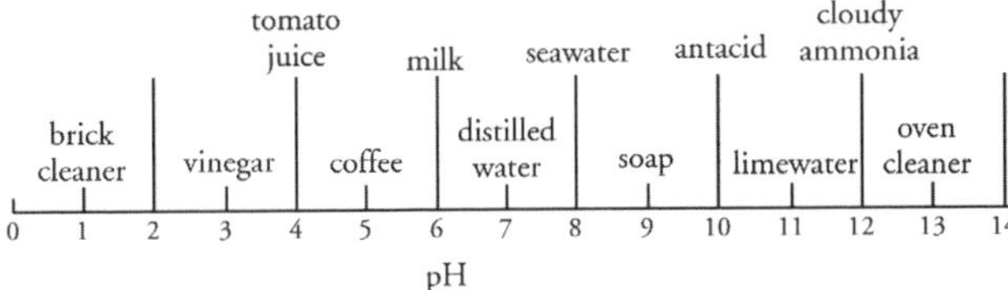

Four students were asked to compare the hydrogen ion concentration, $[H^+]$, of pairs of solutions. Their statements were

Student 1: 'In vinegar $[H^+]$ is four times greater than in cloudy ammonia.'

Student 2: 'The $[H^+]$ is twice as large in antacid as it is in coffee.'

Student 3: 'In soap $[H^+]$ is 10 000 times greater than in oven cleaner.'

Student 4: 'The $[H^+]$ is 1000 times larger in tomato juice than in brick cleaner.'

Which student's statement is correct?

A. Student 1 **B.** Student 2 **C.** Student 3 **D.** Student 4

Question 36

Which one of the following aqueous solutions will have a pH of less than 7?

A. sodium hydroxide
B. potassium chloride
C. ammonium chloride
D. sodium nitrate

Question 37

The partial equation for the reaction of calcium carbonate with sulfuric acid is given below.

$CaCO_3(s) + H_2SO_4(aq) \rightarrow CaSO_4(s) + X + Y$

The products X and Y are

A. CO_2 and H_2O **B.** CO_2 and H_2O_2
C. CO and H_2O **D.** CO_2 and H_2

Question 38

Hydrogen gas is most likely to be produced when a dilute acid is reacted with

A. a metal hydroxide. **B.** a metal hydrogen carbonate.
C. a metal. **D.** a metal carbonate.

Question 39

Which one of the following correctly identifies the gas or gases produced when hydrochloric acid is reacted with either zinc, or sodium hydroxide, or sodium carbonate or sodium hydrogen carbonate?

	Zinc	**Sodium hydroxide**	**Sodium carbonate**	**Sodium hydrogen carbonate**
A.	No gas produced	Hydrogen	Carbon dioxide	Carbon dioxide
B.	Hydrogen	Hydrogen	Carbon dioxide	Carbon dioxide and hydrogen
C.	Carbon dioxide	Carbon dioxide	Hydrogen	No gas produced
D.	Hydrogen	No gas produced	Carbon dioxide	Carbon dioxide

Question 40

Acids and bases are potentially dangerous chemicals and should be handled with care. Which one of the following is the most appropriate method of dealing with a spill of about 10 mL of a strong concentrated acid?

A. Wipe up the acid with a handheld sponge.
B. Pour sodium hydroxide solution onto the spill.
C. Sprinkle sodium hydrogen carbonate powder carefully onto the spill.
D. Pour a large volume of water onto the spilt acid to dilute it.

Question 41

A number of gases are released into the atmosphere by human activity. Some of these will increase the acidity of rainwater. Which one of the following gases is not likely to have this effect?

A. CO_2 **B.** NO_2 **C.** SO_2 **D.** CO

Redox (electron transfer) reactions

Question 42

In the redox reaction shown in the equation below, gold is displaced from a solution of its ions by magnesium atoms.

$2Au^{3+}(aq) + 3Mg(s) \rightarrow 2Au(s) + 3Mg^{2+}(aq)$

Electrons move from

A. gold ions to magnesium atoms and gold ions are reduced.
B. gold ions to magnesium atoms and gold ions are oxidised.
C. magnesium atoms to gold ions and gold ions are reduced.
D. magnesium atoms to gold ions and gold ions are oxidised.

Question 43

In which position in the electrochemical series would chemical species that attract electrons most strongly be found?

A. top left
B. top right
C. lower left
D. lower right

Question 44

The balanced equation for the reaction of magnesium with hydrochloric acid is

$Mg(s) + 2HCl(aq) \rightarrow MgCl_2(aq) + H_2(g)$

This reaction is best classified as

A. redox.
B. acid-base.
C. both acid-base and redox.
D. neither acid-base nor redox.

The following information refers to Questions 45 and 46.

One of the first small-scale energy devices was the Daniel cell. The reaction providing the energy for the cell is

$Cu^{2+}(aq) + Zn(s) \rightarrow Cu(s) + Zn^{2+}(aq)$

Question 45

In the above reaction, a conjugate redox pair is

A. Cu and Zn.
B. Cu^{2+} and Zn^{2+}.
C. Cu^{2+} and Cu.
D. Cu^{2+} and Zn.

Question 46

The half-equation for the reduction process is

A. $Cu^{2+}(aq) + 2e^- \rightarrow Cu(s)$
B. $Zn(s) \rightarrow Zn^{2+}(aq) + 2e^-$
C. $Zn(s) + 2e^- \rightarrow Zn^{2+}(aq)$
D. $Cu^{2+}(aq) \rightarrow Cu(s) + 2e^-$

Question 47

A piece of steel plate is placed in each of four separate containers, each containing a different 0.25 mol L^{-1} aqueous solution. The four solutions are $Pb(NO_3)_2(aq)$, $Zn(NO_3)_2(aq)$, $AgNO_3(aq)$ and $Cu(NO_3)_2(aq)$. It is expected that the piece of steel will be coated with another metal in the solutions of

A. $Pb(NO_3)_2$, $AgNO_3$ and $Cu(NO_3)_2$.
B. $Pb(NO_3)_2$ and $AgNO_3$.
C. $AgNO_3$ and $Cu(NO_3)_2$.
D. $Zn(NO_3)_2$ only.

Question 48

Three metals, R, S and T, have the following properties:

- Metal R does not react with 1 mol L^{-1} H_2SO_4.
- Metal S will react with 1 mol L^{-1} H_2SO_4 to produce H_2, and also reacts with 1 mol L^{-1} RCl_2 solution to produce R.
- Metal T will react with 1 mol L^{-1} H_2SO_4 to produce H_2 but does not react with 1 mol L^{-1} SCl_2 solution.

From this information, the order of reactivity of the metals and H_2, from the highest to the lowest, is

A. $R > H_2 > T > S$ **B.** $H_2 > R > T > S$
C. $S > H_2 > T > R$ **D.** $S > T > H_2 > R$

Question 49

A student investigated the relative activity of the metals Q, R and T by performing three experiments. In each experiment a piece of metal was placed in a solution containing the ions of one of the other metals. The diagrams below show the results of the experiments.

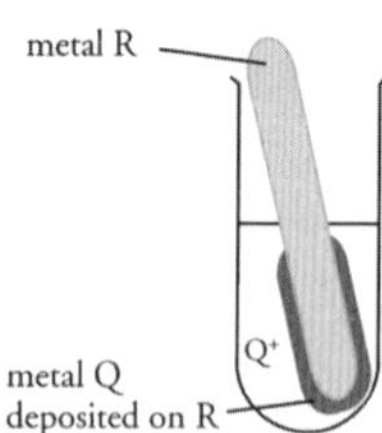

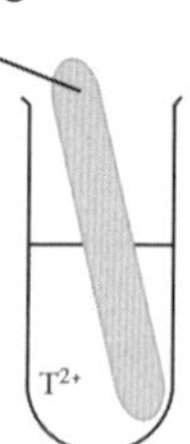

From these results the student determined that the relative activity of the metals was

A. $Q > T > R$ **B.** $R > Q > T$
C. $T > Q > R$ **D.** $T > R > Q$

Question 50

The reductant/oxidant strength of an element depends on its position in the periodic table. Which one of the following elements would be expected to be the strongest reductant?

A. bromine **B.** copper **C.** potassium **D.** zinc

Question 51

Which one of the following metals forms an impervious protective oxide coating in air?

A. iron **B.** aluminium **C.** gold **D.** sodium

Extended response questions

Water as a unique chemical

Question 1

The boiling temperatures of the hydrides of the group 16 elements are:

H_2O 100°C, H_2S –60°C, H_2Se –41°C, H_2Te –2°C.

Explain this trend in the boiling temperatures. (4 marks)

Question 2

For each of the properties of water listed below:

(a) Explain why water has this property.

(b) Describe the importance of the property to life on Earth.

Property 1	Water expands on freezing so that the density of ice is less than that of liquid water.	(2 marks)
Property 2	Water has a high specific heat value.	(2 marks)
Property 3	Water is an excellent solvent.	(2 marks)

(Total = 6 marks)

Question 3

By using of the physical properties of water, explain the following observations.

(a) Water is the preferred liquid used in the radiators of cars. (2 marks)

(b) Fish can live in ponds, lakes and rivers during winter even in countries where the winters are very cold. (2 marks)

(c) Salt contamination of farmland is a major problem in some parts of Australia. (2 marks)

(Total = 6 marks)

Question 4

A heater supplies energy to a block of ice at a constant rate. The ice weighs 18.0 g and is initially at –20°C. The temperature of the ice is monitored every 30 seconds until it has all melted. The resulting water is heated by the same heater until it boils. The water is then heated until it has all vaporised. The time taken to vaporise all of the water is 29.33 minutes. A graph of temperature against time for part of the heating process is produced on the next page.

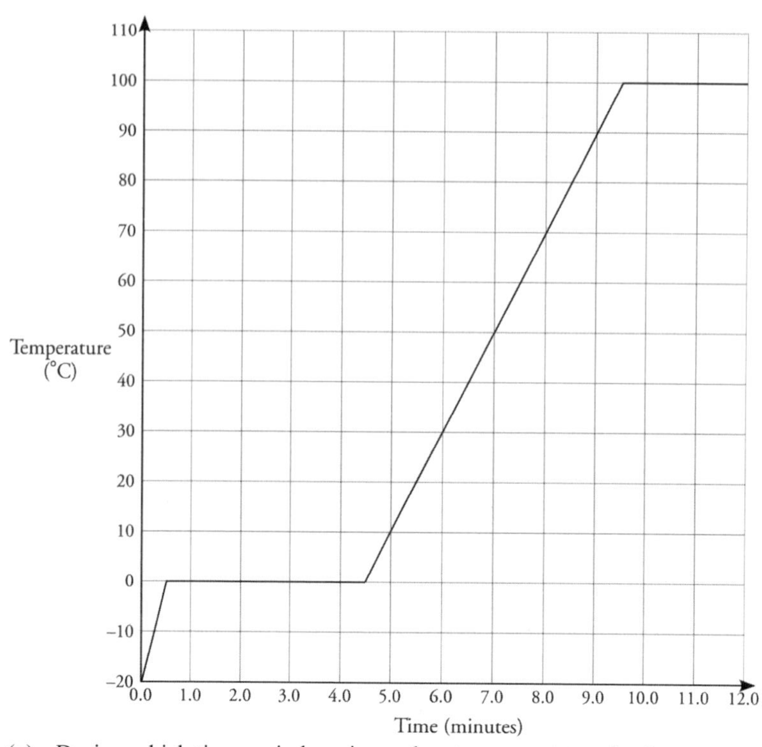

(a) During which time period are ice and water present together? (1 mark)

(b) If the specific heat capacity (specific heat) of water is 4.18 J g^{-1} K^{-1}, calculate the energy, in kJ, used to heat the water from 0°C to 100°C. (2 marks)

(c) Use your answer from part (b) and information from the graph to calculate how much energy, in kJ, the heater delivered each minute. (1 mark)

(d) Using your answer from part (c) and information from the graph, calculate values for:

(i) the heat of fusion of water, in kJ mol^{-1}. (2 marks)

(ii) the heat of vaporisation of water, in kJ mol^{-1}. (2 marks)

(iii) the heat capacity of ice, in J g^{-1} K^{-1}. (2 marks)

(Total = 10 marks)

Question 5

(a) The latent heat of vaporisation of a liquid varies with temperature. For example, at 25°C the heat of vaporisation of water is 44 kJ mol^{-1}, but at 100°C the value is 40 kJ mol^{-1}. Suggest a reason for this variation. (2 marks)

(b) The specific heat capacity of water is 4.18 J g^{-1} $°C^{-1}$ but the value for steam is 2.01 J g^{-1} C^{-1}. Suggest a reason for this difference. (2 marks)

(Total = 4 marks)

Question 6

Some data concerning water, trichloromethane ($CHCl_3$) and butane (C_4H_{10}) is in the table below.

Substance	Molar mass (g mol^{-1})	Boiling temperature (°C)	Heat of vaporisation (kJ mol^{-1})
H_2O	18.0	100	44.0
$CHCl_3$	119.4	61.1	31.0
C_4H_{10}	58.1	–0.5	21.0

(a) Identify which molecules are polar and which are non-polar. (3 marks)

(b) Explain why the boiling temperature and heat of vaporisation of water are higher than those of the other compounds, despite water being a much smaller molecule. (3 marks)

(Total = 6 marks)

Acid–base (proton transfer) reactions

Question 7

(a) The HSO_4^- ion behaves as an acid when dissolved in water, whereas the HCO_3^- ion behaves as a base. Write balanced equations for the reaction of each of these ions with water. (2 marks)

(b) For each equation name the conjugate acid and conjugate base. (2 marks)

(c) Write a balanced equation to show how the HSO_4^- ion would react in a concentrated solution of a strong acid whose formula is HX. (2 marks)

(d) Write a balanced equation to show how the HCO_3^- ion would react in a concentrated solution of a strong base whose formula is ZOH. (2 marks)

(Total = 8 marks)

Question 8

The owner of a swimming pool decides that there are two choices for chlorinating a pool: either a solution of chlorine, Cl_2, or a solution of sodium hypochlorite, NaOCl, could be added. When these substances are added to water HOCl, which is partially responsible for killing bacteria, is produced.

(a) For each substance write an equation for its reaction with water. (2 marks)

(b) For each substance explain how the pH of a swimming pool will be affected if it is added to the pool. (2 marks)

(Total = 4 marks)

Question 9

The dihydrogen phosphate ion ($H_2PO_4^-$) is described as *amphiprotic*. Explain what is meant by this term and give relevant equations to support your explanation. (3 marks)

Question 10

(a) A 1.5 M solution of acid A has a pH of 4.7. Calculate the hydronium ion concentration and hence the hydroxide ion concentration of the acid. (2 marks)

(b) A 1.5 M solution of acid B has a pH of 2.0. Calculate its hydronium ion concentration and compare it with the hydronium ion concentration of acid A. Explain the difference in the hydronium ion concentrations. (2 marks)

(Total = 4 marks)

Question 11

Solutions of malonic acid, $HOOCCH_2COOH$, and nitric acid, HNO_3 of equal concentration are prepared. When the conductivities of the two solutions are measured the conductivity of nitric acid is found to be higher than that of malonic acid.

(a) For each acid write a balanced equation for its reaction with water. (2 marks)

(b) Explain the difference in conductivities of the two solutions. (2 marks)

(c) (i) State the proticity of each acid. (2 marks)

(ii) Explain why your answer to part (c)(i) may differ from the total number of hydrogen atoms in the molecule. (2 marks)

(Total = 8 marks)

Redox (electron transfer) reactions

Question 12

Use the reactivity series of metals to answer the questions below.

(a) Nickel rods are placed in each of the following solutions, copper(II) nitrate solution, zinc nitrate solution, iron(II) nitrate solution, and magnesium(II) nitrate solution.

(i) In which solution would a deposit of metal appear on the nickel rod?

(ii) Write an equation for the reaction.

(iii) Name the oxidant and the reductant. (1 + 1 + 1 = 3 marks)

(b) A solution of iron(II) nitrate exposed to air turns from green to red-brown. Explain this colour change and write an equation for the reaction. (2 marks)

(c) The reactivity series can be used to predict whether a redox reaction will take place. Sometimes a reaction that is predicted to occur does not take place in practice. What are the possible explanations for this? (2 marks)

(Total = 7 marks)

Question 13

Manganese is extracted from the mineral pyrolusite. The first step in this process is the reaction of solid manganese dioxide, MnO_2, with iron(II) sulfate solution, $FeSO_4(aq)$, which also contains a dilute acid. The manganese dioxide reacts to form Mn^{2+} ions and Fe^{2+} ions are converted to Fe^{3+} ions.

(a) Derive the half-equations for the oxidation and reduction reactions. (3 marks)

(b) Identify the oxidant and reductant in this process and give one conjugate redox pair. (2 marks)

(c) Derive the overall equation for the reaction. (2 marks)

(Total = 7 marks)

Question 14

For each of the equations below balance the equation and identify the oxidant, the reductant and the conjugate redox pairs.

(a) $Al(s) + Pb^{2+}(aq) \rightarrow Al^{3+}(aq) + Pb(s)$ (3 marks)

(b) $Fe^{3+}(aq) + I^{-}(aq) \rightarrow Fe^{2+}(aq) + I_2(aq)$ (3 marks)

(Total = 6 marks)

Question 15

Explain the following. Include equations in your answers where relevant. Use your knowledge of the position of the elements in the periodic table and their electron configurations to explain their reactivity.

(a) Zinc reacts with steam producing hydrogen, whereas sodium will react with cold water. (2 marks)

(b) Magnesium reacts rapidly with dilute hydrochloric acid, but copper does not react. (2 marks)

(c) Suggest why gold, silver and copper are believed to be the earliest metals used by humans but metals such as aluminium and potassium were not known until much later. (2 marks)

(Total = 6 marks)

Question 16

(a) The element tin is used to coat steel in 'tin' cans to prevent corrosion from occurring. The layer of tin is plated onto the steel can by electrolysis using a solution of tin(II) nitrate. This is called electroplating. The half-equation for the deposition of the tin is:

$Sn^{2+}(aq) + 2e^{-} \rightarrow Sn(s)$

(i) Justify whether the Sn^{2+} ion is being oxidised or reduced.
(ii) Justify whether the Sn^{2+} ion is the oxidant or the reductant.
(iii)How many electrons are required to plate each tin atom onto the can? (3 marks)

(b) Aluminium is obtained by the electrolysis of molten aluminium oxide dissolved in cryolite to lower the operating temperature. The simplified overall cell reaction is:

$2Al_2O_3(cryolite) \rightarrow 4Al(l) + 3O_2(g)$

(i) Write the oxidation half-reaction and identify the species being oxidised.
(ii) Write the reduction half-reaction and identify the species being reduced.
(iii)How many electrons are transferred for every four atoms of aluminium produced? (3 marks)

(Total = 6 marks)

Question 17

X and Z are two metal elements. When element X is placed in a solution of a salt ZCl_2, metallic Z is precipitated.

(a) Write an ionic equation for this reaction, assuming that both metals form a cation with a charge of 2+. (1 marks)

(b) State which substance is the reductant and which is the oxidant. (1 marks)

(c) State which metal would be placed higher in the activity series of metals. (2 marks)

(Total = 4 marks)

Unit 2 Area of Study 1 test

Multiple choice items

Acid–base (proton transfer) reactions

Question 1

The equation for the reaction between the weak acid, chlorous acid, $HClO_2$, and sodium nitrite, $NaNO_2$, is

$HClO_2(aq) + NaNO_2(aq) \rightarrow NaClO_2(aq) + HNO_2(aq)$

The correct ionic equation for this reaction is

A. $ClO_2^-(aq) + Na^+(aq) \rightarrow NaClO_2(aq)$

B. $HClO_2(aq) + NO_2^-(aq) \rightarrow HNO_2(aq) + ClO_2^-(aq)$

C. $ClO_2^-(aq) + Na^+(aq) \rightarrow NaClO_2(s)$

D. $Na^+(aq) + HClO_2(aq) \rightarrow NaClO_2(aq) + H^+(aq)$

Question 2

The pH of a solution is 3.2 at 25°C. The concentration of hydroxide ions in this solution is closest to

A. $10^{-3.2}$ **B.** $10^{-7.0}$ **C.** $10^{-10.8}$ **D.** 10^{-14}

Question 3

Which one of the substances below is both amphiprotic and diprotic?

A. sulfurous acid, H_2SO_3

B. chloroethanoate ion, $ClCH_2COO^-$

C. dihydrogen arsenate ion, $H_2AsO_4^-$

D. oxalic acid, $(COOH)_2$

Question 4

The following statements refer to the ionic product of water, K_w, which has a value of 10^{-14} mol^2 L^{-2}.

I. This value is only correct at 25°C.

II. The ionic product is valid for any aqueous solution.

III. It only refers to acidic solutions.

IV. It only refers to acidic and/or basic solutions.

Which of the above statements is/are correct?

A. I and II

B. III only

C. I and IV

D. II only

Question 5

A 1.5×10^{-3} mol L^{-1} solution of ethanoic acid is qualitatively best described as

A. strong and concentrated.
B. weak and concentrated.
C. strong and dilute.
D. weak and dilute.

Question 6

A student is asked to compare solutions of two acids. Acid I is 0.50 mol L^{-1} ethanoic acid, CH_3COOH, and acid II is 0.050 mol L^{-1} nitric acid, HNO_3. Which one of the following statements is correct?

A. Acid I is stronger than acid II and acid I is more concentrated.
B. Acid I is weaker than acid II and acid I and more concentrated.
C. Acid I is stronger than acid II and acid I is more dilute.
D. Acid I is weaker than acid II and acid I and more dilute.

Question 7

Separate solutions of sulfuric acid, H_2SO_4, ethanoic acid, CH_3COOH, hydrochloric acid, HCl and lithium hydroxide, LiOH are prepared at 25°C such that they all have the same concentration. Which of the solutions would have the lowest pH?

A. sulfuric acid, H_2SO_4
B. ethanoic acid, CH_3COOH
C. hydrochloric acid, HCl
D. lithium hydroxide, LiOH

The following information refers to Questions 8 and 9.

The pH values and concentrations of four acids are given in the table below.

Acid	**pH**	**Concentration (mol L^{-1})**
I	1.00	0.10
II	0.82	0.10
III	3.77	1.00
IV	2.81	0.01

Question 8

Which acid is the weakest?

A. Acid I
B. Acid II
C. Acid III
D. Acid IV

Question 9

Which acid is diprotic?

A. Acid I
B. Acid II
C. Acid III
D. Acid IV

Question 10

Four solutions have pH values of approximately 1, 6, 7, 13. In alphabetical order, the solutions are carbonic acid, hydrochloric acid, sodium chloride solution and sodium hydroxide solution. The solutions placed in order of increasing pH are

A. sodium hydroxide, sodium chloride, carbonic acid, hydrochloric acid.
B. sodium chloride, sodium hydroxide, carbonic acid, hydrochloric acid.
C. hydrochloric acid, carbonic acid, sodium chloride, sodium hydroxide.
D. carbonic acid, hydrochloric acid, sodium chloride, sodium hydroxide.

Question 11

If a dilute solution of an acid is prepared, then the

A. ratio of solute to solvent is low and the acid is completely ionised.
B. ratio of solute to solvent is low and the acid may be completely ionised.
C. ratio of solute to solvent is high and the acid is completely ionised.
D. ratio of solute to solvent is high and the acid may be completely ionised.

Question 12

The following statements concern a solution of a strong acid.

I. The solution may be dilute.
II. The solution might have a pH greater than 7.
III. The solution could be concentrated.
IV. The acid will be fully ionised. Which of these statements is correct?

A. I, II, III and IV
B. I, III and IV
C. II, III and IV
D. I and III

Question 13

Hydrogen chloride (HCl) dissolves in water to form hydrochloric acid. Which one of the following shows the particles present in largest amounts in hydrochloric acid?

A. water molecules, chloride ions and hydronium ions
B. water molecules, chlorine atoms and hydrogen atoms
C. water molecules and hydrogen chloride molecules
D. hydrogen atoms, chlorine atoms and oxygen atoms

Question 14

Zinc carbonate reacts with hydrochloric acid according to the following equation,

$ZnCO_3(s) + 2HCl(aq) \rightarrow ZnCl_2(aq) + H_2O(l) + CO_2(g)$

Which one of the following equations is the correct ionic equation for this reaction?

A. $Zn^{2+}(s) + 2HCl(aq) \rightarrow ZnCl_2(aq) + 2H^+(l)$
B. $ZnCO_3(s) + 2H^+(aq) \rightarrow Zn^{2+}(aq) + H_2O(l) + CO_2(g)$
C. $CO_3^{2-}(s) + 2H^+(aq) \rightarrow H_2O(l) + CO_2(g)$
D. $2ZnCO_3(s) + 4Cl^-(aq) \rightarrow 2ZnCl_2(aq) + 3CO_2(g)$

Redox (electron transfer) reactions

Question 15

The lead-acid battery is used in most automobiles. The overall equation for the reaction when the battery produces energy is

$Pb(s) + PbO_2(s) + 2H_2SO_4(aq) \rightarrow 2PbSO_4(s) + 2H_2O(l)$

Which one of the following statements about the battery is correct?

A. Lead is reduced when the battery provides energy.
B. The pH in the battery falls as the reaction proceeds.
C. The reduction reaction produces water.
D. The overall reaction is as an acid-base reaction only.

Question 16

Which one of the following is a redox reaction?

A. $Ba^{2+}(aq) + SO_4^{2-}(aq) \rightarrow BaSO_4(s)$
B. $SO_2(g) + H_2O(l) \rightarrow H^+(aq) + HSO_3^-(aq)$
C. $2Cu^{2+}(aq) + 4I^-(aq) \rightarrow 2CuI(s) + I_2(aq)$
D. $NaHCO_3(aq) + HCl(aq) \rightarrow NaCl(aq) + H_2O(l) + CO_2(g)$

Question 17

The equations for two redox reactions are given below.

$2Ag^+(aq) + Cu(s) \rightarrow Cu^{2+}(aq) + 2Ag(s)$

$2Fe^{3+}(aq) + 2I^-(aq) \rightarrow 2Fe^{2+}(aq) + I_2(aq)$

In these reactions the reducing agents (reductants) are

A. Cu and Fe^{3+}
B. Ag^+ and Fe^{3+}
C. Ag^+ and I^-
D. Cu and I^-

Question 18

Part of the electrochemical series is shown below.

$Ni^{2+}(aq) + 2e^- \rightarrow Ni(s)$

$Mg^{2+}(aq) + 2e^- \rightarrow Mg(s)$

The atoms and ions above are in their correct relative positions as in the Electrochemical Series. Which of the possible pairs of chemical species would be predicted to undergo a spontaneous electron transfer reaction?

A. Ni^{2+} and Mg.
B. Ni^{2+} and Mg^{2+}
C. Ni and Mg^{2+}
D. Ni and Mg

Question 19

Which one of the metals below could not be used as the anode in the sacrificial electrochemical protection of an iron cathode?

A. zinc
B. chromium
C. tin
D. magnesium

Question 20

Using your knowledge of the reactivity series of metals it would be expected that lead would be able to reduce

A. all of Ag^+, Al^{3+}, Cu^{2+}, Fe^{2+}.
B. Al^{3+} and Fe^{2+}.
C. Ag^+ and Cu^{2+}.
D. Cu^{2+} and Fe^{2+}.

Question 21

Nickel rods are placed into solutions of aluminium nitrate, lead nitrate, magnesium nitrate and silver nitrate, which all have the same concentration. In which of the following will the nickel react with all solutions?

A. magnesium nitrate solution
B. magnesium nitrate solution and aluminium nitrate solution
C. lead nitrate solution and silver nitrate solution
D. aluminium nitrate solution, lead nitrate solution, magnesium nitrate solution and silver nitrate solution

Extended response questions

Acid–base (proton transfer) reactions

Question 1

A solution of hydrochloric acid and a solution of ethanoic acid both have a pH of 3.0.

(a) How will the concentrations of these two solutions differ, if at all? (3 marks)
(b) Calculate the concentration of OH^- in these solutions. (1 mark)
(Total = 4 marks)

Question 2

Below is a list of fourteen substances.

Hydrochloric acid, sulfuric acid, phosphoric acid, magnesium oxide, copper(II) oxide, sodium hydroxide, aluminium hydroxide, copper, aluminium, sodium, zinc, sodium hydrogen carbonate, magnesium carbonate, potassium carbonate.

Write balanced formula equations and ionic equations for each of the reactions below using chemicals from the above list.

(a) A monoprotic acid reacting with a group III metal (2 marks)
(b) A triprotic acid reacting with a group I metal hydroxide (2 marks)
(c) A monoprotic acid reacting with a metal carbonate solution (2 marks)
(d) A metal hydrogen carbonate solution reacting with a diprotic acid (2 marks)
(e) A divalent metal oxide reacting with a diprotic acid to give a blue solution. (2 marks)
(Total = 10 marks)

Question 3

A solution of methanoic acid has the same pH as a solution of hydrochloric acid. However, the concentration of methanoic acid is much higher than that of hydrochloric acid. Explain these observations. (Total = 3 marks)

Question 4

Arsenic acid, H_3AsO_4, is a weak triprotic acid similar in its structure and properties to phosphoric acid. Write equations for its successive ionisation in aqueous solution.

(Total = 3 marks)

Question 5

Write a balanced formula equation and an ionic equation for each of the following reactions.

(a) The decomposition of baking soda, sodium hydrogen carbonate when heated. (1 mark)

(b) In industrial areas, rainwater is often contaminated with small amounts of sulfuric acid. What is the reaction of iron with dilute sulfuric acid? (2 marks)

(c) The reaction of an antacid, magnesium hydroxide with hydrochloric acid in the stomach. (2 marks)

(d) The reaction of nitric acid and calcium carbonate, producing calcium nitrate used in fireworks. (2 marks)

(Total = 7 marks)

Question 6

Write a balanced chemical equation describing how each of the solids below reacts with dilute hydrochloric acid.

(a) Copper carbonate (1 mark)

(b) Zinc (1 mark)

(c) Magnesium sulfite, $MgSO_3$ (1 mark)

(d) Calcium sulfide, CaS (1 mark)

(Total = 4 marks)

Redox (electron transfer) reactions

Question 7

Classify each of the equations given below as one or more of the following reaction types: *acid-base, redox, dissociation, ionisation, precipitation.*

(a) $Ag^+(aq) + Cl^-(aq) \rightarrow AgCl(s)$ (1 mark)

(b) $2Cu^+(aq) \rightarrow Cu(s) + Cu^{2+}(aq)$ (1 mark)

(c) $CaF_2(s) \rightarrow Ca^{2+}(aq) + 2F^-(aq)$ (1 mark)

(d) $Pb(NO_3)_2(aq) + 2KI(aq) \rightarrow 2KNO_3(aq) + PbI_2(s)$ (1 mark)

(e) $HCN(aq) + H_2O(l) \rightarrow CN^-(aq) + H_3O^+(aq)$ (1 mark)

(f) $HClO_4(aq) + LiOH(aq) \rightarrow LiClO_4(aq) + H_2O(l)$ (1 mark)

(g) $O_2(g) + 2H_2O(l) + 4e^- \rightarrow 4OH^-(aq)$ (1 mark)

(Total = 7 marks)

Question 8

(a) Which metal is expected to be higher in the activity series: cobalt, Co, or strontium, Sr? Give an explanation for your answer. (2 marks)

(b) A series of experiments between a metal and a metal cation were carried out. The results are shown in the table below.

Experiment	Metal	Cation	Result
1	Zn	$V^{2+}(aq)$	No reaction
2	V	$Ni^{2+}(aq)$	Ni produced
3	Ni	$Zn^{2+}(aq)$	No reaction
4	Ni	$Sn^{2+}(aq)$	Sn produced

Use these results to produce the order of these four metals in the reactivity series. (3 marks)

(Total = 5 marks)

Question 9

A student performed the experiment shown in the diagram below as part of an investigation into the relative reactivity of metals. Initially the beaker contained 200.0 mL of 0.150 mol L^{-1} nickel chloride solution. After several hours the dark green colour of the solution had become lighter and a silvery grey deposit had formed on the piece of magnesium metal and on the bottom of the beaker. A small number of bubbles of gas also formed on the surface of the magnesium during this time.

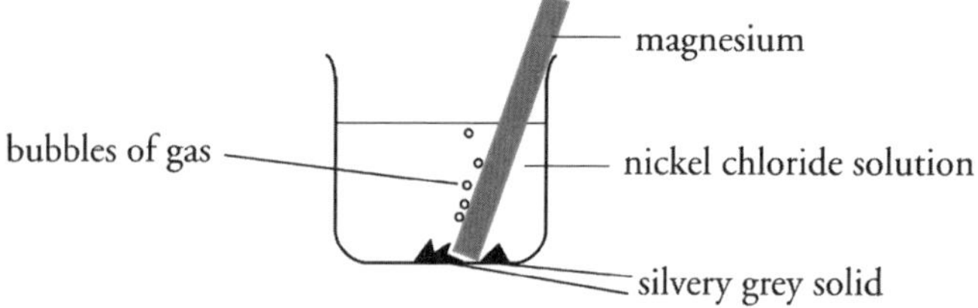

(a) Give an explanation for the changes observed by the student. (3 marks)

(b) Give a balanced oxidation–reduction equation for the production of the silvery grey solid. (1 mark)

(c) Identify the gas that is produced in this experiment and give a balanced equation for its formation. (2 marks)

The silvery grey solid was removed from the piece of magnesium and the beaker and was washed and dried. The mass of the solid was 0.880 g. The piece of magnesium was also washed and dried. The mass of magnesium had decreased by 0.401 g.

(d) Use the mass of silvery grey solid to calculate the expected loss in mass of the piece of magnesium. (2 marks)

(e) Explain why your answer to part (d) differs from 0.401 g. (1 mark)

(Total = 9 marks)

Chapter 5

Unit 2 Area of Study 2 – How are chemicals measured and analysed?

Multiple choice items

Measuring solubility and concentration

Question 1

A saturated solution is formed when 0.30 g of a salt dissolves in 15 mL of water. The solubility of the salt in g/100 g of water is

A. 0.045
B. 2.0
C. 4.5
D. 30

Question 2

The maximum solubility of potassium bromide, KBr, at 25°C is 68 g/100 g H_2O. What mass of water will just dissolve 1.00 mole of KBr at this temperature?

A. 57 g
B. 81 g
C. 168 g
D. 175 g

Question 3

The solubilities of four compounds, at 25°C, are given in the table below.

Compound	Solubility (g/100 mL solution)
Potassium chloride, KCl	30.7
Potassium nitrate	31.9
Sodium bromide, NaBr	58.3
Sodium chloride, NaCl	31.7

If saturated solutions of each of these compounds are prepared at 25°C, which one would have the lowest concentration in mol L^{-1}?

A. potassium chloride solution
B. potassium nitrate solution
C. sodium bromide solution
D. sodium chloride solution

Question 4

The solubility of potassium nitrate in water at 70°C is approximately 140 g per 100 g of water. Which one of the following changes to a saturated potassium nitrate solution, will cause some potassium nitrate to crystallise?

A. increasing the temperature above 70°C at constant volume.
B. decreasing the temperature below 70°C at constant volume.
C. maintaining the temperature at 70°C and adding water to the solution.
D. decreasing the temperature below 70°C and adding water to the solution.

Question 5

When the temperature of solutions containing dissolved salts or dissolved gases increases the solubility of

A. both gases and salts increases.
B. gases increases and of salts decreases.
C. gases decreases and of salts increases.
D. both gases and salts decreases.

Question 6

The solubility of sodium nitrate at 60°C is 124 g/100 g H_2O and at 20°C is 88.1 g/100 g H_2O. 150 g of water is saturated with sodium nitrate at 60°C. What mass of sodium nitrate will be precipitated if this solution is cooled to 20°C?

A. 23.9 g
B. 35.9 g
C. 53.8 g
D. 132 g

Question 7

The mass of potassium nitrate, KNO_3, in grams, present in 0.75 L of a 2.2 mol L^{-1} potassium nitrate solution is closest to

A. 34.5
B. 167
C. 222
D. 296

Question 8

Household bleach contains 35.0 g of sodium hypochlorite, NaClO, per litre of bleach. What volume of water must be added to 200 mL of bleach to change the concentration of NaClO to 5.00 g per litre?

A. 1.20 L
B. 1.4 L
C. 0.28 L
D. 0.08 L

Question 9

When a solution of bleach is diluted, the number of moles of bleach

A. increases.

B. decreases.

C. remains constant.

D. varies according to the amount of dilution.

Question 10

A solution of ammonia, NH_3, contains 3.70×10^{-4} mole of ammonia dissolved in 100 mL of solution. What is the concentration of the solution in g L^{-1}?

A. 6.29×10^{-4}

B. 6.29×10^{-2}

C. 6.29

D. 62.9

Question 11

What is the concentration, in mol L^{-1}, of a solution that contains 2.00 g of silver nitrate, $AgNO_3$, dissolved in 300 mL of solution?

A. 0.00354

B. 0.0118

C. 0.0392

D. 6.67

Question 12

A solution of copper chloride contains 5.70 g of copper chloride, $CuCl_2$, in 750 mL of solution. What is the concentration of chloride ion in the solution in g L^{-1}?

A. 2.01

B. 3.01

C. 4.01

D. 7.60

Question 13

What is the concentration of chloride ions, in mol L^{-1}, in a 1.2 mol L^{-1} solution of aluminium chloride, $AlCl_3$?

A. 4.8.

B. 3.6.

C. 2.4.

D. 1.2.

Question 14

200 mL of a 2.0 mol L^{-1} solution of sodium nitrate is diluted to 500 mL. The concentration of the diluted solution, in mol L^{-1}, is

A. 0.40
B. 0.80
C. 2.0
D. 5.0

Question 15

Lead chloride, $PbCl_2$, has a solubility of 1.08 g in 100 g of H_2O at 25°C. This corresponds to a concentration of (assume the density of the solution is 1.00 g mL^{-1})

A. 0.388 mol L^{-1}.
B. 108 g L^{-1}.
C. 1080 mg L^{-1}.
D. 10800 ppm.

Question 16

Which of the following sodium chloride (NaCl) solutions contains the largest number of moles of sodium chloride?

A. 400 mL of a 3.0 mol L^{-1} solution
B. 300 mL of a 40.0 g L^{-1} solution
C. 300 mL of a 0.4 mol L^{-1} solution
D. 400 mL of a 0.25 g mL^{-1}solution

Question 17

Which one of the following solutions contains the smallest amount of nitrate ion?

A. 600 mL of 0.45 mol L^{-1} sodium nitrate, $NaNO_3$
B. 500 mL of 0.30 mol L^{-1} calcium nitrate, $Ca(NO_3)_2$
C. 300 mL of 0.30 mol L^{-1} aluminium nitrate, $Al(NO_3)_3$
D. 250 mL of 0.25 mol L^{-1} thorium nitrate, $Th(NO_3)_4$

Question 18

An aqueous solution is labelled '0.75 mol L^{-1} $CaBr_2$'. The best explanation of this label is that the solution contains

A. 0.75 mol of calcium bromide added to 1.0 L of distilled water.
B. 150 g of calcium bromide added to 1.0 L of distilled water.
C. 0.15 g of calcium bromide per 1.0 mL of solution.
D. 0.75 g of calcium bromide per 1.0 mL of solution.

Question 19

Which one of the following solutions has the lowest concentration of chloride ions?

A. 100 mL of a solution containing 0.05 mol of potassium chloride
B. 100 mL of a solution containing 0.03 mol calcium chloride
C. 100 mL of a solution containing 0.04 mol aluminium chloride
D. 100 mL of a solution containing 0.02 mol tin(IV) chloride

Question 20

260 mL of 0.50 mol L^{-1} potassium sulfate solution is added to 430 mL of 1.70 mol L^{-1} aluminium sulfate solution. The concentration of sulfate ions, in mol L^{-1}, in the final solution is

A. 3.56.
B. 3.37.
C. 2.32.
D. 1.25.

Question 21

An aqueous solution of ethanol has a concentration of 40%(m/m). If the density of the solution is 0.932 g mL^{-1}, then the concentration expressed as %(m/v) is

A. 37.3
B. 40
C. 42.9
D. 55.9

Analysis for acids and bases

Question 22

A 0.0491 mol L^{-1} solution of sodium carbonate was used to standardise a solution of hydrochloric acid. A 20.00 mL aliquot of the sodium carbonate solution was placed in a conical flask and titrated with the hydrochloric acid solution from a burette. The correct indicator for this reaction would be one that changes colour when the number of mole of hydrogen ions added

A. results in the pH of the solution in the flask being 7.
B. just exceeds the number of mole of CO_3^{2-} ions present originally.
C. just exceeds double the number of mole of CO_3^{2-} ions present originally.
D. equals the number of mole of CO_3^{2-} ions present originally.

Question 23

A student wishes to determine the concentration of ethanoic (acetic) acid in vinegar. The student titrates a 20.00 mL sample of a standard sodium hydroxide solution with a diluted vinegar solution from a burette. Four experiments were carried out and the following titration results were obtained: 21.65 mL, 22.35 mL, 22.30 mL and 22.35 mL. The discrepancy in the first titration could be due to the student washing

A. the conical flask with sodium hydroxide solution only.
B. the pipette with water only.
C. the burette with water only.
D. the pipette with sodium hydroxide solution only.

Question 24

Anhydrous sodium carbonate, Na_2CO_3, is a good primary standard. What mass of sodium carbonate, when dissolved in water in a 250 mL volumetric flask, is needed to make a 0.0650 mol L^{-1} solution?

A. 0.01625 g
B. 1.722 g
C. 6.890 g
D. 27.56 g

Question 25

0.148 g of a metal carbonate exactly reacts with 20.00 mL of 0.100 mol L^{-1} hydrochloric acid. The formula of the metal carbonate is most likely to be

A. Li_2CO_3
B. Na_2CO_3
C. $MgCO_3$
D. $SrCO_3$

Question 26

0.1851 g of a pure dicarboxylic acid, $Z(COOH)_2$ was added to ~20.00 mL of water and titrated with 0.136 mol L^{-1} NaOH solution from a burette. To reach the endpoint a titre of 20.62 mL was required. The equation for the reaction is

$Z(COOH)_2(aq) + 2NaOH(aq) \rightarrow Z(COONa)_2(aq) + 2H_2O(l)$

The identity of the dicarboxylic acid is most likely to be

A. $CH_2(COOH)_2$
B. $C_2H_4(COOH)_2$
C. $C_3H_6(COOH)_2$
D. $C_4H_8(COOH)_2$

Question 27

200 mL of 0.10 mol L^{-1} hydrochloric acid, 200 mL of 0.20 mol L^{-1} hydrochloric acid and 100 mL of 0.40 mol L^{-1} hydrochloric acid are mixed together. The concentration of hydrochloric acid in the resulting solution, in mol L^{-1}, is

A. 0.10
B. 0.20
C. 0.70
D. 5.0

Question 28

What volume of water must be added to 100 mL of 2.00 mol L^{-1} nitric acid to change its concentration to 0.100 mol L^{-1}?

A. 100 mL
B. 190 mL
C. 1.90 L
D. 2.00 L

Measuring gases

Question 29

Neon gas at 20°C and standard atmospheric pressure is placed in a 1.0 L closed container. Under these conditions

A. all neon atoms have the same kinetic energy.
B. the average kinetic energy of neon atoms is different from that of other gases under the same conditions.
C. the average kinetic energy of neon atoms is proportional to the temperature.
D. the percentage of atoms with high kinetic energy is higher than it would be at the same pressure and volume and a temperature of 40°C.

Question 30

Equal volumes of sulfur dioxide and oxygen are at the same temperature and pressure. Both gas samples

A. contain equal masses.
B. have all molecules moving with the same velocity.
C. contain equal numbers of atoms.
D. have the same number of molecules.

Question 31

Under standard laboratory conditions, SLC, the volume occupied by

A. one mole of chlorine gas, Cl_2, is approximately double the volume occupied by one mole of argon, Ar.
B. 39.95 g of argon is approximately the same as the volume occupied by 4.00 g of helium.
C. one mole of ammonia is exactly the same as the volume occupied by one mole of helium.
D. one mole of all real gases is exactly the same as there are no interparticle forces of attraction.

Question 32

100 mL of ethane gas was mixed with 500 mL of oxygen gas at 20°C and 1 atmosphere pressure, and sparked. The reaction shown by the following equation occurred.

$2C_2H_6(g) + 7O_2(g) \rightarrow 4CO_2(g) + 6H_2O(l)$

What would be the total volume of gas present when the reaction had cooled to the original temperature and pressure?

A. 200 mL
B. 350 mL
C. 550 mL
D. 650 mL

Question 33 [VCAA 2014 SA Q8]

When hydrochloric acid is added to aluminium sulfide, the highly toxic gas hydrogen sulfide is evolved. The equation for this reaction is

$Al_2S_3(s) + 6HCl(aq) \rightarrow 2AlCl_3(aq) + 3H_2S(g)$

If excess hydrochloric acid is added to 0.200 mol of aluminium sulfide, then the volume of hydrogen sulfide produced at standard laboratory conditions (SLC) will be

A. 1.63 L
B. 4.90 L
C. 7.44 L
D. 14.9 L

Question 34 [VCAA 2014 SA Q9]

An aerosol can with a volume of 300.0 mL contains 2.80 g of propane gas as a propellant. The warning label says the aerosol may explode at temperatures above 60.0°C. What is the pressure in the can at a temperature of 60.0°C?

A. 5.87×10^{-1} kPa
B. 1.06×10^{2} kPa
C. 5.87×10^{2} kPa
D. 2.58×10^{4} kPa

Question 35 [VCAA 2015 SA Q4]

The emergency oxygen system in a passenger aircraft uses the decomposition of sodium chlorate to produce oxygen. At 76.0 kPa and 292 K, each adult passenger needs about 1.60 L of oxygen per minute. The equation for the reaction is

$2NaClO_3(s) \rightarrow 2NaCl(s) + 3O_2(g)$
$M(NaClO_3) = 106.5 \text{ g mol}^{-1}$

The mass of sodium chlorate required to provide the required volume of oxygen for each adult passenger per minute is

A. 3.56 g
B. 5.34 g
C. 7.85 g
D. 53.7 g

Question 36 [VCAA 2018 SA Q10]

Bioethanol, C_2H_5OH, is produced by the fermentation of glucose, $C_6H_{12}O_6$, according to the following equation.

$C_6H_{12}O_6(aq) \rightarrow 2C_2H_5OH(aq) + 2CO_2(g)$

The mass of C_2H_5OH obtained when 5.68 g of carbon dioxide, CO_2, is produced is

A. 0.168 g
B. 0.337 g
C. 2.97 g
D. 5.94 g

Analysis for salts

Question 37

7.329 g of barium chloride, $BaCl_2.6H_2O$, is dissolved in enough water to make 600 mL of solution. The concentration, in mol L^{-1}, of chloride ions in the solution is closest to

A. 0.0500
B. 0.0704
C. 0.100
D. 0.117

Question 38

Which one of the following liquids is least likely to conduct electricity?

A. mercury
B. an aqueous solution of methanol
C. molten sodium chloride
D. a barium chloride solution

Question 39 [VCAA 2010 SA Q9]

The graph shows the absorption spectra of three food dyes: Blue No. 1, Red No. 2 and Yellow No. 4.

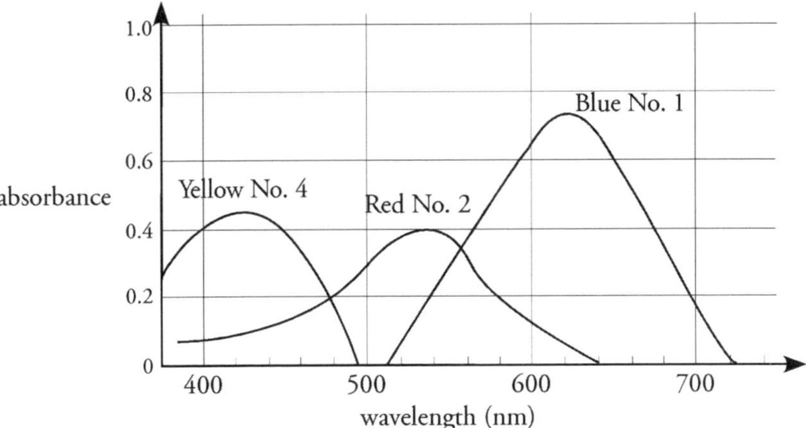

Which one of the following is the best wavelength to determine the concentration of Red No. 2 dye in a solution containing a mixture of all three dyes?

A. 430 nm
B. 500 nm
C. 540 nm
D. 620 nm

Question 40

Sodium carbonate is reacted with of silver nitrate according to the following equation:

$Na_2CO_3(aq) + 2AgNO_3(aq) \rightarrow Ag_2CO_3(s) + 2NaNO_3(aq)$

If 20.0 mL of 0.150 mol L^{-1} sodium carbonate solution is added to 30.00 mL of 0.250 mol L^{-1} silver nitrate solution, the maximum mass of silver carbonate, in grams, that would be precipitated is

A. 0.414.
B. 0.827.
C. 1.65.
D. 2.07.

Question 41

A solution contains 7.70 g of potassium iodide. What is the least volume of an exactly 2.00 mol L^{-1} lead nitrate solution that would be required to ensure complete precipitation of the lead ions as lead iodide?

A. 46.4 mL
B. 36.6 mL
C. 23.2 mL
D. 11.6 mL

Question 42 [VCAA 2009 E1 SA Q3]

The UV-visible spectrum of a solution of a certain compound is shown below.

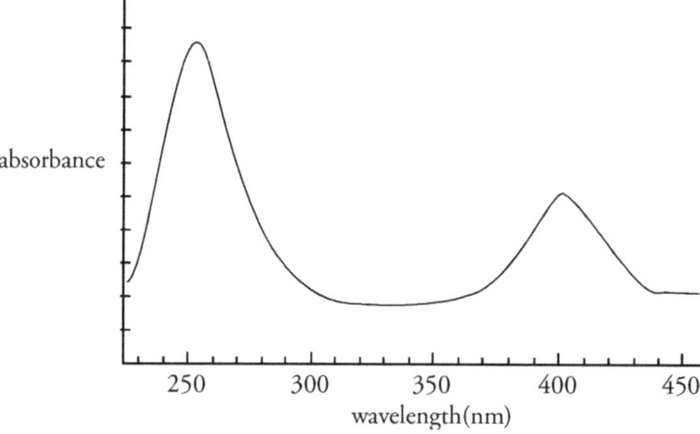

Consider the statements below about this compound and its UV-visible spectrum.

I. The amount of light absorbed by a solution of this compound depends on its concentration.
II. The amount of light absorbed by a solution of this compound depends on the wavelength of light used.
III. The spectrum is a result of electrons falling back from higher to lower electronic energy levels.
IV. The concentration of a solution of this compound can only be determined by UV-visible spectroscopy at 250 nm.

Which of the above statements are true?

A. I and II **B.** II and III
C. I, II and III **D.** I, II and IV

Question 43
The equation for the reaction of methane with oxygen is

$CH_4(g) + 2O_2(g) \rightarrow CO_2(g) + 2H_2O(l)$

What mass of carbon dioxide is produced when 3.2 g of methane and 3.2 g of oxygen are allowed to react?

A. 2.2 g
B. 4.4 g
C. 6.4 g
D. 8.8 g

Question 44
The amount of chlorine in a pesticide may be determined by precipitation of the chlorine as silver chloride, AgCl. If 1.75 g of pesticide reacts to give 0.177 g of AgCl, then the percentage, by mass, of chlorine in the pesticide is

A. 0.0705%
B. 2.50%
C. 10.1%
D. 40.9%

Question 45
Uranium hexafluoride, UF_6, is used in the production of uranium fuel rods for nuclear power stations. The number of mole of fluorine atoms in 5.84 g of UF_6 is closest to

A. 0.00277
B. 0.0166
C. 0.0995
D. 0.116

Extended response questions

Measuring solubility and concentration

Question 1

The solubility of sodium nitrate, $NaNO_3$, at 20°C is 88 g/100 g H_2O and is 135 g /100 g at 70°C. A saturated solution is prepared from sodium nitrate and 40 g of water at 70°C. The solution is then cooled to 20°C.

(a) What mass of $NaNO_3$ dissolves at 70°C? (1 mark)

(b) What mass of $NaNO_3$ will precipitate from the solution at 20°C? (2 marks)

(c) What mass of water must be added to the mixture at 20°C to just dissolve all of the $NaNO_3$? (2 marks)

(Total = 5 marks)

Question 2

The graph below shows the variation of solubility with changing temperature for three compounds, A, B and C.

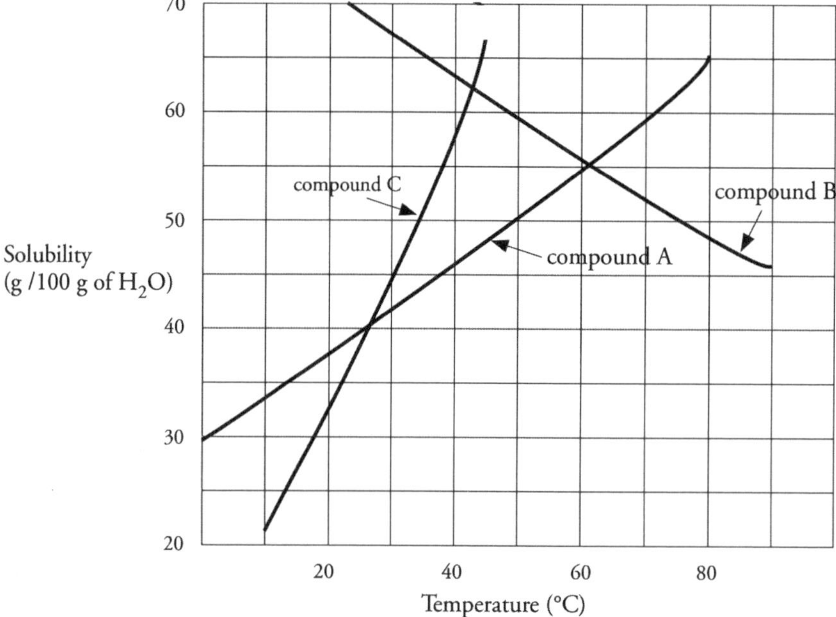

(a) Which of the compounds A, B and C, is a gas? Give a reason for your answer. (2 marks)

(b) What is the solubility of compound B at 35°C? (1 mark)

(c) What volume of water at 60°C is needed to make a saturated solution from 50 g of compound A? (2 marks)

(d) If 80 g of compound C is added to 60 g of water at 40°C, what mass of compound C would remain undissolved? (3 marks)

(Total = 8 marks)

Question 3

A solution of ethanol in water is made by dissolving 15.3 g of ethanol in 120 mL of water. The density of ethanol is 0.785 g mL^{-1}.

(a) Calculate the volume of the ethanol before it is dissolved. (1 mark)

(b) Calculate the expected volume of the ethanol solution. (1 mark)

(c) The volume of the ethanol solution is found to be only 135 mL. Give a possible explanation for this observation. (1 mark)

(d) Calculate the concentration of the ethanol solution in the following units:

(i) molarity (1 mark)

(ii) g L^{-1} (1 mark)

(iii) % m/m (1 mark)

(Total = 6 marks)

Analysis for acids and bases

Question 4

The concentration of a sample of dilute sulfuric acid was determined by volumetric analysis and by precipitation.

(a) Volumetric analysis:

50.0 mL of the sulfuric acid was accurately diluted to 250 mL in a standard flask. A 20.0 mL aliquot of the diluted acid was placed in a conical flask and titrated with a standard 0.100 mol L^{-1} solution of sodium hydroxide. The average titre was 22.60 mL.

(i) Write a balanced equation for the reaction.

(ii) Calculate the concentration of the undiluted sulfuric acid in mol L^{-1}.

(1 + 4 = 5 marks)

(b) Precipitation:

50.0 mL of the undiluted sulfuric acid was reacted with an excess of barium chloride solution. The precipitate formed was filtered, washed, dried and weighed. The mass of the precipitate was 7.96 g.

(i) Write a balanced equation for the reaction.

(ii) Calculate the concentration of the sulfuric acid in mol L^{-1}. (1 + 4 = 5 marks)

(c) State a possible error in each analysis, which could lead to a difference in the calculated molarities. (2 marks)

(Total = 12 marks)

Question 5

A scientist wishes to determine the percentage purity of a sample rock that contains copper carbonate. The scientist weighs 1.052 g of the rock into a flask and reacts it with sulfuric acid. The copper(II) carbonate in the mixture exactly reacts with 23.50 mL 0.2516 mol L^{-1} sulfuric acid.

(a) Write a balanced equation for the reaction between copper carbonate and sulfuric acid. (2 marks)

(b) Calculate the mass of copper carbonate that reacted with the acid. (2 marks)

(c) Calculate the percentage of copper carbonate in the rock sample. (1 mark)

(d) Calculate the mass of water, in grams, formed in the reaction. (2 marks)

(Total = 7 marks)

Question 6

Concentrated hydrochloric acid, HCl, is often used to adjust the pH of swimming pools. The concentration of one brand is claimed by its manufacturer to be 380 g of HCl per litre. A student decides to check this claim using the following method:

10.00 mL of the concentrated acid was diluted to 250 mL in a volumetric flask. The dilute acid solution was placed in a burette. 20.00 mL of 0.168 M sodium carbonate solution was pipetted into a conical flask. An indicator was added, and the base was neutralised by the acid from the burette. 18.39 mL of the acid was required.

$Na_2CO_3(aq) + 2HCl(aq) \rightarrow 2NaCl(aq) + H_2O(l) + CO_2(g)$

(a) Calculate the number of mole of Na_2CO_3 in the conical flask. (1 mark)

(b) How many mole of HCl was added from the burette? (1 mark)

(c) How many mole of HCl was in the volumetric flask? (1 mark)

(d) Calculate the mass of HCl in the volumetric flask. (1 mark)

(e) Calculate the concentration of the undiluted HCl in g L^{-1}. (1 mark)

(f) Suggest one safety warning that should be included on the label of the container of concentrated acid. (1 mark)

(Total = 6 marks)

Question 7

The label on a container of 'Mr Muscle' oven cleaner states that it contains 4.33% (by mass) of sodium hydroxide, NaOH, as the active ingredient. A student wishes to confirm the accuracy of this statement and determines the percentage by mass of NaOH in the cleaner by reacting it with 0.05134 M sulfuric acid.

23.74 g of the oven cleaner is dissolved in water and made up to a volume of 250 mL. The student then titrates 20.00 mL aliquots of this solution with the sulfuric acid, using a suitable indicator. An average titre of 20.28 mL was obtained.

(a) Write the equation for this reaction. (1 mark)

(b) Give two safety precautions that the student should take when carrying out this determination. (2 marks)

(c) Calculate the:

(i) amount of sulfuric acid used in the titrations. (1 mark)

(ii) number of mole of NaOH in the 20.00 mL aliquots. (1 mark)

(iii)mass of NaOH in the 250 mL solution. (2 marks)

(iv)percentage of NaOH in the oven cleaner. (1 mark)

(Total = 8 marks)

Measuring gases

Question 8

Complete the following unit conversions.

(a) 200 L to mL (1 mark)

(b) 4.62 atm to kPa (1 mark)

(c) 25°C into K (1 mark)

(d) 9.62×10^6 Pa into kPa (1 mark)

(Total = 4 marks)

Question 9

Calculate the following.

(a) The moles of N_2 gas at 42.0°C needed to exert a pressure of 100 kPa in a 5.00 L vessel. (1 mark)

(b) The volume that 5.0 g of H_2 gas would occupy at SLC. (2 marks)

(c) The temperature required to have 2.00 mol of gas exert a pressure of 200 kPa in a 1.5 L vessel. (1 mark)

(Total = 4 marks)

Question 10

20 mL of propane, C_3H_8, is burned in excess oxygen, according to the equation:

$C_3H_8(g) + 5O_2(g) \rightarrow 3CO_2(g) + 4H_2O(g)$

All gas volumes are measured at SLC.

(a) What is the total volume of gas produced during the reaction? (3 marks)

(b) Which of the product(s) would contribute to the enhanced greenhouse effect? Explain. (2 marks)

(Total = 5 marks)

Question 11

Iron(III) oxide is decomposed, to produce iron, according to the following equation:

$2Fe_2O_3(s) \rightarrow 4Fe(l) + 3O_2(g)$

An average human consumed approximately 6.0 mL of oxygen gas every minute. The oxygen gas is at 28°C and 100 kPa of pressure in the lungs.

(a) What mass of iron(III) oxide would be required to produce the amount of oxygen consumed by an average human in a day? (4 marks)

(b) At this temperature and pressure, what is the molar volume of oxygen gas? (2 marks)

(Total = 6 marks)

Analysis for salts

Question 12

20.00 mL of a 0.105 mol L^{-1} solution of barium hydroxide is pipetted into a beaker. Small amounts of sulfuric acid are added to the beaker from a burette and at each addition the electrical conductivity of the solution in the beaker is measured. A graph of electrical conductivity against volume of acid is plotted, as shown in the diagram below.

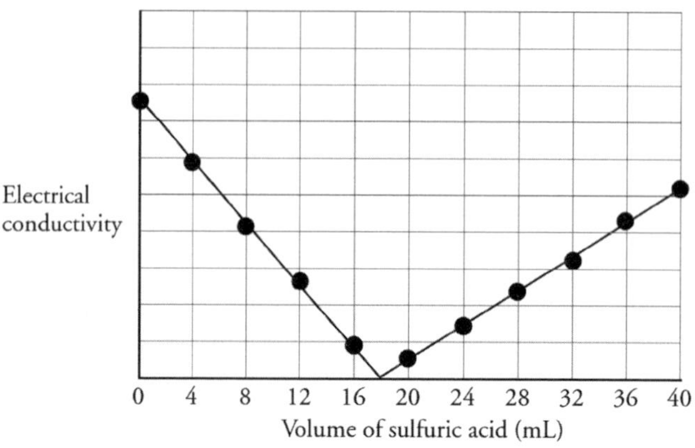

The lowest conductivity occurred at a volume of 18.00 mL.

(a) Write a balanced equation for the reaction of barium hydroxide with sulfuric acid. (2 marks)

(b) Explain why the conductivity of the solution in the beaker falls and then rises again. (3 marks)

(c) Calculate the concentration of the sulfuric acid in mol L^{-1}. (2 marks)

(Total = 7 marks)

Question 13

50.0 mL of a 0.250 mol L^{-1} zinc chloride solution is added to 50.0 mL of a 0.500 mol L^{-1} potassium carbonate solution.

(a) Write the equation for the reaction. (1 mark)

(b) Calculate the mass of precipitate produced. (2 marks)

(c) Calculate the concentration of the potassium ions in the final solution. (2 marks)

(Total = 5 marks)

Question 14

200 mL of a 3.00 mol L^{-1} solution of iron(III) sulfate is mixed with 120 mL of a 5.00 mol L^{-1} solution of sodium hydroxide. A precipitate of iron(III) hydroxide forms.

(a) Write a balanced equation for the reaction. (1 mark)

(b) Determine which reactant is in excess. (3 marks)

(c) Calculate the final concentration of the reactant in excess. (2 marks)

(d) Calculate the mass of the precipitate formed. (2 marks)

(Total = 8 marks)

Question 15

75.0 mL of a 0.800 mol L^{-1} potassium chloride solution is reacted with 50.0 mL of 1.20 mol L^{-1} silver nitrate solution.

(a) Write a balanced equation for the reaction. (1 mark)

(b) Which reagent is in excess, and by how many moles? (2 marks)

(c) Name the insoluble product, and state how many grams of it are obtained. (2 marks)

(d) Write the ionic equation for the reaction and give the formulas of the spectator ions. (2 marks)

(Total = 7 marks)

Question 16

Potassium permanganate, $KMnO_4$, has been used in some water treatment plants to remove compounds of iron and manganese, control taste and odour, remove colour and to control biological growth. After the water has been treated, the amount of residual $KMnO_4$ must be low or health problems will result. The amount of $KMnO_4$ remaining can be measured using UV-visible spectrometry. The absorption spectrum of potassium permanganate in the visible region is shown below.

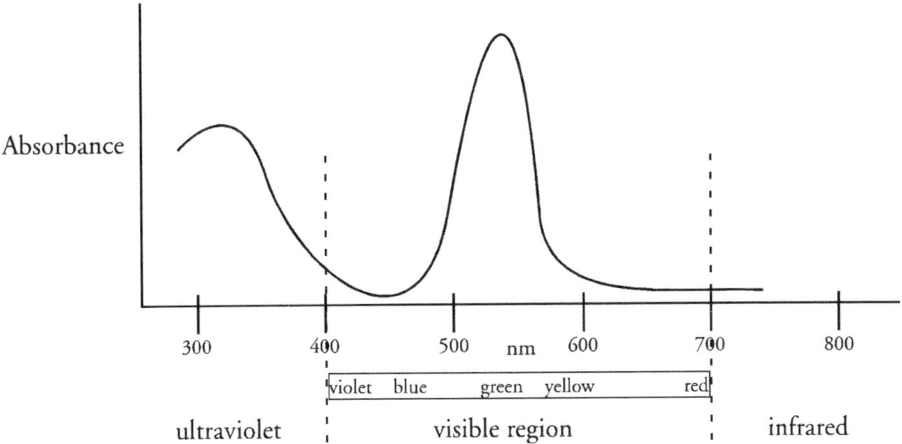

(a) Use this spectrum to explain why solutions of potassium permanganate are purple. (1 mark)

The absorbance of a series of standard solutions of potassium permanganate was measured and the results are shown below.

$KMnO_4$ concentration (ppm)	**Absorbance**
10	0.29
15	0.44
20	0.58
30	0.87

The absorbance of a sample of treated water was 0.64.

(b) Plot a graph of absorbance against concentration for potassium permanganate and thus determine the concentration of $KMnO_4$ in the treated water. (2 marks)

(c) How much potassium permanganate would a person ingest if they drank 500 mL of the treated water? (2 marks)

(Total = 5 marks)

Question 17

Phosphate salts have many uses, for example they are important fertilisers and improve the action of detergents. Wastewater will contain some of this phosphate which can then become part of the natural water supply. If too much phosphate is present, the growth of blue-green is promoted and eutrophication of the water supply may occur. The amount of phosphate in water can be determined using UV-visible spectroscopy. The phosphate present in water is reacted with ammonium molybdate and a reducing agent. A blue colour is produced and the absorbance of the solution is measured.

In a typical experiment, a set of standard solutions were prepared and the absorbance of each measured. These results were used to produce the calibration graph below.

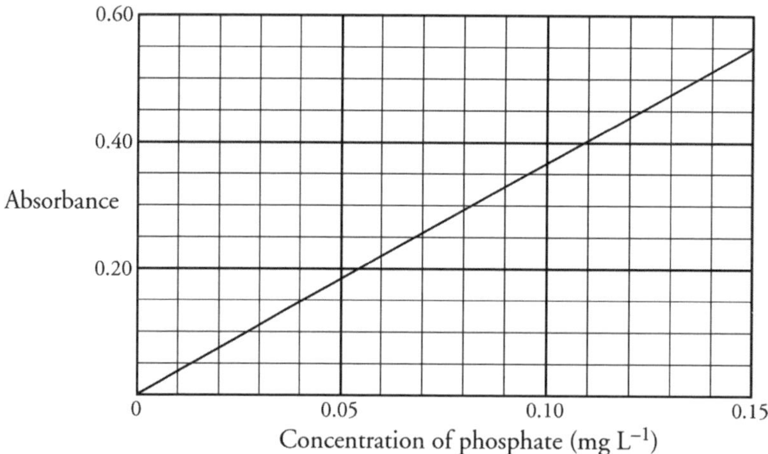

Three water samples were taken from each of three streams and in each case any phosphate present was converted into the blue substance and its absorbance measured. The results are given in the table below.

Stream	Measured absorbances	Average absorbance	Average phosphate concentration (mg L^{-1})
A	0.15, 0.18, 0.12		
B	0.22, 0.26, 0.30		
C	0.45, 0.52, 0.51		

(a) Complete the table above by calculating the average absorbance and average phosphate concentration for each stream. (3 marks)

To prevent excessive growth of blue-green algae and thus eutrophication of the water supply, the amount of phosphate present should not exceed 0.10 ppm.

(b) Which of the above streams may be in danger of eutrophication? (1 mark)

(c) Suggest likely reasons for the variation in the phosphate concentrations in the streams. (1 mark)

(Total = 5 marks)

Unit 2 Area of Study 2 test

Multiple choice items

Analysis of substances in water

Question 1

As the temperature increases the solubility of carbon dioxide in water

A. increases and the pH of the solution decreases.
B. increases and the pH of the solution increases.
C. decreases and the pH of the solution decreases.
D. decreases and the pH of the solution increases.

Question 2

How many ppm of nickel are present in hydrated nickel sulfate, $NiSO_4.6H_2O$?

A. 3.40×10^5 ppm.
B. 8.77×10^3 ppm.
C. 2.23×10^5 ppm.
D. 3.79×10^5 ppm.

Question 3

A 4.120 g sample of copper carbonate contains an unreactive impurity. When an excess of hydrochloric acid is added to the sample, 1.23 g of carbon dioxide is evolved. What is the mass of impurity in the sample?

A. 0.666 g.
B. 1.23 g.
C. 2.34 g.
D. 3.46 g.

Question 4

The solubility of ammonium chloride, NH_4Cl, at 25°C is 39.0 g/100 g H_2O. If 150 g of ammonium chloride is added to 250 g of water at 25°C, the mass of solid that remains undissolved is closest to

A. 53 g
B. 98 g
C. 110 g
D. 134 g

Question 5

A student titrates 20.00 mL of a sodium hydroxide solution with 0.0496 mol L^{-1} sulfuric acid. The volume of required for reaction is 22.56 mL. The concentration of the sodium hydroxide solution, in mol L^{-1}, is

A. 0.0280
B. 0.0559
C. 0.0879
D. 0.112

Question 6

Carbon monoxide reacts with oxygen to produce carbon dioxide.

$2CO(g) + O_2(g) \rightarrow 2CO_2(g)$

If 40.0 g of carbon monoxide and 20.0 g of oxygen are allowed to react, the mass of carbon dioxide formed will be

A. 27.5 g
B. 40.0 g
C. 55.0 g
D. 60.0 g

Question 7

The solubility of lead nitrate in water is 52.3 g/100 g H_2O at 20°C and 88.0 g/100 g H_2O at 60°C. If 50.0 g of water is saturated with lead nitrate at 60°C, what mass of lead nitrate will be precipitated if the solution is cooled to 20°C?

A. 17.9 g
B. 26.2 g
C. 35.7 g
D. 52.3 g

Extended response questions

Analysis of substances in water

Question 1

An impure sample of silver oxide was analysed as follows. 1.634 g of the sample was dissolved in dilute nitric acid. The solution was filtered to remove any insoluble residue and reacted with an excess of sodium chloride solution. The silver chloride precipitate was collected washed with distilled water and dried. The mass of dry AgCl was 1.717 g.

(a) Write balanced equations for the two reactions that occurred. (2 marks)

(b) Why was the silver chloride washed? (1 mark)

(c) What is the percentage purity of silver oxide in the sample? (3 marks)

(Total = 6 marks)

Question 2

(a) Calculate the molarity of OH^- ions in a solution of calcium hydroxide, $Ca(OH)_2$ made by completely dissolving 4.5 g of calcium hydroxide in 500 mL of water. (3 marks)

(b) What volume of the calcium hydroxide solution would react completely with 100 mL of 0.10 mol L^{-1} hydrochloric acid? (3 marks)

(c) The same calcium hydroxide solution was reacted in a separate experiment with 100 mL of 0.10 mol L^{-1} phosphoric acid.

(i) Write a balanced equation for the reaction. (1 mark)

(ii) What would be the volume ratio of calcium hydroxide solution reacting in this reaction when compared to the volume reacting with the hydrochloric acid? (1 mark)

(iii)What difference in a property of calcium chloride and calcium phosphate would be observed in these two experiments? (1 mark)

(Total = 9 marks)

Question 3

100.0 mL of a 1.50 M solution of iron(III) sulfate is mixed with 60.00 mL of a 2.50 M solution of sodium hydroxide. A precipitate of iron(III) hydroxide forms.

(a) Write a balanced equation for the reaction. (1 mark)

(b) Determine which reactant is in excess. (3 marks)

(c) Calculate the concentration of the excess reactant. (2 marks)

(d) Calculate the mass of the precipitate formed. (2 marks)

(Total = 8 marks)

Question 4

The solubilities at 20°C and molar masses of potassium iodide, potassium nitrate, sodium iodide and sodium nitrate are given in the table below.

Compound	**Solubility at 20°C (g / 100 g H_2O)**	**Molar mass ($g\ mol^{-1}$)**
KI	144.0	166.0
KNO_3	31.6	101.1
NaI	179.0	149.9
$NaNO_3$	88.1	85.0

34.0 g of sodium nitrate is dissolved in 50.0 g of water at 20°C. In a separate container, 66.4 g of potassium iodide is also dissolved in 50.0g of water at 20°C. The two solutions are mixed at 20°C.

Calculate the mass of any compound that precipitates from the mixed solutions.

(Total = 3 marks)

Chapter 6

Unit 2 Examination

Section A

Question 1

The equation for the reaction of ethanoic acid, CH_3COOH, with hydroxide ion is given below.

$CH_3COOH(aq) + OH^-(aq) \rightleftharpoons CH_3COO^-(aq) + H_2O(l)$

In this reaction the base and the conjugate base are

A. $OH^-(aq)$ and $CH_3COO^-(aq)$

B. $OH^-(aq)$ and $H_2O(l)$

C. $CH_3COOH(aq)$ and $CH_3COO^-(aq)$

D. $CH_3COO^-(aq)$ and $H_2O(l)$

Question 2

A solution of barium hydroxide, $Ba(OH)_2$, has a pH of 11.0 at 25°C. The concentration of barium hydroxide, in mol L^{-1}, is closest to

A. 5.0×10^{-4} **B.** 1.0×10^{-3}

C. 3.0 **D.** 11.0

Question 3

Nitric acid, HNO_3, is a strong acid. A solution of nitric acid is prepared with a concentration of 0.15 mol L^{-1}. Nitrous acid, HNO_2, is a weak acid. A solution of this acid is prepared with a concentration of 0.25 mol L^{-1}. Which one of the following correctly gives the concentration of H_3O^+ in each solution?

	Concentration of $H_3O^+(aq)$ in HNO_3	Concentration of $H_3O^+(aq)$ in HNO_2
A.	0.15 mol L^{-1}	0.25 mol L^{-1}
B.	0.15 mol L^{-1}	less than 0.25 mol L^{-1}
C.	less than 0.15 mol L^{-1}	0.25 mol L^{-1}
D.	less than 0.15 mol L^{-1}	less than 0.25 mol L^{-1}

Question 4

Deionised water is rarely found in the natural environment because

A. rainwater is deionised as it flows over rocks.

B. water is purified by evaporation to form clouds.

C. water is an excellent solvent.

D. water is immiscible with non-polar liquids.

Question 5

Which one of the following compounds is likely to have the highest boiling temperature?

A. C_2H_6 **B.** H_2O_2

C. CH_3OH **D.** N_2H_4

Question 6

The mass of lead iodide precipitate formed when 200.0 mL of 1.50 mol L^{-1} potassium iodide solution reacts with 150.0 ml of a 0.500 mol L^{-1} lead nitrate solution is closest to

A. 138 g
B. 35.0 g
C. 2.80×10^2 g
D. 69.0 g

Question 7

Which of the following compounds, when in the liquid state, is **most** likely to be miscible with water?

A. CH_3COOH
B. CCl_4
C. $C_7H_{15}OH$
D. C_8H_{18}

Question 8

$2H_2PO_4^-(aq) \rightleftharpoons HPO_4^{2-}(aq) + H_3PO_4(aq)$

In the above reaction, the $H_2PO_4^-$ ion acts as

A. an acid.
B. an amphiprotic substance.
C. a reductant.
D. an oxidant.

Question 9

200 mL of 0.300 M nitric acid (HNO_3) is reacted with 100 mL of 0.500 M barium hydroxide solution ($Ba(OH)_2$). Which reactant is **in excess** and by how many moles?

A. nitric acid by 0.0100 mol
B. nitric acid by 0.0200 mol
C. barium hydroxide solution by 0.0100 mol
D. barium hydroxide solution by 0.0200 mol

Question 10

What volume of water must be added to 20.0 mL of 9.0 M hydrochloric acid to produce a concentration of 1.5 mol L^{-1}.

A. 100 mL
B. 120 mL
C. 140 mL
D. 160 mL

Question 11

0.010 mol L^{-1} solutions containing sodium chloride, carbon dioxide, sodium hydroxide and ammonia are all tested with a pH meter. Which of the following lists states the most likely pH values to be shown by the meter?

	NaCl(aq)	**CO_2(aq)**	**NaOH(aq)**	**NH_3(aq)**
A.	7.0	2.0	12.0	12.0
B.	6.0	7.0	11.0	7.0
C.	8.0	5.5	11.0	12.0
D.	7.0	5.5	12.0	10.6

Question 12

What would be the final pH of a mixture of 200 mL of 0.60 M potassium hydroxide solution and 200 mL of 1.00 M hydrochloric acid?

A. 1.0 **B.** 0.70
C. 0.30 **D.** 0.40

Question 13

Ammonia gas dissolves in water and then reacts as shown in the following equation:

$NH_3(aq) + H_2O(l) \rightleftharpoons NH_4^+(aq) + OH^-(aq)$

This reaction is best described as

A. ionisation. **B.** dissociation.
C. redox. **D.** hydration.

Question 14

Sulfur dioxide reacts with oxygen to form sulfur trioxide.

$2SO_2(g) + O_2(g) \rightleftharpoons 2SO_3(g)$

If 10.0 g of sulfur dioxide are allowed to react with 10.0 g of oxygen, what will be the mass of sulfur trioxide produced when the reaction is complete?

A. 20.0 g **B.** 10.0 g
C. 12.5 g **D.** 25.0 g

Question 15

Which of the following metals forms an impervious protective oxide coating in air?

A. aluminium **B.** sodium
C. gold **D.** iron

Question 16

Reactive metals are often joined to less reactive metals to protect them from corrosion. Which of the following metals could not be used in the sacrificial electrochemical protection of a piece of nickel?

A. magnesium **B.** iron
C. tin **D.** zinc

Question 17

In normal phase HPLC, a polar stationary phase, such as silica or alumina, is used along with a non-polar or low polarity solvent such as hexane. An alternative method is called reversed phase HPLC. In this case the stationary phase is non-polar, usually a long-chain hydrocarbon. Which one of the following liquids is **unlikely** to be used as the mobile phase in the reversed phase method?

A. water **B.** octane
C. methanol **D.** ethanol

Question 18

Lithium nitride, Li_3N, is a highly reactive substance and reacts with hydrogen according to the following equation

$Li_3N(s) + 2H_2(g) \rightarrow LiNH_2(s) + 2LiH(s)$

This reaction is best described as

A. an acid-base reaction.
B. a redox reaction
C. both acid-base and redox
D. neither acid-base nor redox

Question 19

200 mL of methane gas was mixed with 600 mL of oxygen gas at 20°C and 1.5 atmosphere pressure, and sparked. The reaction shown by the following equation occurred.

$CH_4(g) + 2O_2(g) \rightarrow CO_2(g) + 2H_2O(l)$

What would be the total volume of gas present when the reaction had cooled to the original temperature and pressure?

A. 200 mL **B.** 350 mL **C.** 400 mL **D.** 650 mL

Question 20

2.0 L of oxygen is in one vessel and 1.0 L of hydrogen is in another vessel. Both vessels are at the same temperature and pressure. How would the amount of oxygen compare to the amount of hydrogen?

A. There would be equal masses of both.
B. There would be equal moles of both.
C. The mass of oxygen would be twice that of hydrogen.
D. The moles of oxygen would be twice that of hydrogen.

Section B

Question 1

(a) A chemist made the following observations using clean metal surfaces.

Metal X dissolved in YNO_3 solution, forming a deposit of metal Y.
Metal Z did not react with $X(NO_3)_2$ solution.
Metal Y did not react with $Z(NO_3)_2$ solution.

Place metals X, Y and Z in order of increasing reactivity (least reactive first). (2 marks)

(b) Tin (Sn) rods are placed in each of four equimolar aqueous solutions of $AuNO_3$, $CuSO_4$, $FeSO_4$ and $ZnCl_2$.

(i) Describe and explain what you would expect to see in each of these experiments. (2 marks)

(ii) Give equations for any reactions that occur. (2 marks)

(c) Write an equation for a reaction in which a metal reacts with an aqueous solution of $SnCl_2$. (1 mark)

(Total = 7 marks)

Question 2

The boiling temperatures of the group 14 and group 15 hydrides are given in the table below, along with their molar masses and number of electrons per molecule.

Compound	Boiling temperature (°C)	Molar mass ($g\ mol^{-1}$)	Number of electrons
CH_4	–161	16.0	10
SiH_4	–112	32.1	18
GeH_4	–88	76.6	36
SnH_4	–52	122.7	54
NH_3	–33	17.0	10
PH_3	–88	34.0	18
AsH_3	–63	78.0	36
SbH_3	–17	124.8	54

(a) Which group of contains polar molecules? Give an explanation for your answer. (3 marks)

(b) Explain why the boiling temperature of SbH_3 is greater than that of SnH_4. (2 marks)

(c) Explain why the boiling temperature of NH_3 is so large for such a small molecule. Draw a diagram to support your answer. (2 marks)

(d) Give an explanation for the increase in boiling temperatures in group 14. (1 mark)

(Total = 8 marks)

Question 3

Hydrazine, N_2H_4, and hydrogen peroxide, H_2O_2, react together according to the following equation:

$N_2H_4(l) + 2H_2O_2(l) \rightarrow N_2(g) + 4H_2O(g)$

(a) Derive the oxidation half-equation. (1 mark)

(b) Derive the reduction half-equation. (1 mark)

(c) Calculate the mass of steam produced when 500 kg of hydrazine and 500 kg of hydrogen peroxide are allowed to react. (3 marks)

(Total = 5 marks)

Question 4

A student is asked to demonstrate a redox reaction and is given access to pieces of copper and magnesium and solutions of magnesium nitrate and copper sulfate.

(a) Which chemicals should the student choose? Give a reason for your answer. (2 marks)

(b) Write a balanced ionic equation for the reaction that will occur when the appropriate chemicals are mixed. (1 mark)

(c) Identify the conjugate redox pairs in the equation in part b). (1 mark)

(Total = 4 marks)

Question 5

Write full and ionic equations for the following reactions.

(a) Calcium nitrate solution reacting with sodium phosphate solution (2 marks)

(b) Potassium hydrogen carbonate solution reacting with sulfuric acid (2 marks)

(Total = 4 marks)

Question 6

The specific heat of water is 4.18 J g^{-1} °C^{-1} and the specific heat of steel is 0.46 J g^{-1} °C^{-1}. The density of water is 1.0 g mL^{-1}. On a hot day the temperature of the water in a car radiator rises from 18°C to 29°C.

(a) If the capacity of the radiator is 10.0 L, calculate the energy in joules required to cause this temperature increase. (2 marks)

(b) The same amount of energy is absorbed by an empty steel radiator of mass 10.0 kg. What is the temperature increase of the radiator if its initial temperature is also 18°C? (2 marks)

(c) Explain why the specific heat of water is significantly higher than the specific heat of steel. (2 marks)

(Total = 6 marks)

Question 7

(a) Perchloric acid, $HClO_4$, is a strong acid and propanoic acid, C_2H_5COOH, is a weak acid. Write balanced equations demonstrating the reaction of both acids with water. (2 marks)

(b) Using 5.0 mol L^{-1} and 0.10 mol L^{-1} solutions of each acid as examples, explain carefully how perchloric acid can be strong and dilute, and propanoic acid can be weak and concentrated. (4 marks)

(c) If 250 mL of 0.500 mol L^{-1} perchloric acid is added to 300 mL of 0.200 mol L^{-1} potassium hydroxide solution, calculate the pH of the final solution? (3 marks)

(Total = 9 marks)

Question 8

The major acidic component of vinegar is ethanoic acid, CH_3COOH. A student determines the concentration of ethanoic acid in vinegar by the following method. The student weighed 39.62 g of vinegar into a volumetric flask and made up the volume to 250.0 mL. The diluted vinegar was placed in a burette and titrated against

20.00 mL of 0.1056 mol L^{-1} sodium hydroxide solution using phenolphthalein as indicator. The average of three concordant results was 18.62 mL.

(a) Calculate the amount of sodium hydroxide (in mol) used in the titration. (1 mark)

(b) Calculate the amount of ethanoic acid (in mol) in the 250 mL flask. (1 mark)

(c) Calculate the mass of ethanoic acid in 250 mL. (1 mark)

(d) Calculate the volume of vinegar used if the density of vinegar is 1.01 g mL^{-1}. (1 mark)

(e) Calculate %(m/v) of ethanoic acid in vinegar. (1 mark)

(f) Which liquids should be used to wash the following pieces of equipment?

(i) the burette

(ii) the 250 mL volumetric flask

(iii) the pipette (3 marks)

(Total = 8 marks)

Question 9

The specific heat of water is 4.18 J g^{-1} $°C^{-1}$ and at 100°C the latent heat of vaporisation of water is 40.0 kJ mol^{-1}. Calculate the total amount of energy required to heat 100 g of water from 20°C to 100°C and then to completely convert all of the water to steam.

(Total = 3 marks)

Question 10

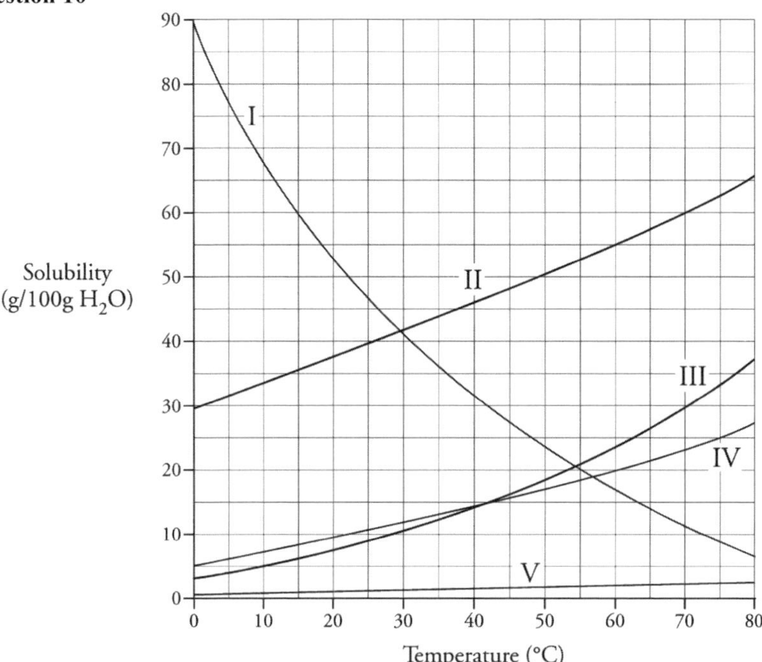

The solubility curves for five compounds are shown on the graph above. Use the graph to complete the questions below.

(a) Which curve is most likely to be that of a gas? (1 mark)

(b) Which substance is most likely to be lead chloride? (1 mark)

(c) What mass of substance III will dissolve in 75.0 g of water at 70°C? (1 mark)

(d) One substance is ammonium chloride whose solubility at 25°C is 24.0 g per 60 g of water. Which curve is that for ammonium chloride? (1 mark)

(e) Apart from substance I, which two substances and at what temperature have the same solubility? (1 mark)

(f) 45 g of each compound is added to 250 g of water in separate containers at 30°C. Which compound or compounds will remain undissolved? (2 marks)

(Total = 7 marks)

Chapter 7

Answers: Unit 1 Area of Study 1

Multiple choice items

Elements and the periodic table

Question	Answer	Comments
1.	**A.**	This is the definition of mass number.
2.	**C.**	40 is the mass number (protons + neutrons) and 20 is the atomic number (protons = no of electrons in a neutral atom).
3.	**D.**	All these particles have more protons than electrons.
4.	**A.**	The mass number and atomic number are placed before the element symbol, with the mass number on top. For this atom the mass number is 29 + 35 = 64 and the atomic number = 29.
5.	**D.**	Neutral atoms of phosphorus have 15 electrons.
6.	**A.**	The mass number of this particle is 27 + 28 = 55 and its atomic number is 27. It has two more protons than electrons (27 to 25) and thus carries a charge of 2+.
7.	**B.**	Number of neutrons = mass number – atomic number
8.	**B.**	Isotopes have the same atomic number but different mass numbers.
9.	**B.**	A is the ground state configuration of element 6. C is the configuration of an excited state of an anion, while D is the configuration of a cation.
10.	**C.**	All d subshells contain 5 orbitals each of which can take two electrons.
11.	**A.**	Mg^{2+} has ten electrons. The anion must also have ten electrons and the element will have eight protons.
12.	**B.**	These elements have *similar* chemical properties but not the same. The outer-shell electron configuration is the same for each element (s^2p^5).
13.	**D.**	Element 16 is sulfur. Selenium is in the same vertical group as sulfur and thus is expected to have similar chemical properties.
14.	**B.**	The size of the atoms increases going down group 1, hence the atomic radius increases. When K is compared to Li the outer-shell electron is further from the nucleus and less firmly held. Thus, the ionisation energy decreases from Li to K.
15.	**D.**	Chemical properties are largely determined by the outer-shell electron configuration. Elements are arranged in order of increasing atomic number.

16.	**C.**	As the atomic number increases across a period, the attraction between the nucleus and the outer-shell electrons increases and thus the size of the atom decreases. The electrons are also more firmly held and so the first ionisation energy increases.
17.	**C.**	In going across the periodic table, metallic character decreases (Na, Mg, Al are metals and P, S, Cl are non-metals) as does the atomic radius. Na, Mg and Al are good reducing agents, S and Cl are not.
18.	**D.**	In going down a group of elements in the periodic table, more electron shells are needed to accommodate the electrons. Only two shells are needed for the electrons of Be; Mg needs three shells; Ca four shells and Sr five shells. If more shells are used, then the atom increases in size.
19.	**C.**	All group I elements form 1+ cations (1 electron in the outer shell) and there is no tendency to form 2+ cations. Going from Li to Cs, the outer-shell electrons become further from the nucleus, have less attraction to the nucleus and hence are more easily removed.
20.	**B.**	The metals in A, B and C are lithium, sodium, magnesium, aluminium, and iron.
21.	**A.**	The size of an atom or ion will be determined by the nuclear charge and the number of electron shells. Na^+ and F^- have electrons in two shells, while Cl^- and K^+ use three shells. Na^+ has a nuclear charge of 11+, while the nuclear charge of F^- is 9+.
22.	**C.**	The nuclear charge of K is greater than that of Na. The K atom has electrons in four shells, whereas Na has electrons in three shells. Thus K atoms will be larger than Na atoms. The ions, K^+ and Na^+ will be smaller than their respective atoms. Actual values are Na^+ 102 pm, Na 186 pm, K^+ 138 pm and K 227 pm.
23.	**D.**	The element has four electrons in the outer shell. It cannot be carbon because carbon has only six electrons in total. This element has at least eight electrons.
24.	**B.**	All the inert gases except helium have the outer-shell configuration s^2p^6.

Covalent substances

Question	Answer	Comments
25.	**A.**	A covalent bond between two atoms in a molecule consists of a shared pair of electrons, one originating from each atom. These shared electrons are attracted to the nucleus of both atoms in the molecule.

26.	A.	PF_3 is a covalent molecule formed when a P atom shares three of its five outer-shell electrons, one with each of three F atoms. In the molecule, the P atom forms three covalent bonds and has one non-bonding electron pair, i.e. there are eight outer-shell electrons around P.
27.	D.	F atoms have seven outer-shell electrons so only share one electron to gain a full outer electron shell. C, N and O atoms all share more than one electron to gain full outer shells.
28.	C.	Nitrogen atoms have five outer-shell electrons, so share three electrons with other atoms to gain the stability of a full outer shell. Thus they form three covalent bonds.
29.	B.	Non-metals achieve the stability of a full outer shell by sharing electrons between two atoms. A covalent bond consists of a shared pair of electrons, one originally from each atom.
30.	A.	Metals have metallic bonding, metals reacting with non-metals produce salts having ionic bonding, positive and negative ions are called cations and anions respectively and non-metals share electron in covalent bonding.
31.	C.	Diamond exists as a covalent network lattice in which each carbon atom forms four strong covalent bonds to four other carbon atoms. Methane is a molecular substance whose molecules have strong covalent bonds within the molecule but weak dispersion forces between them. The bonds, which must be overcome when a change of state occurs, are covalent bonds in diamond but dispersion forces in methane, thus methane has a much lower melting and boiling point.
32.	C.	The number of bonding pairs plus the number of non-bonding pairs of electrons determine the shape of the molecule. The electron pairs repel each other and get as far apart as possible.
33.	A.	In *A* the C atom forms three C–H bonds and one C–P bond, while the P atom forms two more bonds to H. *B* is CH_3CN which has a triple bond, *C* has a C to O double bond. In *D* each N forms one single bond to O and one double bond to O.
34.	B.	H_2O and H_2S are both V shaped molecules. CO_2 is linear, NH_3 is triangular pyramidal, BF_3 is triangular planar and CH_4 is tetrahedral.
35.	B.	Ammonia is a triangular pyramid. Nitrogen atoms form three covalent bonds to three hydrogen atoms and there is also a non-bonding electron pair on the nitrogen atom.
36.	C.	C_2H_2, HCl and N_2 are all linear molecules. PCl_3 has a triangular pyramid shape.
37.	D.	Fluorine is the most electronegative element so the difference in electronegativity between F and H is greater than that between C, N and O and hydrogen.

38. **D.** PH_3 is an asymmetrical triangular pyramid and the molecule is polar with a permanent dipole. CO_2, CH_4, and CF_4 are all symmetrical and non-polar as they have no permanent dipole.

39. **D.** C to O have different electronegativities and the C=O bonds are polar covalent bonds. Since CO_2 is a linear molecule the bond polarities cancel out and the molecule is non-polar.

40. **D.** The electronegativity of the halogens decreases in the order $F > Cl > Br > I$. The smallest electronegativity difference will be between C and I. This will give the smallest molecular dipole.

41. A. All four molecules are quite polar and their dipoles decrease in the order $CH_3F > CH_3Cl > CH_3Br > CH_3I$ (6.2, 6.2, 6.0 and 5.4D). However, there are also dispersion forces that will contribute to the intermolecular attractions. These are dependent on the number of electrons present (18e, 26e, 44e and 62e). Thus, there is a larger change in dispersion forces. The boiling points (in °C) are $CH_3F = -78 < CH_3Cl = -24 < CH_3Br = 3.6 < CH_3I = 42$

42. **C.** Molecular substances have weak intermolecular bonding, but covalent network and layer lattices have strong covalent bonding throughout. Thus, molecular substances have much lower melting and boiling points than covalent lattices.

43. **B.** Molecular substances often (but not always) have low boiling temperatures. Some elements (e.g. O_2, N_2, F_2 etc.) are composed of molecules. Many molecular substances are liquids (H_2O, Br_2) or solids (I_2) at room temperature. They generally do not conduct electricity.

44. **B.** HF is very soluble in water because it forms hydrogen bonds with water molecules. Butan-1-ol is slightly soluble in water. The –OH group forms hydrogen bonds with water molecules but the $CH_3CH_2CH_2CH_2-$ part of the molecule does not. Both O_2 and propane are only slightly soluble in water since they are either non-polar or only slightly polar molecules and do not readily form bonds to water molecules.

45. A. Both methanol and ethanol exhibit hydrogen bonding and have one –OH group per molecule. The magnitude of the dispersion forces will be higher in ethanol as it is a larger molecule.

46. **B.** The four molecules have the same number of electrons and similar molar masses. Hence the dispersion forces between the molecules in these substances will be similar. $C_3H_7NH_2$ and $C_2H_5NHCH_3$ will also have hydrogen bonding between their molecules. This will be greater for $C_3H_7NH_2$. The boiling temperatures (in °C) are $C_4H_{10} = -0.5$; $C_3H_7NH_2 = 48.5$; $C_2H_5NHCH_3 = 36.5$ and $(CH_3)_3N = 2.9$.

47.	**C.**	All the molecules have intermolecular dispersion forces but aminomethane contains a –N–H bond and is the only molecule that also exhibits hydrogen bonding. Its boiling point is expected to be (and is) higher than that of the other alternatives.
48.	**C.**	Three electrons from each carbon atom form covalent bonds with three other carbon atoms in the same layer. The remaining electron from each carbon atom is delocalised through the layer.
49.	**B.**	In diamond, each carbon is covalently bonded to four other carbon atoms. In graphite, carbon nanotubes and buckyballs each carbon is covalently bonded to three other carbon atoms. In each of these forms, the carbon atoms are in rings and the fourth electron from each carbon is delocalised around the ring or throughout the layer.

Reactions of metals

Question	Answer	Comments
50.	**C.**	The melting temperatures of both II and VI are below 0°C and their boiling temperatures are both higher than 50°C.
51.	**A.**	I has the highest melting and boiling temperatures so is most likely to have the strongest bonding, and thus most likely to have the greatest strength.
52.	**D.**	The metal structure model considers the outer-shell electrons of metal atoms to be delocalised. Thus, positive metal ions exist in a regular array with bands (a 'sea') of delocalised electrons between them. Forces of attraction exist between the positive metal ions and the delocalised electrons.
53.	**A.**	When metals react, they lose electrons. Going down groups 1 and 2 the outermost (valence) electrons get further from the nucleus and are thus easier to remove. Hence the reactivity increases going down the group.
54.	**D.**	When metals are bent or stretched the inter particle bonds must be overcome and then reform in the new position. Statements I, II and III are true but not relevant the properties of malleability and ductility.
55.	**C.**	Delocalised outer-shell electrons in metals are able to move through the metal under the influence of an applied potential difference. This makes the metal an electrical conductor.
56.	**A.**	The attractive forces between particles must be overcome for the metal to melt or boil. The stronger the forces of attraction the higher the melting or boiling points.

57.	**B.**	Density is defined as mass per unit volume. The greater the number of particles, and therefore mass, in a given volume of metal, the greater its density.
58.	**A.**	Metals with low reactivity are easiest to obtain from their ores or to be found uncombined.
59.	**D.**	Calcium will react with cold water. Copper and silver do not react with steam.
60.	**B.**	Calcium in the most reactive metal in this group and iron is the least rcactivc.
61.	**A.**	This is the activity series of metals.
62.	**C.**	Mercury is the least reactive metal (lowest on the activity series).
63.	**C.**	The most reactive metals are the most difficult to extract from their ores.
64.	**C.**	Magnesium is a reactive metal and is therefore found naturally only as its compounds.
65.	**C.**	Their low reactivity meant that they were known as elements long before the more reactive metals.

Reactions of ionic compounds

Question	Answer	Comments
66.	**A.**	Hard and brittle with high melting and boiling temperatures indicates that the attractive forces between particles are strong and much energy is needed to overcome them.
67.	**B.**	Electrical conductors must contain either electrons or ions which are able to move. Solid ionic compounds are crystalline with ions in fixed positions, and no delocalised electrons. When the ionic compound melts, the ionic bonds are overcome and the ions are able to move. Thus, the molten salt is a conductor.
68.	**C.**	M atoms have 2 outer-shell electrons, X atoms have 7 outer-shell electrons. When ionic bonds form, M atoms donate 2 electrons, one to each of 2 X atoms, so that all three atoms have the stability of full outer electron shells. Thus, the formula is MX_2.
69.	**A.**	Metal atoms lose their outer-shell electrons to gain the extra stability of full shells, but gain a positive charge as the number of protons in the atom exceeds the number of electrons.
70.	**C.**	The element is unlikely to be carbon or silicon as these elements form covalent oxides. Magnesium only forms one ionic oxide, MgO, but manganese, which is a transition metal forms both Mn^{2+} and Mn^{4+} ions so can have oxides MnO and MnO_2.

71.	B.	Calcium atoms have two outer-shell electrons and fluorine atoms have seven. A calcium atom will therefore donate two electrons, one to each of two fluorine atoms so that all atoms have the stability of full outer shells. Thus, the formula is CaF_2.
72.	D.	The formulas of the ions are NH_4^+ and SO_4^{2-}.
73.	B.	Two aluminium atoms each donate three outer-shell electrons, two to each of three oxygen atoms so that all ions formed have the stability of full outer shells. Both aluminium and oxide ions then have the same electron configuration which is that of neon.
74.	D.	If a solid precipitates rapidly from solution small crystals will form. To form large crystals the process must happen slowly.
75.	C.	PbI_2 is insoluble and forms a precipitate. The spectator ions, K^+ and NO_3^- are omitted from the equation.
76.	C.	Strontium carbonate is insoluble in water. The lithium and chloride ions are spectator ions.
77.	C.	Lead sulfate is not soluble in water. All the other sulfates are soluble as are all the potassium salts.
78.	D.	K^+ and Cl^- ions are spectator ions.
79.	A.	$MgSO_4$ is soluble in water but $MgCO_3$ is not soluble. $BaSO_4$ and $BaCO_3$ are both insoluble in water. In the other answers one of the cations either gives a precipitate with a test solution or does not produce a precipitate, contrary to the results.
80.	D.	K_2CO_3, $ZnSO_4$ and NH_4Cl are all soluble in water.
81.	C.	KOH and $MgCl_2$ are both soluble in water. $Ca(OH)_2$ and $PbCl_2$ are partly soluble in water. AgI and $CuCO_3$ are insoluble.

Separation and identification of components of mixtures

Question	Answer	Comments
82.	A.	Since the stationary phase is polar, the most polar molecules will be attracted more strongly and will travel the smallest distance.
83.	D.	Polar molecules will be attracted to the polar solvent molecules and will thus move more rapidly through the column than non- polar molecules.
84.	B.	I and III would slow down components and therefore they would spend more time in the column. With II, the components would all flow through more quickly and the retention time decreased.
85.	D.	As the stationary phase is non-polar, non-polar components will have a high affinity for it and this will increase their retention time. Small molecules will generally have shorter retention times as described in the question information.

Extended response questions

Elements and the periodic table

Question 1

(a) Oxygen, O (the atom has eight electrons) (1 mark)
(b) The process would release energy, since the electron has moved from a subshell of high energy to one of lower energy (4s to 3s). (2 marks)
(c) $1s^22s^22p^4$ (1 mark)
(Total = 4 marks)

Question 2

(a) Magnesium, calcium and barium have similar chemical properties. (1 mark)
(b) Barium atoms are larger than magnesium atoms and thus the outer-shell electrons are less strongly held than the outer-shell electrons in Mg atoms. (2 marks)
(c) $1s^22s^22p^63s^23p^64s^2$ (1 mark)
(d) The electron configuration of a calcium ion, Ca^{2+}, is $1s^22s^22p^63s^23p^6$; i.e. the Ca atom has lost the two outer-shell electrons (4s electrons). (1 mark)
(e) A magnesium atom has the electron configuration $1s^22s^22p^63s^2$ and has electrons in three shells. The electron configuration of a Mg^{2+} ion is $1s^22s^22p^6$ and only two shells are used. The outermost electrons of a Mg atom are thus further from the nucleus and the atom is larger than the cation. (1 mark)
(Total = 6 marks)

Question 3

(a) 'Alkali' metals and 'alkaline earth' metals. These metals are generally highly reactive, soft and have relatively low melting temperatures. (1 mark)
(b) Lithium, Li; sodium, Na; potassium, K; rubidium, Rb; caesium, Cs; magnesium, Mg; calcium, Ca; strontium, Sr; barium, Ba. (2 marks)
(c) (i) Silicon, Si
(ii) Phosphorus, P (2 marks)
(d) Selenium is in group 16 (group VI) and period 4. (1 mark)
(Total = 6 marks)

Question 4

(a) Lithium (Li), beryllium (Be), and carbon in the form of graphite, are all solids at room temperature that conduct heat and electricity. (3 marks)
(b) (i) Phosphorus, P, and sulfur, S, are solid non-metals.
(ii) Chlorine, Cl, and argon, Ar, are gaseous non-metals. (2 marks)
(c) Caesium, Cs, is the most reactive 'alkali' metal and lithium, Li, is the least reactive. (2 marks)
(Total = 7 marks)

Question 5

(a) Increases. F has electrons in two shells, Cl uses three shells, Br uses four shells and I uses five shells. Going from one period to the next adds on an extra shell of electrons and increases the volume and radius of the atom. (2 marks)

(b) Decreases. These elements will react by gaining an electron or by sharing an electron. To gain an electron a substance must be able to remove an electron from another material. The strength with which an atom can attract electrons will determine how reactive it is. F attracts extra electrons more strongly than Cl. The extra electron goes into the second shell on F but into the third shell on Cl and so is more strongly held on F. (2 marks)

(c) Decreases. All these elements have a core charge of +7. However, electrons attracted by F atoms will be attracted to the second shell, but for iodine any electrons will be attracted to the fifth shell, which is further from the nucleus. The attraction for iodine will be weaker than that for fluorine. (2 marks)

(Total = 6 marks)

Question 6

(a) The relative mass of an atom will depend upon the number of neutrons present as well as the number of protons. An element with a smaller atomic number (number of protons) can have a greater relative mass if it has isotopes that have a larger number of neutrons. (In the case of argon and potassium, 99.6% of naturally occurring argon is the $^{40}_{18}Ar$ isotope, while 93% of potassium occurs as the $^{39}_{19}K$ isotope. (2 marks)

(b) A series of transition metals results from the progressive filling of a d–subshell as the atomic number increases. These subshells consist of 5 orbitals, each of which can take 2 electrons. Hence 10 elements result and the subshell electron configuration increases from d^1 to d^{10}. (2 marks)

(Total = 4 marks)

Covalent substances

Question 7

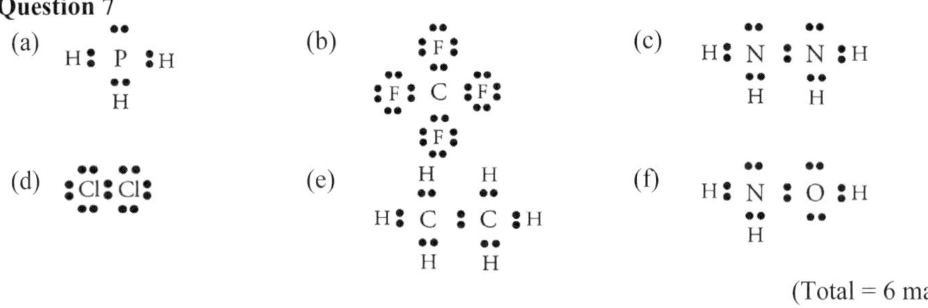

(Total = 6 marks)

Question 8

	Molecule	Shape	Polar/non-polar
(a)	F_2	linear	non-polar
(b)	CH_2O	triangular planar	polar
(c)	CCl_4	tetrahedral	non-polar
(d)	HCN	linear	polar
(e)	BF_3	triangular planar	non-polar

(Total = 10 marks)

Question 9

(a) H—C≡C—H

or

N≡C—C≡N

(b) 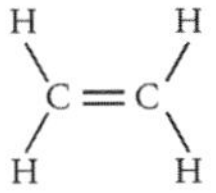 $H_2C=CH_2$

or C_2F_4

(c) 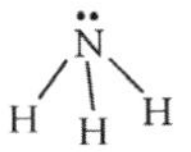 NH_3 (N with a lone pair, bonded to three H)

or NF_3

(d) 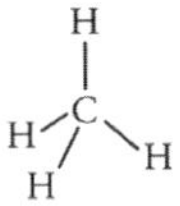 CH_4 (C bonded to four H)

or CF_4

(Total = 4 marks)

Question 10

CF_4 is a symmetrical molecule. Although each C–F bond is polar because of the molecular symmetry, the bond polarities cancel each other out.

(2 marks)

Question 11

(a) $1s^22s^22p^63s^23p^4$ (1 mark)

(b) There are 6 electrons in the outer shell of a sulfur atom. To form a double bond, the sulfur atom shares two electrons with each oxygen atom. In SO_2 the number of electrons around the sulfur atom is 6 + 4 = 10. In SO_3 the number is 6 + 6 = 12. (2 marks)

(c) In both SO_2 and SO_3 there are three groups of electrons. In SO_2 there are 4 in each double bond plus 2 in a lone pair. In SO_3 there are 4 electrons in each double bond. The valence structures are

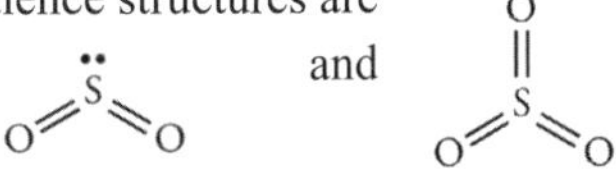

(2 marks)

(d) In periods 3–6 the atoms are larger and can accommodate more than 8 electrons around the central atom. Also these elements have the d subshell available to accommodate the extra electrons (3d for sulfur). (1 mark)

(Total = 6 marks)

Question 12

(a) H—C≡N—

(b) 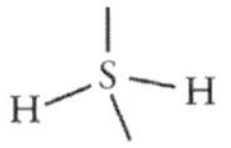 H—S—H

(c) 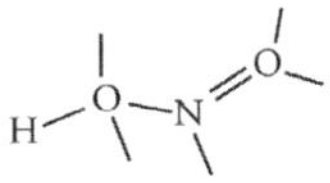 H—O—N=O

(d) 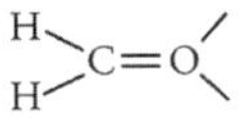 $H_2C=O$

(e) 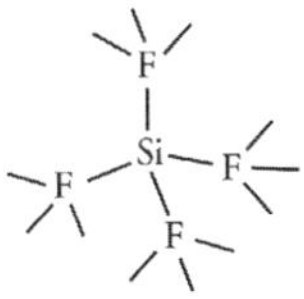 SiF_4 (Si bonded to four F)

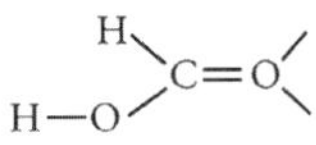

(f) H—O—C(H)=O

(Total = 6 marks)

Question 13

(a) Methane, CH_4, is a non-polar molecule. The only forces of attraction between the

molecules are dispersion forces. These are very weak and hence methane is a gas at room temperature. Water is a polar molecule. As well as dispersion forces there are hydrogen bonds between the molecules. Hence the intermolecular attractions are much greater in water and it is a liquid. (2 marks)

(b) Iodine is a non-polar molecule. It does not form hydrogen bonds to water molecules and thus has low solubility in water. The dispersion forces between the iodine molecules are comparable to the dispersion forces between the hexane molecules. Hence iodine is soluble in hexane. (1 mark)

(Total = 3 marks)

Question 14

(a)

	CH_3Cl	CH_3Br	CH_3I
Number of electrons	26	44	62

(3 marks)

(b) The attractive forces due to dipole-dipole bonding should be approximately the same for each compound since the dipoles are approximately the same. However, the dispersion forces will increase from CH_3Cl to CH_3Br to CH_3I since the number of electrons is increasing in this order. (2 marks)

(Total = 5 marks)

Question 15

(a)

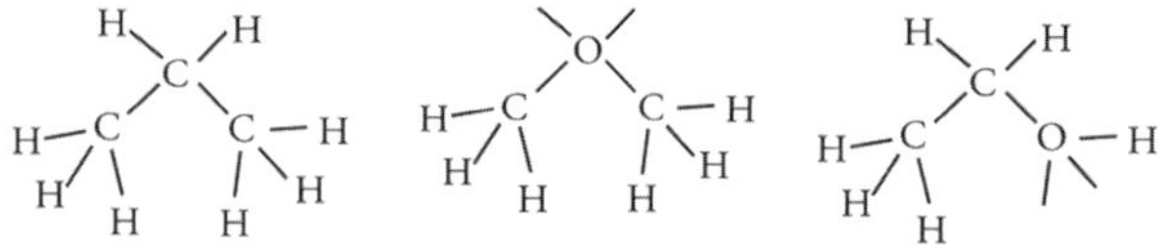

propane dimethyl ether ethanol

(3 marks)

(b) Dimethyl ether and ethanol are isomers. They both have the molecular formula, C_2H_6O. (1 mark)

(c) Propane has $(3 \times 6) + 8 = 26$ electrons
Dimethyl ether has $(2 \times 6) + 6 + 8 = 26$ electrons
Ethanol has $(2 \times 6) + 6 + 8 = 26$ electrons (1 mark)

(d) The size of the dispersion forces between molecules depends on the number of electrons in the molecule and the shape of the molecule. These three molecules have the same number of electrons and very similar molecular shapes. The size of the dispersion forces should be approximately the same for the three molecules. (2 marks)

(e) The only attractive force between propane molecules will be dispersion forces. Dimethyl ether will have similar dispersion forces acting between its molecules. Dimethyl ether molecules also have a small molecular dipole. Oxygen has a higher electronegativity than carbon. The C–O bonds are polar with the oxygen atom being slightly negative and the carbon atom slightly positive. The small molecular dipole in dimethyl ether means that the intermolecular forces are slightly larger in dimethyl ether than they are in propane. Thus, there is a small increase in boiling temperature. Ethanol contains an O–H bond. Hydrogen bonding occurs between ethanol molecules, so the intermolecular forces are larger in ethanol than dimethyl ether. Hence the boiling temperature of ethanol is higher than that of dimethyl ether. (3 marks)

(Total = 10 marks)

Question 16

(a) Methane and ammonia have similar atomic masses so would be expected to have similar boiling points if dispersion forces were the only intermolecular forces operating. (1 mark)

(b) The boiling points are very different, and the boiling point of methane is much lower than that of ammonia. This is because ammonia is a polar molecule whereas methane is non-polar. The attractive forces between ammonia molecules results from dispersion forces and hydrogen bonding. In methane the only attractive forces between the molecules are dispersion forces.

$^{\delta+}H_3–N^{\delta-}$--------$^{\delta+}H_3–N^{\delta-}$ (3 marks)

(Total = 4 marks)

Question 17

(a) Allotropes are different physical forms of the same chemical element. Their chemical bonding may differ in strength, nature and direction. (1 mark)

(b) In diamond each carbon atom is covalently bonded to four other carbon atoms. There is covalent bonding between the atoms throughout the lattice. In graphite each carbon atom is covalently bonded to three other carbon atoms. The carbon atoms are arranged in layers. There are dispersion forces between the layers. (2 marks)

(c) (i) Diamond has strong bonding throughout its structure. Graphite has weak bonding between the layers. (1 mark)

(ii) In graphite one electron from each carbon atom is delocalised throughout the layer. This allows conduction of electricity. Diamond has no delocalised electrons. (1 mark)

(iii) The distance between the layers of atoms in graphite is greater than the length of the covalent bonds in diamond. Hence the atoms in diamond are closer together and the density is greater. (1 mark)

(iv) Neither diamond nor graphite melt to a liquid when heated, but at a very high temperature all the bonds are broken and the solid becomes a gas. In graphite the presence of delocalised electrons within each layer means that the bonding in the layers is slightly stronger than the bonding between the atoms in diamond. (1 mark)

(d) (i) The strong bonding between carbon atoms in diamond make it harder than the rock etc. which it cuts. (1 mark)

(ii) Diamond transmits and reflects light. It also produces a white light spectrum, making it attractive as jewellery. (1 mark)

(iii) Because diamond is so hard it can be cut to produce a very fine edge, which is more accurate where precision is needed in an operation. (1 mark)

(iv) The weak bonding between the layers of carbon atoms in graphite is overcome when a pencil is moved across paper leaving a trail of carbon on the paper. (1 mark)

(v) The very high melting point of graphite makes it a suitable container for other high melting point substances. (1 mark)

(vi) The ability of graphite layers to 'slide' over each other makes it suitable as a lubricant. (1 mark)

(vii) Graphite is an electrical conductor but also is relatively inert chemically. It can be shaped so is suitable as an electrode. (1 mark)

(viii) Graphite is black, opaque and can exist as a very fine powder in suspension in a solvent. (1 mark)

(ix) Graphite absorbs neutrons produced in nuclear reactions. If some of the neutrons are absorbed in this way, they are prevented from taking part in further nuclear reactions and the speed of the nuclear reaction is reduced. (1 mark)

(Total = 16 marks)

Reactions of metals

Question 18

(a) Potassium: $1s^22s^22p^63s^23p^64s^1$
Chromium: $1s^22s^22p^63s^23p^63d^54s^1$ (2 marks)

(b) Both potassium and chromium have metallic bonding. The positive nuclear charge of chromium is greater than that of potassium, therefore electrons are more strongly attracted to the nucleus and the chromium atom has a smaller radius than the potassium atom. Potassium only has one 4s electron which is delocalised but chromium has both the 3d and 4s electrons. This means that the metallic bonding in chromium is stronger than that in potassium as positive metal ions and delocalised electrons are closer and the number of delocalised electrons is higher. (2 marks)

(c) Potassium and chromium:
– are both reductants and react chemically by forming positive ions
– both have a metallic lustre (potassium rapidly oxidises in air). (2 marks)

(Total = 6 marks)

Question 19

(a) The metallic bonding in aluminium produces a malleable metal, which is insufficiently strong and rigid to be suitable for bridge building. (1 mark)

(b) 'Silver' coins are an alloy of copper and nickel, which is silver in appearance but not as expensive to produce as coins made of the element silver. (1 mark)

(c) Recycling aluminium requires less energy than producing it from bauxite. Recycling involves melting the discarded pieces of aluminium and recasting. Production from bauxite involves electrolysis of a molten salt, which is very energy intensive. (1 mark)

(d) A pure iron sword would corrode when left exposed to air and moisture. (1 mark)

(e) Titanium is light and strong and does not corrode, essential requirements when the joint cannot easily be replaced and must function for many years. (1 mark)

(Total = 5 marks)

Question 20

(a) In the diagram opposite, each metal atom has lost an electron to form a positive ion. These ions are in a regular array. The electrons lost from each atom have formed an electron 'sea' which is spread throughout the lattice. (3 marks)

(b) (i) When a potential difference is applied across a piece of metal the delocalised electrons move towards the positive terminal and away from the negative terminal in equal numbers and thus an electric current flows in the metal. (2 marks)

(ii) Ions and electrons in a metal are able to move relative to one another as the bonding between them is not rigid or fixed in its direction. Layers of metal ions can move to change the shape of a metal and metallic bonds are not broken. Thus the metal is malleable and ductile. (2 marks)

(iii) Metallic bonding is the force of attraction between layers of positive metal ions and layers of delocalised outer-shell electrons surrounding them. (2 marks)

(Total = 9 marks)

Question 21

(a) $2Cr(s) + 3O_2(g) \rightarrow 2Cr_2O_3(s)$ (2 marks)

(b) $Pb(s) + 2Cl_2(g) \rightarrow PbCl_4(s)$ (2 marks)

(c) $2K(s) + 2H_2O(l) \rightarrow 2KOH(aq) + 2H_2(g)$ (2 marks)

(d) $2Al(s) + 6H_2O(g) \rightarrow 2Al(OH)_3(s) + 3H_2(g)$ (2 marks)

(e) $2Fe(s) + 6HCl(aq) \rightarrow 2FeCl_3(aq) + 3H_2(g)$ (2 marks)

(f) $2Al(s) + 3H_2SO_4(aq) \rightarrow Al_2(SO_4)_3(aq) + 3H_2(g)$ (2 marks)

(Total = 12 marks)

Question 22

(a) Both oxygen and water are necessary for iron objects to rust. In the desert there is little or no water and deep in the ocean there is little or no oxygen. (2 marks)
(However, in the deep ocean, sulfate-producing bacteria may cause iron to corrode.)

(b) Aluminium forms a surface oxide layer which is strongly bonded to the aluminium beneath it, and which protects the metal from further reaction. (2 marks)

(c) Sodium reacts violently with water forming sodium hydroxide and hydrogen so cannot be stored in water. (2 marks)

(d) The purposes of alloying gold are to make it harder and more resistant to wear, and to change its colour for use as jewellery by alloying with, for example, copper or platinum. (2 marks)

(Total = 8 marks)

Question 23

Atoms of tin and lead are of different sizes. The lack of uniform bonding strength throughout an alloy resulting from the presence of atoms of at least two elements, results in the alloy having a lower boiling point than the pure metal. Thus the solder could be melted and used to join metals without the risk of melting them. (3 marks)

Question 24

(a) *Advantages:* Iron is relatively cheap and strong.
Disadvantages: Pure iron corrodes in air and is heavy as a building material. (4 marks)

(b) (i) Galvanising. The iron is dipped into a bath of molten zinc, which forms a protective coating from the air and prevents corrosion. Scratched coatings still give cathodic protection as the iron and zinc are in contact and the zinc acts as a sacrificial anode.
(ii) Alloying. Iron can be alloyed with various other elements to produce steel. Steel has a low carbon and manganese content which increase its strength. Alloy steel contains up to 10% of other metals to give the steel the required properties; e.g. stainless steel, which is corrosion resistant, contains about 10% chromium. (4 marks)

(Total = 8 marks)

Reactions of ionic compounds

Question 25

(a) (i) Na^+ and F^-
(ii) Mg^{2+} and O^{2-} (2 marks)

(b) All of the ions, Na^+, F^-, Mg^{2+} and O^{2-}, have the same electron configuration, $1s^22s^22p^6$. (1 mark)

© Although all four ions have the same electron configuration, the attractive force between magnesium and oxide ions is higher that between sodium and fluoride ions (approximately four times higher). The charge on the ions results from the transfer of two electrons in magnesium oxide rather than one in the case of sodium fluoride. (2 marks)

(Total = 5 marks)

Question 26

(a) Cr_2O_3
(b) KNO_3
(c) $MgCO_3$
(d) $HgCl_2$
(e) $Al(OH)_3$
(f) Li_3PO_4
(g) $NaHCO_3$
(h) CaF_2
(i) Ba_3N_2
(j) $FeSO_4$

(Total = 10 × ½ = 5 marks)

Question 27

(a) Lithium bromide
(b) Aluminium sulfate
(c) Lead(II) sulfide
(d) Chromium(III) bromide
(e) Zinc nitrate
(f) Potassium oxide
(g) Nickel(II) hydroxide
(h) Copper(II) phosphate
(i) Iron(III) chloride
(j) Silver iodide
(k) Tin(II) carbonate
(l) Scandium(III) oxide

(Total = 12 × ½ = 6 marks)

Question 28

(a) +4 (b) +2
(c) +1 (d) +3
(e) +3 (f) +2
(g) +3 (h) +2 (Total = 8 × 1 = 8 marks)

Question 29

Solid magnesium chloride exists as a crystalline ionic lattice in which each ion is surrounded by ions of opposite charge. The ionic bonds between ions are fixed in length, strength and direction. There are no delocalised electrons.

For an electric current to flow, a substance must contain charged particles that are free to move. When magnesium chloride melts or dissolves in water, the crystal structure breaks down and the ions are able to move and carry an electric current. (Total = 3 marks)

Question 30

(a)	Li_3P	Li^+ $1s^2$	P^{3-} $1s^22s^22p^63s^23p^6$	(2 marks)
(b)	Na_2S	Na^+ $1s^22s^22p^6$	S^{2-} $1s^22s^22p^63s^23p^6$	(2 marks)
(c)	K_2O	K^+ $1s^22s^22p^63s^23p^6$	O^{2-} $1s^22s^22p^6$	(2 marks)
(d)	CaF_2	Ca^{2+} $1s^22s^22p^63s^23p^6$	F^- $1s^22s^22p^6$	(2 marks)
(e)	$AlCl_3$	Al^{3+} $1s^22s^22p^6$	Cl^- $1s^22s^22p^63s^23p^6$	(2 marks)
(f)	Mg_3N_2	Mg^{2+} $1s^22s^22p^6$	N^{3-} $1s^22s^22p^6$	(2 marks)

(The electron configurations of all the ions are those of the inert gas nearest to the element in the periodic table; i.e. the nearest stable electron configuration.) (Total = 12 marks)

Question 31

As the radius of the cation increases, the melting point of the fluoride decreases. The increasing radius of the cation causes the centre of positive charge and the centre of negative charge to move further apart. This decreases the strength of the ionic bonding. Less energy is then required to overcome the bond and the melting point decreases. (2 marks)

Question 32

(a)

pair 1: No pair 2: Yes pair 3: Yes pair 4: Yes pair 5: Yes (5 × 1 = 5 marks)

(b) pair 2: $AgNO_3(aq) + KI(aq) \rightarrow KNO_3(aq) + AgI(s)$ (1 mark)

pair 3: $Pb(NO_3)_2(aq) + MgCl_2(aq) \rightarrow Mg(NO_3)_2(aq) + PbCl_2(s)$
(Note that lead(II) chloride is only insoluble in cold water.) (1 mark)

pair 4: $Na_2CO_3(aq) + CuCl_2(aq) \rightarrow 2NaCl(aq) + CuCO_3(s)$ (1 mark)

pair 5: $6KOH(aq) + Al_2(SO_4)_3(aq) \rightarrow 3K_2SO_4(aq) + 2Al(OH)_3(s)$ (1 mark)

(c)

	Spectator ions	Ionic equation	
pair 2	K^+ and NO_3^-	$Ag^+(aq) + I^-(aq) \rightarrow AgI(s)$	(1 mark)
pair 3	Mg^{2+} and NO_3^-	$Pb^{2+}(aq) + 2Cl^-(aq) \rightarrow PbCl_2(s)$	(1 mark)
pair 4	Na^+ and Cl^-	$CO_3^{2-}(aq) + Cu^{2+}(aq) \rightarrow CuCO_3(s)$	(1 mark)
pair 5	K^+ and SO_4^{2-}	$3OH^-(aq) + Al^{3+}(aq) \rightarrow Al(OH)_3(s)$	(1 mark)

(Total = 13 marks)

Question 33

The result from test tube A shows that neither sulfate nor carbonate anions are present. Test tube B suggests that the anion present is Cl^-.
The reaction is given by $Ag^+(aq) + Cl^-(aq) \rightarrow AgCl(s)$.

Test tube C shows that neither Ba^{2+} nor Pb^{2+} nor Ca^{2+} nor Sr^{2+} are present. The cation present has a soluble sulfate and an insoluble carbonate. This excludes cations from group 1 metals and Ag^+. Many transition metal cations can be excluded since the initial solution is colourless. The possible cations are Mg^{2+}, Zn^{2+}, Al^{3+}.

(4 marks)

Answers: Unit 1 Area of Study 1 test

Multiple choice items

Elements and the periodic table

Question	Answer	Comments
1.	**A.**	The isotope of Sr has 38 protons and 52 neutrons, while the isotope of Zr has 40 protons and 50 neutrons.
2.	**A.**	$_{12}Mg^{2+}$ has 10 electrons (electron configuration of neon). The other alternatives have 18 electrons (electron configuration of argon).
3.	**B.**	The atomic number is subtracted from the mass number.
4.	**D.**	The calcium ion has two less electrons than the neutral atom, which has 20 electrons.
5.	**D.**	The ionisation energies of electrons in the same shell increase as more electrons are removed, but there is a much larger difference in ionisation energy between that of the last electron in a shell and the first electron to be removed from the next inner shell. **D** has three outer-shell electrons with similar energies and a large jump to the ionisation energy of the fourth electron.
6.	**A.**	The graphs show two electrons of similar ionisation energy for elements I and II, then a larger energy difference from the ionisation energy of the third electron.
7.	**B.**	Lines in an *emission* spectrum, are caused by electrons moving from a *higher* energy shell to a *lower* energy shell.
8.	**B.**	Due to the increasing positive charge on the nucleus, from left to right across the periodic table, the atomic radius decreases and the electronegativity increases.
9.	**C.**	All ions have the same number of electrons (18) but the S^{2-} has the smallest nuclear charge.
10.	**D.**	This is the definition of the unit.

Covalent substances

Question	Answer	Comments
11.	**B.**	Carbon and chlorine are both non-metals. The other alternatives are all metal and non-metal so will react by electron transfer.
12.	**C.**	This structure has four bonds to each nitrogen.
13.	**D.**	A polar bond occurs when it forms between two atoms having different electron attracting abilities (electronegativities).
14.	**C.**	Hydrogen bonding is stronger than dispersion forces or dipole-dipole bonding and occurs between polar molecules in which hydrogen is bonded to oxygen, nitrogen or fluorine.
15.	**D.**	The strength of dispersion forces between molecules depends on the number of electrons per molecule.
16.	**A.**	**B** has a double bond between carbon and oxygen, while **D** has a triple bond between nitrogen and carbon. Graphite has one electron per carbon atom delocalised over the layers, while in diamond each carbon has four single bonds to four other diamonds.

Reactions of metals and ionic compounds

Question	Answer	Comments
17.	**C.**	This is a characteristic of metals, which causes much of their typical behaviour.
18.	**A.**	The (+5 × 2) charge balances the (–2 × 5) charge on the oxide ions.
19.	**A.**	This electron configuration contains 17 electrons (group 17 element), which will react by accepting an electron to achieve a full outer shell. The other alternatives all donate electrons when forming compounds.
20.	**C.**	**A** and **B** cause structural changes, **D** produces an alloy. **C** is using the metal as an electrical conductor but when the current no longer flows the metal is unchanged.
21.	**B.**	Ions form by outer shell electron transfer from metal to non-metal atoms so that both atoms gain full outer shells and a positive or negative charge. The positive and negative ions in the crystal are then bonded by electrostatic forces of attraction.
22.	**C.**	In **A**, $Li(NO_3)_2$ should be $LiNO_3$; in **B**, AgO should be Ag_2O; in **D**, $CuBr_3$ should be CuBr or $CuBr_2$ and $NaCO_3$ should be Na_2CO_3.
23.	**D.**	The strength of ionic bonds is such that temperatures higher than room temperature are needed to overcome them and cause melting. The arrangement is alternate positive and negative ions as each ion is surrounded in the lattice by and attracted to oppositely charged ions.

24. **D.** These are reactive metals and the energy required to produce the pure metal is too great for a chemical process.

25. **B.** In reaction **B**, Ca^{2+} ions dissolve from calcium containing rocks by the action of acidic rainwater. Thus, the ions are going into solution, not being precipitated from solution, as is the case with the other reactions.

26. **A.** Lead sulfate is not soluble in water, hence the ionic bonding between these ions will be the strongest.

Extended response questions

Elements and the periodic table

Question 1

(a) The atomic number is an integer and is the number of protons in the nucleus of an atom. It is given the symbol *Z*. All atoms of the same element have the same atomic number; e.g. all atoms of oxygen have an atomic number of 8. (2 marks)

(b) The mass number is an integer and is the sum of the number of protons and the number of neutrons. It is given the symbol A. Many atoms of oxygen have a mass number of 16. This means that these atoms have 8 protons and 8 neutrons in the nucleus. (2 marks)

(c) Atoms that have the same atomic number but different mass numbers are called isotopes. Isotopes have the same number of protons but different numbers of neutrons; e.g. $^{16}_{8}O$ and $^{17}_{8}O$ are isotopes of oxygen. Both have eight protons. The first has eight neutrons but the second atom has nine neutrons. (2 marks)

(Total = 6 marks)

Question 2

(a) $1s^2 2s^2 2p^6 3s^2 3p^6 3d^6 4s^2$ (1 mark)

(b) Iron is classified as a transition metal because it has a partially filled d subshell. (1 mark)

(c) The electron configuration of Fe^{3+} is $1s^2 2s^2 2p^6 3s^2 3p^6 3d^5$. (1 mark)

(Total = 3 marks)

Question 3

(a) Electronegativity is the ability of an atom to attract electrons. Metals have low electronegativities (~0.7 to ~1.9) and non-metals have higher values (typically ~2.0 to 4.0). (2 marks)

(b) Core charge is the effective nuclear charge felt by the outer-shell electrons. It is the difference between the nuclear charge (atomic number) and the number of inner-shell electrons. It is also equal to the number of electrons in the outer shell. For sulfur (Z = 16), the core charge is +6 (16 – 10). (2 marks)

(c) The first ionisation energy is the amount of energy needed to remove one electron from an atom in the gaseous phase. Ionisation energy usually has units of kJ mol^{-1}. Normally, one of the outer-shell electrons would be removed first. (2 marks)

(Total = 6 marks)

Question 4

(a) (i) F

(ii) Ne

(iii) F

(iv) Co

(v) S (5 marks)

(b) The core charge increases from Na to Cl (+1 to +7). Hence the ability of an atom to attract another electron increases in the same order. (2 marks)

(Total = 7 marks)

Covalent substances

Question 5

(a) (1 mark)

```
   H  H
   ••  ∘∘
H : C : S :
   ••  ∘∘
   H
```

(b) 5 (1 mark)

(c) 2 (1 mark)

(d) (1 mark)

```
   H          H
    \        /
H — C — S
    /
   H
```

(e) Polar (1 mark)

(f) Less (1 mark)

(g) Methanol, CH_3OH, has a similar structure to methyl sulfide. Oxygen and sulfur are both in group 16, electronegativity decreases down the group, thus the electron attracting ability of sulfur is less than that of oxygen. The S–H bond will be less polar than the O–H and the molecule is less polar (also the C–S is less polar than the C–O bond). (1 mark)

(Total = 7 marks)

Question 6

(a) :N≡N:

(i) linear (ii) non-polar

(b) H—C≡C—H

(c)

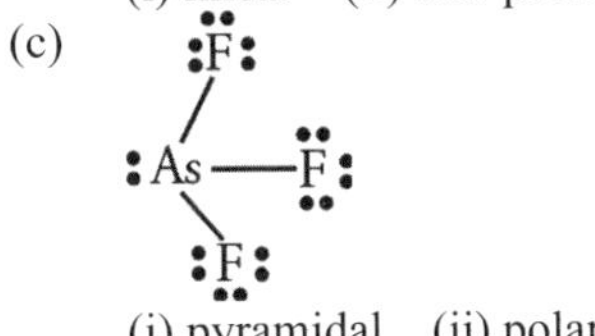

(i) pyramidal (ii) polar

(d)

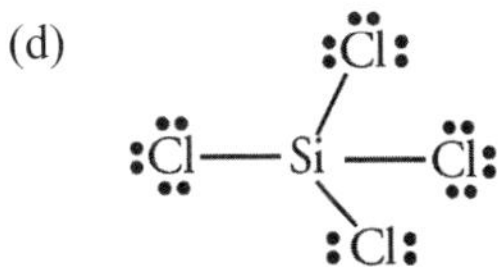

(i) tetrahedral (ii) non-polar

(e) H—F: (with lone pairs on F)

(i) linear (ii) polar

(Total = 5 × 2 = 10 marks)

Question 7

(a) (i) No. of electrons in $C_2H_6 = 6 + 6 + 6 = 18$
No. of electrons in $NH_2NH_2 = 7 + 2 + 7 + 2 = 18$ (1 mark)
(ii) $M_r(C_2H_6) = 12.01 + 12.01 + 6.048 = 30.068 = 30.1$
$M_r(NH_2NH_2) = (2 \times 14.01) + (4 \times 1.008) = 32.052 = 32.1$ (1 mark)

(b) Ethane is a non-polar molecule with dispersion forces as the only attraction between molecules. Hydrazine is a polar molecule which contains a N-H bond (enabling hydrogen bonding). The attractive forces between hydrazine molecules are hydrogen bonds, dipole-dipole bonds and dispersion forces. (3 marks)

(c) Hydrogen bonding is the strongest form of weak bonding. As the two molecules have similar masses and the same number of electrons their dispersion forces will be similar. Therefore, hydrazine has the higher boiling point because of its additional hydrogen bonding. (3 marks)

(Total = 8 marks)

Reactions of metals and ionic compounds

Question 8

(a) The ionic bond between a Ca^{2+} and an O^{2-} ion where both ions carry double charge is stronger than that between K^+ and F^- where both ions carry only a single charge. Therefore, more energy is required to overcome the bonding and cause melting.
(2 marks)

(b) K^+ is a larger ion than Li^+, thus the ionic bond between the metal and the non- metal ion is weaker in KF than in LiF. (2 marks)

(Total = 4 marks)

Question 9

(a) XY
(b) R_3Q
(c) MG_3 (Total = 3 marks)

Question 10

(a) Large lead atoms are in a close-packed structure in the metal, giving it a high density. A lead weight of fixed volume is therefore very heavy. (2 marks)

(b) Copper is a very good conductor of electricity as its outer-shell electrons are delocalised and can flow easily through the metal when a potential difference is applied. The 'sea' of delocalised electrons also gives the metal its ductility as the layers of positive ions can be moved relative to each other to stretch the metal into a wire and the metallic bonds will reform in the new position. (2 marks)

(c) Copper is a good conductor of heat as the close-packed arrangement of the atoms allows kinetic energy to pass through the metal. This spreads the heat evenly over the saucepan base for even cooking. (2 marks)

(d) Tungsten is a transition element and has a very high melting point due to its strong metallic bonding. It can withstand the high temperatures produced in the filaments of electric light globes. (2 marks)

(e) Silver reacts slowly with oxygen at room temperature and gold is unreactive. These elements have high atomic numbers and their valence electrons are strongly attracted to the atomic nucleus. Thus, they are poor reductants. They are suitable for use in jewellery as they retain their metallic lustre. (2 marks)

(Total = 10 marks)

Question 11

(a) $Mg(s) + 2H_2O(g) \rightarrow Mg(OH)_2(s) + H_2(g)$ (2 marks)

(b) $Ca(s) + 2HCl(aq) \rightarrow CaCl_2(aq) + H_2(g)$ (2 marks)

(c) $4Na(s) + O_2(g) \rightarrow 2Na_2O(s)$ (2 marks)

(Total = 6 marks)

Question 12

(a) Chromium(III) oxide

(b) Potassium sulfate

(c) Copper(I) chloride

(d) Barium carbonate (Total = 4 marks)

Answers: Unit 1 Area of Study 2

Multiple choice items

Quantifying atoms and compounds

Question	Answer	Comments
1.	**A.**	Atomic masses are scaled against the mass of a ^{12}C atom. An atom of ^{24}Mg has approximately twice the mass of a ^{12}C atom. If a ^{12}C atom is given a relative mass of 24, then the relative mass of a ^{24}Mg atom would be ~48.
2.	**B.**	This is the definition of relative atomic mass. RAMs have no units. The answers **A**, **C** and **D** all have the units of mass.
3.	**C.**	If the % of the lighter isotope is x then the % of the heavier isotope is $100 - x$. $192.2 = \frac{191x + (100 - x)193}{100} \therefore -80 = -2x \therefore x = 40\%$
4.	**A.**	Definition.
5.	**C.**	A is the relative formula mass of the substance. It has the same numerical value as the molar mass but has no units.
6.	**C.**	$n(Fe_2(SO_4)_3) = 40.0 \div 400 = 0.1$ mol. Each mole of iron sulfate contains 12 mole of O atoms. n(O atoms) $= 0.1 \times 12 = 1.20$ mol
7.	**C.**	n(N atoms) $= 0.15 \times 3 = 0.45$ mol mass of N $= 0.45 \times 14 = 6.3$ g
8.	**C.**	Formula mass = (RAM X × 2) + (16 × 5) = 182 (RAM X × 2) = 182 – 80 = 102 RAM X = 102 ÷ 2 = 51.0

9.	**D.**	Formula mass Cr_2O_3 = (52 × 2) + (16 × 3) = 152 g mol^{-1}
10.	**D.**	Formula mass Li_2SO_4 = (6.9 × 2) + 32.1 + (16 × 4) = 109.9 $n(Li_2SO_4)$ = 2.20 ÷ 109.9 = 0.0200
11.	**B.**	Formula mass Mn_2O_3 = (54.9 × 2) + (16 × 3) = 157.8 $n(Mn_2O_3)$ = 5.00 ÷ 157.8 = 0.0317 mol n(O) = 3 × 0.0317 = 0.0951; mass O = 0.0951 × 16 = 1.52 g
12.	**A.**	In this compound 126.9 g of iodine combines with 5 × 19 g of fluorine. Formula mass of compound = 126.9 + 95 = 221.9 % F = (95 ÷ 221.9) × 100 = 42.81
13.	**A.**	% C = (mass C ÷ molar mass compound) × 100. For the four compounds the values are A = 40.0%; B = 38.71%; C = 39.1%; D = 37.5%
14.	**D.**	% O = 100 – 18.78 – 28.98 = 52.24% Mass O = (6.4 × 52.24) ÷ 100 = 3.34 g
15.	**B.**	Mass sulfur = 5.65 – 1.72 – 1.64 = 2.29 % sulfur = (2.29 ÷ 5.65) × 100 = 40.5
16.	**A.**	Molar mass of propanoic acid = 36 + 6 + 32 = 74 g mol^{-1}. Mass of 1.5 mole = 74 × 1.5 = 111 g.
17.	**B.**	Molar mass of methane = 12 + 4 = 16 g mol^{-1}. n(H) = (4 × 4) ÷ 16 = 1.0 mol; i.e. 6 × 10^{23} atoms.
18.	**D.**	Each molecule of ethane contains 8 atoms. Thus 0.1 mole contains 0.1 × 6 × 10^{23} × 8 atoms. 1 mole of ethane weighs 24 + 6 = 30 g. Thus 1.0 g is (1 ÷ 30) mol and contains (2 ÷ 30) mole of C. One molecule of ethane would weigh 30 ÷ (6 × 10^{23}) g; that is, 5 × 10^{-23} g
19.	**C.**	% H = 100 – 80 = 20 n(H) 20 ÷ 1 = 20; n(C) = 80 ÷ 12 = 6.67 ratio n(H):n(C) = 20:6.67 = 3:1
20.	**C.**	Mass Sn reacted = 3.561 – 2.374 = 1.187 g n(Sn) = 1.187 ÷ 118.7 = 0.0100 mol n(I) = 5.076 ÷ 126.9 = 0.0400 mol Simplest ratio n(I) : n(Sn) is 0.0400 : 0.0100, i.e. 4 : 1
21.	**D.**	Molar mass of $C_3H_6O_3$ = 36 + 6 + 48 = 90 %C = (36 ÷ 90) × 100 = 40%
22.	**B.**	% C in each compound *A* = 50%; *B* = 63.2%; *C* = 60%; *D* = 51.8%.
23.	**C.**	% O in each compound is CH_4O = 50%; $C_2H_4O_2$, = 53.3%; $C_3H_8O_3$ = 52.2; $C_4H_8O_3$ = 46.2%

Families of organic compounds

Question	Answer	Comments
24.	**D.**	Definitions of the functional groups.
25.	**C.**	Saturated hydrocarbon molecules (alkanes) have the general formula C_nH_{2n+2} where n is the number of carbon atoms. This formula is consistent with each carbon atom forming four single bonds to hydrogen atoms. When $n = 3$ the formula is C_3H_8.
26.	**B.**	Unsaturated hydrocarbon molecules with one double bond (alkenes) have the general formula C_nH_{2n} where n is the number of carbon atoms. This formula is consistent with each molecule containing one >C=C<. When $n = 3$ the formula is C_3H_6.
27.	**B.**	Alkenes have two hydrogen atoms less than an alkane.
28.	**A.**	Alkynes have the general formula C_nH_{2n-2}. B and C are alkenes and D is an alkane.
29.	**D.**	There are five carbon atoms in the longest chain of the alcohol. Smallest numbers are achieved from the LHS. For the name of the acid, the C from the COOH group must be included.
30.	**D.**	A are isotopes, B are members of a homologous series and C are ions. D are isomers.
31.	**C.**	Structural formulas show all the chemical bonds in the molecule. For this molecule a semi-structural formula would be $CH_3CH_2CH_2CH_2CH_3$. The molecular formula (and in this case also the empirical formula) is C_5H_{12}.
32.	**C.**	Members of a homologous series have the same functional group and therefore similar chemical properties. Their physical properties show a gradual change as the formula and mass of the molecule increase by increments of $-CH_2$ for each successive member of the series.
33.	**A.**	Butene has the formula C_4H_8 and there are three isomers with this formula. The formula of butane is C_4H_{10} and there are two isomers. The compounds will have different boiling temperatures and different chemical properties.
34.	**D.**	The semi-structural formula of the compound is $CH_3CH(CH_3)CH(CH_3)CH_3$ and the molecular formula is C_6H_{14}. Only single C–C and C–H are present.
35.	**D.**	Octanol contains eight carbon atoms + two methyl groups = 10
36.	**C.**	The general equation for complete combustion of a hydrocarbon is C_xH_y + oxygen $\rightarrow xCO_2 + y/2H_2O$ Since equal numbers of moles of CO_2 and H_2O are formed: $x = y/2$ and $y = 2x$, i.e. $n(\text{H}) = 2n(\text{C})$ If $n(\text{C}) = 5$ mol, then $n(\text{H}) = 10$ mol and formula is C_5H_{10}.

Polymers and society

Question	Answer	Comments
37.	D.	The polymer chain can be broken at the points indicated by the dotted lines to find out which monomer was used to make the polymer. $\vdots\, CH_2-CH(CH_3)\, \vdots\, CH(CH_3)-CH_2\, \vdots\, CH_2-CH(CH_3)\, \vdots\, CH_2-CH(CH_3)\, \vdots$
38.	B.	This structure has a CH_3– group on every carbon atom in the chain. Since propene has the structure $CH_3CH{=}CH_2$, in the polymer there must be $–CH_2–$ groups in the chain.
39.	C.	If the polymer chains are shorter and have more branches then the material will have a lower melting temperature, a lower density, have less crystalline areas and will have a lower average molar mass.
40.	B.	It is difficult to change the shape of thermosetting polymers since the chains are extensively cross linked.
41.	A.	There is no hydrogen bonding between the chains since the H atoms are not bonded to a highly electronegative atom. There is no cross linking between the chains. The setting of a 'white' glue can be reversed by using water.
42.	A.	In HDPE the polymer chains have very little branching and thus pack close together. The dispersion forces between the chains are thus stronger than those in LDPE. HDPE is harder, stronger and less flexible than LDPE. LDPE has more branching and the chains are pushed further apart.
43.	B.	When the chain length increases the average molar mass increases and the melting temperature increase.
44.	B.	A high degree of crystallinity results in an increase in melting temperature. Side branches lower the degree of crystallinity. The polymer chains are usually longer.

Extended response questions

Quantifying atoms and compounds

Question 1

(a) No. of neutrons = 71 – 31 = 40 (1 mark)

(b) Mass of one atom of ^{69}Ga = $\dfrac{68.9256}{6.02 \times 10^{23}} = 1.14 \times 10^{-22}$ g (1 mark)

(c) Expected peak height is $\frac{12.0 \times 39.892}{60} = 7.96\ (\sim 8.0)$ (1 mark)

Peak should be placed at 71 (70.9247). (1 mark)

(d) RAM(Ga) = (68.9256 × 0.60108) + (70.9247 × 0.39892) = 69.723 (2 marks)

(Total = 6 marks)

Question 2

% ^{87}Rb isotope = 100 – 72.17 = 27.83%

$$\frac{72.17 \times 84.912}{100} + \frac{27.83 \times \text{RIM}}{100} = 85.468$$

27.83 × RIM = 8546.8 – 6128.1

Hence RIM = $\frac{2418.7}{27.83} = 86.91$ (3 marks)

Question 3

The mass spectrometer will measure the relative mass of the individual bromine molecules. Br_2 molecules will consist of either two ^{79}Br atoms or two ^{81}Br atoms or one ^{79}Br atom and one ^{81}Br atom.

All three combinations will be present in molecular bromine and so the mass spectrum will show peaks at 158, 160 and 162. (3 marks)

Question 4

(a) In the periodic table the elements are placed in order of increasing atomic number. The atomic numbers of argon and potassium are 18 and 19 respectively. Hence argon is placed before potassium. For argon to have a higher relative mass than potassium the isotopes of argon must contain more neutrons than the isotopes of potassium.
(The major isotopes of argon and potassium are $^{40}_{18}$Ar and $^{39}_{19}$K, respectively.) (2 marks)

(b) Many naturally occurring elements are mixtures of isotopes. Relative atomic mass is the weighted mean of the relative isotopic masses. While relative isotopic masses may have values close to whole numbers, if there are different amounts of two or more isotopes making up the atoms of an element, then non-integer values of RAM are possible.

(2 marks)

(c) RAM is the weighted mean of the relative masses of the isotopes. The relative mass of ^{151}Eu will be close to 151 and that of ^{153}Eu close to 153. If the % of each isotope in naturally occurring europium is approximately the same (i.e. ~50) then the RAM will be 152. (2 marks)

(Total = 6 marks)

Question 5

(a) number of protons = 82; number of neutrons = 125 (1 mark)

(b) The relative mass of an element is the weighted mean of the relative masses of the naturally occurring isotopes. (1 mark)

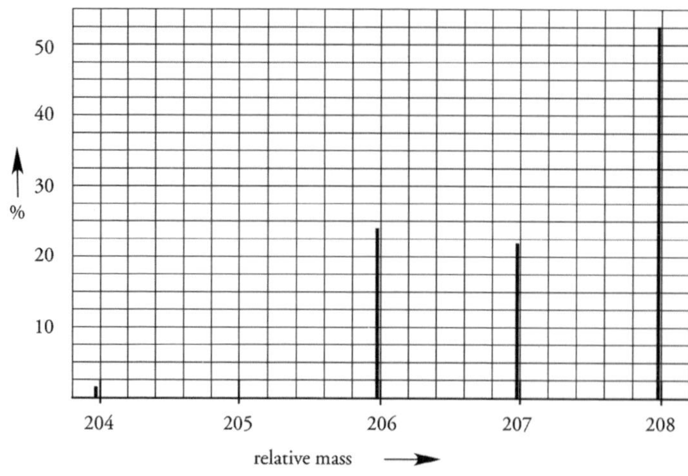

(3 marks)

(c) $RAM(Pb) = \frac{(203.973 \times 1.4) + (205.975 \times 24.1) + (206.976 \times 22.1) + (207.977 \times 52.4)}{100}$

$= 207.2$ (3 marks)

(Total = 8 marks)

Question 6

(a) Mass of oxygen in the indium oxide = 6.06 – 5.0
= 1.06 g $n(\text{In}) = 5.0 \div 75 = 0.0667$;
$n(\text{O}) = 1.06 \div 16 = 0.0663$
Ratio $n(\text{In}):n(\text{O}) = 0.0667:0.0663 = 1:1$
The scientists had assumed that the formula of indium oxide was InO. (3 marks)

(b) From the later formula, $\frac{n(\text{In})}{n(\text{O})} = \frac{2}{3}$ and $n(\text{O}) = 0.0663$ mol, hence

$n(\text{In}) = \frac{0.0663 \times 2}{3} = 0.0442$ mol

$RAM(\text{In}) = \frac{5.0}{0.0442} = 113$ (3 marks)

(Total = 6 marks)

Question 7

(a) Relative formula mass of bornite = 2(63.5) + 55.8 + 4(32.1) = 311.2 (1 mark)

(b) $\%Cu = \frac{2 \times 63.5 \times 100}{311.2} = 40.81\%$

$\%Fe = \frac{55.8 \times 100}{311.2} = 17.93\%$

$\%S = \frac{4 \times 32.1 \times 100}{311.2} = 41.26\%$ (3 marks)

(c) Mass of copper $= \frac{1000 \times 40.81}{100} = 408.1$ g (2 marks)

(Total = 6 marks)

Question 8

(a) $\%N\ (\text{urea}) = \dfrac{2\times14\times100}{12+16+2(14+2)} = 46.67\%$

$\%N\ ((NH_4)_2SO_4) = \dfrac{2\times14\times100}{2(14+4)+32.1+4(16)} = 21.20\%$

$\%N\ (NH_4NO_3) = \dfrac{2\times14\times100}{14+4+14+3(16)} = 35\%$ (3 marks)

(b) $n(N) = \dfrac{2\times100}{80} = 2.5$ mol (2 marks)

(c) $n(N) = \dfrac{2\times500}{132} = 7.58$ mol

Mass(N) = 7.58 × 14 = 106 g $\left(\text{or } \dfrac{21.2\times500}{100}\right)$ (2 marks)

(Total = 7 marks)

Question 9

(a) Molar mass of propane = 36 + 8 = 44 g mol^{-1} (1 mark)
(b) $n(C_3H_8) = 11 \div 44 = 0.25$ mol (1 mark)
(c) Number of molecules = $0.25 \times 6 \times 10^{23} = 1.5 \times 10^{23}$ (1 mark)
(d) $n(H) = n(C_3H_8) \times 8 = 0.25 \times 8 = 2.0$ mol (1 mark)
(e) Number of atoms in each molecule = 3 + 8 = 11
Total number of atoms = $11 \times 1.5 \times 10^{23} = 1.65 \times 10^{24}$ (1 mark)
(Total = 5 marks)

Question 10

(a) The relative molecular mass is the mass of 1 molecule of a substance compared to the mass of 1 atom of ^{12}C taken as 12 exactly. (2 marks)
(b) The molar mass is the mass, in grams, of 1 mole of a substance. (2 marks)
(Total = 4 marks)

Question 11

(a) $n(C) = (1.2 \times 10^{23}) \div (6 \times 10^{23}) = 0.2$ mol (1 mark)
(b) Mass C = 0.2 × 12 = 2.4 g (1 mark)
(c) Each molecule of ethane contains 2 atoms of carbon, thus the number of molecules will be half the number of atoms of carbon.
Number of molecules = $(1.2 \times 10^{23}) \div 2 = 6 \times 10^{22}$ (1 mark)
(d) Every 2 atoms of carbon are combined with 6 atoms of hydrogen.
Number of hydrogen atoms = $3 \times (1.2 \times 10^{23}) = 3.6 \times 10^{23}$ (1 mark)
(e) $n(C_2H_6) = n(C) \div 2 = 0.1$ mol
Mass (C_2H_6) = 0.1 × 30 = 3.0 g (2 marks)
(Total = 6 marks)

Question 12

(a) Relative formula mass of Na_2CO_3 = 2(23) + 12 + 3(16) = 106 (1 mark)
(b) Mass Na_2CO_3 = 0.25 × 106 = 26.5 g (1 mark)
(c) $n(Na) = 2 \times 0.25 = 0.50$ mol (1 mark)

(d) $n(O) = 3 \times 0.25 = 0.75$ mol
Mass oxygen = $0.75 \times 16 = 12.0$ g (2 marks)
(Total = 5 marks)

Question 13

(a) Mass oxygen = 15.00 – 3.89 = 11.11 g (1 mark)
(b) $n(N) = 3.89 \div 14 = 0.278$ mol
$n(O) = 11.11 \div 16 = 0.694$ mol (2 marks)
(c) Ratio $n(O) : n(N) = 0.694 \div 0.278 = 2.5:1$; simplest ratio is 5:2
Hence, the empirical formula is N_2O_5. (2 marks)
(Total = 5 marks)

Question 14

$n(O) = (9 \times 10^{22}) \div (6 \times 10^{23}) = 0.15$ mol;
$n(H) = 0.40 \div 1.0 = 0.40$ mol.
Ratio $n(C) : n(H):n(O) = 0.15:0.40:0.15 = 1:2.67:1$; simplest whole number ratio is 3:8:3 and the empirical formula is $C_3H_8O_3$. (3 marks)

Question 15

(a) To allow more air into the crucible to react with the magnesium. (1 mark)
(b) Mass of Mg = 15.86 – 15.67 = 0.19 g; $n(Mg) = 0.19 \div 24.3 = 0.007819$ mol
Mass of O = 15.96 – 15.86 = 0.10 g; $n(O) = 0.10 \div 16 = 0.00625$ mol
Ratio $n(Mg) : n(O) = 0.007819/0.00625 : 1.0 = 1.25 : 1$ or 5 : 4
Empirical formula of magnesium oxide is Mg_5O_4. (3 marks)
(c) The mass of oxygen is too low for the mass of Mg. Either some of the magnesium remained unreacted or some magnesium oxide escaped from the crucible during the heating process. (2 marks)
(Total = 6 marks)

Question 16

(a) To remove the remaining zinc iodide. (1 mark)
(b) Mass of zinc reacting = 26.58 – 26.04 = 0.54 g
$n(Zn) = 0.54 \div 65.4 = 0.008257$ mol
Mass of iodine = 28.66 – 26.58 = 2.08 g
$n(I) = 2.08 \div 126.9 = 0.01639$ mol
Ratio $n(Zn) : n(I) = 0.008257 : 0.01639 = 1.0 : 1.99$ i.e. 1 : 2
The empirical formula of zinc iodide ZnI_2. (3 marks)
(Total = 4 marks)

Question 17

(a) $n(H) = 0.12 \div 1.0 = 0.12$ mol; $n(C) = 0.48 \div 12 = 0.04$ mol
(2 marks)
(b) Ratio $n(H) : n(C) = 0.12:0.04 = 3:1$; hence empirical formula is CH_3.
(2 marks)

(c) The formula CH_3 has a molar mass of 12 + 3 = 15 g mol^{-1}. Since the actual molar mass is 30.0 g mol^{-1} then the molecular formula must be 2× the empirical formula. Molecular formula is C_2H_6.

(Alternatively, let molecular formula = $(CH_3)_x = C_xH_{3x}$. then $30.0 = 12x + 3x$ and $x = 2$)

(2 marks)

(Total = 6 marks)

Question 18

(a) % oxygen = 100 – 50.0 – 8.33 – 19.44 = 22.23% (1 mark)

(b)

	carbon	hydrogen	nitrogen	oxygen
%	50.0	8.33	19.44	22.23
no. mole	50.0 ÷ 12 = 4.17	8.33 ÷ 1.0 = 8.33	19.44 ÷ 14 = 1.39	22.23 ÷ 16 = 1.39
÷ smallest	4.17 ÷ 1.39 = 3.0	8.33 ÷ 1.39 = 5.99 = 6.0	1.0	1.0

Hence, the empirical formula is C_3H_6NO. (3 marks)

(c) Molar mass of compound = 21.6 ÷ 0.15 = 144 g mol^{-1}. (1 mark)

(d) Molecular formula is $(C_3H_6NO)_x$

Hence $36x + 6x + 14x + 16x = 144$ i.e. $72x = 144$ and $x = 2$

Molecular formula is $C_6H_{12}N_2O_2$. (2 marks)

(Total = 7 marks)

Question 19

(a) $n(CO_2) = 3.14 \div 44 = 0.0714$ mol (1 mark)

(b) 1 mole of CO_2 contains 1 mole of C; hence n(C) = 0.0714 mol (1 mark)

(c) Mass of C = 0.0714 × 12 = 0.856 g (1 mark)

(d) Mass of H = 1.00 – 0.856 = 0.144 g (1 mark)

(e) n(H) = 0.144 ÷ 1.0 = 0.144 mol; n(C) = 0.0714 mol

Ratio n(H):n(C) = 0.144:0.0714 = 2.02:1; or 2:1

Empirical formula is CH_2. (2 marks)

(f) Molar mass of compound = 14.0 ÷ 0.25 = 56.0 g mol^{-1}. Molecular formula is $(CH_2)_x$.

Hence $56.0 = 12x + 2x$ and $x = 4$

Molecular formula is $(CH_2)_4$ or C_4H_8. (2 marks)

(Total = 8 marks)

Families of organic compounds

Question 20

(a) and (b) There are five alkene isomers with the formula C_5H_{10}.

$CH_3CH_2CH_2CH{=}CH_2$ 1-pentene

$CH_3CH_2CH{=}CHCH_3$ 2-pentene

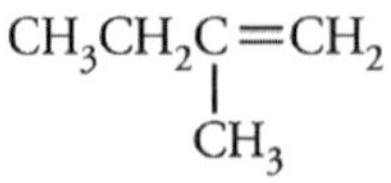

$CH_3CH_2C(CH_3)=CH_2$ 2-methyl-1-butene

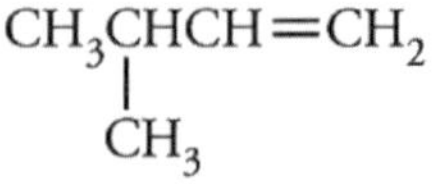

$CH_3CH(CH_3)CH=CH_2$ 3-methyl-1-butene

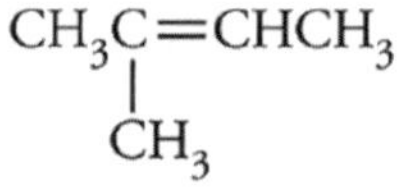

$CH_3C(CH_3)=CHCH_3$ 2-methyl-2-butene

(any 3 for 3 + 3 = 6 marks)

(c) $2C_5H_{10}(l) + 15O_2(g) \rightarrow 10CO_2(g) + 10H_2O(l)$ (2 marks)

(Total = 8 marks)

Question 21

(a) 2-methylpentane
(b) 3-methylbut-1-ene
(c) 2-methylhept-4-yne
(d) 3-methylpentan-2-ol
(e) 3,3-dimethylbutanoic acid (Total = 6 marks)

Question 22

(a) $CH_3CH(CH_3)CH(CH_3)CH_2CH_2CH_2CH_3$

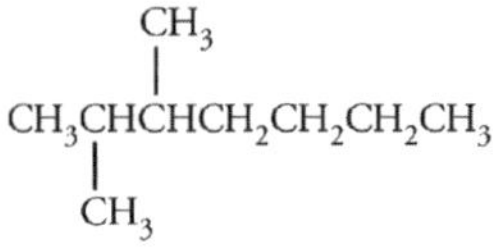

(b) $CH_3CH(CH_3)CH=CHCH_2CH_2CH_3$

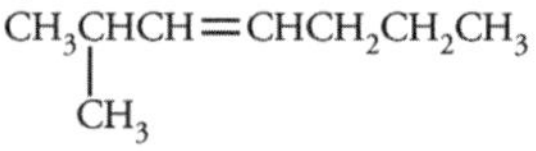

(c) $CH_3CH(CH_3)C\equiv CCH_2CH_3$

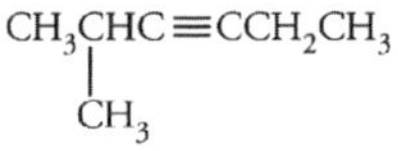

(d) $CH_3C(OH)(CH_3)-CH(CH_3)CH_3$

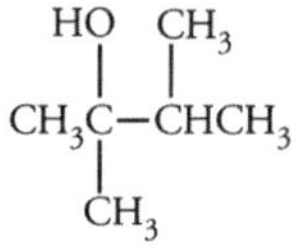

(e) $CH_3CH(CH_3)COOH$

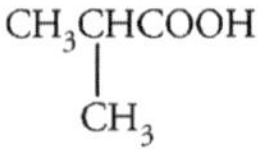

(Total = 5 marks)

Question 23

(a) $CH_3CH(OH)CH_3$ (1 mark)

(b) $CH_3CH(CH_3)COOH$ or $CH_3CH_2COOCH_3$ or $CH_3COOCH_2CH_3$ or $HCOOCH_2CH_2CH_3$ (1 mark)

(c) $(CH_3)_2CHCH=CH_2$ or $CH_3CH_2CH_2CH=CH_2$ or $CH_3CH_2CH=CHCH_3$ or $(CH_3)_2CHCH=CH_2$ or $CH_3CH_2C(CH_3)=CH_2$ (1 mark)

(d) $CH_3CH(CH_3)CH_2CH_3$ or $(CH_3)_4C$ (1 mark)

(e) $H_3CC\equiv CCH_3$ or $CH_2=CHCH=CH_2$ or $CH_2=C=CHCH_3$ (1 mark)

(Total = 5 marks)

Question 24

(a) Ethane
(b) Propan-1-ol or 1-propanol
(c) Propene
(d) Methanoic acid

Question 25

(a) A + H_2 → 2-methylpropane, whose molecular formula is C_4H_{10}. Hence the molecular formula of A must be C_4H_8.

Also, B + H_2 → butane whose molecular formula is also C_4H_{10} and the molecular formula of B must be C_4H_8. (2 marks)

(b) A and B are alkenes whose functional group is >C = C<. (1 mark)

(c) 2-methylpropane has the semi-structural formula $CH_3CH(CH_3)_2$ and must have been formed from the hydrogenation of $CH_2{=}C(CH_3)_2$. The structural formula of A is

```
  H   H
   \ /
H - C         H
     \       /
      C = C
     /       \
H - C         H
   / \
  H   H
```

(1 mark)

(d) When HBr is added to $(CH_3)_2CH{=}CH_2$ it can be done in two ways. This is possible because the groups at the two ends of the double bond are different. The two products C and D have the structural formulas

```
    H   H                          H   H
     \ /                            \ /
  H - C           H               H - C           H
       \         /                     \         /
H - C - C  -  C - H            H - C - C  -  C - H
   / \  |     \                   / \  |     \
  H   H H      Br                H   H Br     H
```

(2 marks)

(e) Butane can be made by hydrogenation of two alkenes. These alkenes are $CH_3–CH{=}CH–CH_3$ and $CH_2{=}CH–CH_2–CH_3$. (2 marks)

(f) The correct structure of B is $CH_3–CH{=}CH–CH_3$. This molecule is symmetrical; the two ends of the double bond have the same groups attached, H and CH_3. There is only one possible product when HBr adds across the double bond, no matter to which carbon atom of the double bond the Br and H are added. (1 mark)

Compound E has the structure $CH_3CH_2CHBrCH_3$. (1 mark)

(Total = 10 marks)

Polymers and society

Question 26

(a)

```
  H    H     H    H     H    H
  |    |     |    |     |    |
—C  —  C  —  C  — C  —  C  — C—
  |    |     |    |     |    |
  H   C6H5   H   C6H5   H   C6H5
```

(2 marks)

(b)

```
  F   F   F   F   F   F
  |   |   |   |   |   |
—C — C — C — C — C — C—
  |   |   |   |   |   |
  F   F   F   F   F   F
```

(2 marks)

(Total = 4 marks)

Question 27

(a) $H_2C=CH(CN)$ — H and H on one carbon; H and CN on the other

(b) $CH_3CH=CHCH_3$ — CH_3 and H on one carbon; H and CH_3 on the other

(Total = 4 marks)

Question 28

(a) (i) Polymer III (1 mark)

(ii) Polymer I (1 mark)

(iii) Polymer II (1 mark)

(b)

Polymer	Properties	Uses
Cross-linked polymer	Stiff, hard, strong, brittle, good electrical insulators, resists chemicals	Electrical insulation, knobs, handles, tableware, casting, encapsulation of other materials
High density polyethene	Hard, stiff, strong, able to be sterilised	Plastic bottles, tubing, toys, buckets, containers, fuel tanks, dustbins, water pipes
Low density polyethene	Flexible, somewhat soft	Cling film, bags, squeeze bottles, cable insulation, flexible water pipes

(6 marks)

(Total = 9 marks)

Question 29

Advantages: lightweight, can be coloured, easily molded, cheap to produce, good strength and toughness, many are chemically inert and resist corrosion, many are good thermal and electrical insulators, water resistant, thermoplastics can be recycled. (2 marks)

Disadvantages: At low temperatures they are often brittle, many burn easily giving off toxic fumes, often UV sensitive, can be deformed under mechanical load, many are derived from crude oil which is a non- renewable resource. (2 marks)

(Total = 4 marks)

Answers: Unit 1 Area of Study 2 test

Multiple choice items

Quantifying atoms and compounds

Question	Answer	Comments
1.	**A.**	$n(KCl) = n(K) = 0.25$ mass K = $0.25 \times 39.1 = 9.78$ g
2.	**B.**	mass H in compound = $n(H)$ in compound × 1 For A mass H = $(20 \div 16) \times 4 = 5$ g

		For B mass H = (36 ÷ 18) × 2 = 4 g For C mass H = (10 ÷ 2) × 2 = 10 g For D mass H = (40 ÷ 58) × 10 = 6.9 g
3.	**B.**	$n(Na_3PO_4)$ = 16.4 ÷ 164 = 0.1 mol; n(Na) = 3 × 0.1 = 0.3
4.	**D.**	% O = 100 – 38.8 = 61.2 n(Cl) = 38.8 ÷ 35.5 = 1.093; n(O) = 61.2 ÷ 16 = 3.825 ratio n(Cl):n(O) = 1.093:3.825 = 1:3.5 or 2:7
5.	**A.**	Mass of nitrogen in oxide = 8.8 – 3.2 – 5.6 g n(N) = 5.6 ÷ 14 = 0.4; n(O) = 3.2 ÷ 16 = 0.2 ratio n(N):n(O) = 0.4:0.2 = 2:1
6.	**A.**	If the percentage of the lighter isotope = x, then the percentage of the heavier isotope = 100 – x and $203x + (100 - x)205 = 204.4 \times 100$ $-2x = 20440 - 20500 = -60$ and hence x = 30%.
7.	**C.**	For each of the answers the number of atoms present is A = $0.10 \times 2 \times 6 \times 10^{23} = 1.2 \times 10^{23}$ B = $4 \times 6 \times 10^{22} = 2.4 \times 10^{23}$ C = $(1.0 \div 18) \times 3 \times 6 \times 10^{23} = 1 \times 10^{23}$ D = $0.05 \times 14 \times 6 \times 10^{23} = 4.2 \times 10^{23}$
8.	**C.**	% Cl = 100 – 45.53 = 54.47% mass Cl = (6.25 × 54.47) ÷ 100 = 3.40 g
9.	**B.**	Definition of Avogadro's number

Families of organic compounds and polymers in society

Question	Answer	Comments
10.	**C.**	Carboxylic acids have the general formula $C_nH_{2n+1}COOH$ or $C_nH_{2n}O_2$. Doubling C (to get 2 O atoms) would give molecular formula $C_4H_8O_2$. Doubling D would give a di-alcohol.
11.	**C.**	The isomers are $CH_3CH_2CH(CH_3)COOH$, $(CH_3)_3CCOOH$ and $CH_3CH(CH_3)CH_2COOH$.
12.	**B.**	Organic compounds are named by finding the longest carbon chain in the molecule and naming it after the corresponding alkane. This chain is then numbered. Each side chain or substituted group on the longest chain is then identified by the smallest possible number. Double bonds in the longest chain are similarly identified.
13.	**D.**	Vinyl alcohol, CH_2=CHOH, undergoes addition polymerisation to make the polymer. The large number of OH groups in the molecule makes it water soluble.
14.	**C.**	Heating a thermoplastic polymer weakens the bonds between the polymer chains. The material softens and its strength is lowered.

15. **B.** In cross-linked polymers there are covalent bonds between the polymer chains. There is very little movement of the chains relative to one another and these polymers are rigid. Cling film, ropes and carry bags all change shape when used.

16. **A.** Elastomers are partially cross-linked polymers. There are a small number of covalent bonds between the polymer chains.

17. **B.** The monomer used to make this polymer has the structure $CH_3CH_2CF{=}CHF$ and the molecular formula $C_4H_6F_2$. There is no hydrogen bonding between the chains since the H atoms are not bonded to a highly electronegative atom. C has both F atoms on the same carbon atom.

18. **A.** Incinerating the plastics will release CO_2 and other gases into the atmosphere.

19. **C.** In a fire, thermoplastic materials first melt and then burn. This can be a significant disadvantage.

Extended response questions

Quantifying atoms and compounds

Question 1

(a) A. Bombarding electrons produce positive ions from injected gas molecules.
B. An applied electric field determines the path of the positive ions through the spectrometer.
C. An applied magnetic field deflects positive ions towards the collector/detector.

(3 marks)

(b) The line at 86 relative mass units would be due to $^{12}C(^{1}H)_2{}^{35}Cl(^{37}Cl)^+$ ions. The line at 88 relative mass units would be due to $^{12}C(^{1}H)_2(^{37}Cl)_2^+$ ions. (2 marks)

(c) In a sample of chlorine there are more atoms of ^{35}Cl than ^{37}Cl. In CH_2Cl_2 those molecules containing two ^{35}Cl atoms will be more common than those containing one ^{35}Cl and one ^{37}Cl. Similarly, molecules containing two ^{37}Cl will be least common.

(2 marks)

(Total = 7 marks)

Question 2

No. of atoms of He produced in 10 days = $6.2 \times 10^{10} \times 60 \times 60 \times 24 \times 10 = 5.357 \times 10^{16}$

n(He) produced in 10 days = $3.68 \times 10^{-7} \div 4.0 = 9.2 \times 10^{-8}$ mol

No. of atoms of He in 1.0 mol = $5.357 \times 10^{16} \div 9.2 \times 10^{-8} = 5.82 \times 10^{23}$

(Total = 4 marks)

Question 3

(a) RFM (malachite) = $(63.54 \times 2) + 12.01 + (16 \times 5) + (1.01 \times 2) = 221.1$ (4 sig. fig)

(1 mark)

(b) $\frac{127.08}{221.1} \times 100\% = 57.5\%$ (2 marks)

(c) $\frac{57.5}{100} \times 500$ kg = 287 kg (3 sig. fig) (3 marks)

(Total = 6 marks)

Question 4

n(Cu) = 0.203 ÷ 63.55 = 0.003194 mol

Mass O = 0.256 – 0.203 = 0.053 g

n(O) = 0.053 ÷ 16.0 = 0.003313

Ratio n(O) : n(Cu) = 0.003313 : 0.003194 = 1.04 : 1.0; i.e. 1 : 1

Empirical formula of copper oxide is CuO. (Total = 3 marks)

Families of organic compounds and polymers in society

Question 5

(a) 3-methylhexane
(b) 3,3-dimethylbut-1-ene
(c) methanol
(d) 4-methylpentan-1-ol
(e) ethanoic acid

(Total = 5 × 1 = 5 marks)

Question 6

(a) butane
(b) 2-methylpropan-1-ol
(c) 2-chloropent-2-ene
(d) fluoromethanoic acid

(Total = 4 × 1 = 4 marks)

Question 7

(a)

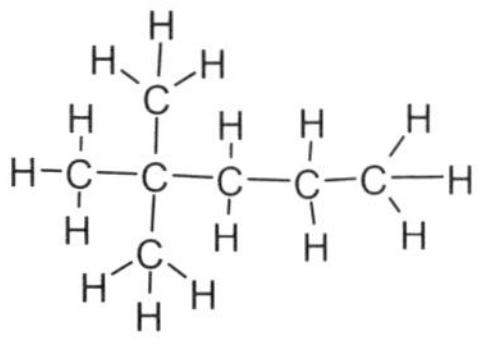

(b)

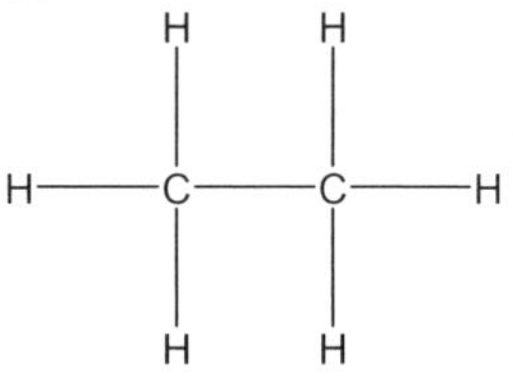

(c)

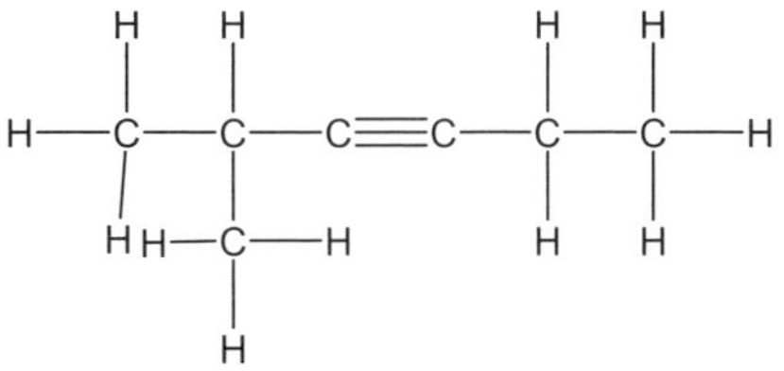

(d)

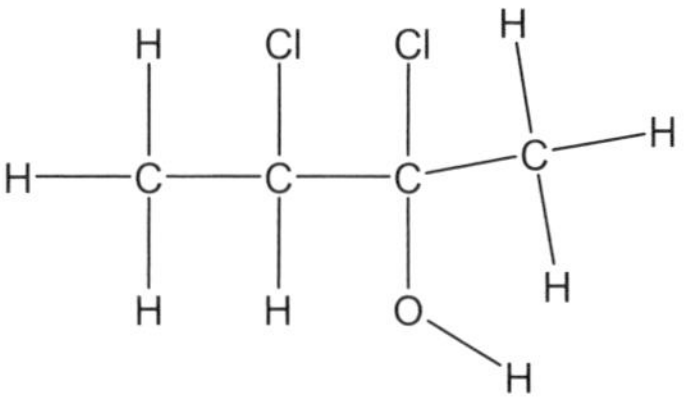

(e)

```
   H  H  H  H   O
   |  |  |  |  //
H—C—C—C—C—C
   |  |  |  |  \
   H  H  H  H   O—H
```

(Total = 5 × 1 = 5 marks)

Question 8

```
  H  Cl  H  Cl  H  Cl
  |  |   |  |   |  |
—C—C—C—C—C—C—
  |  |   |  |   |  |
  H  Cl  H  Cl  H  Cl
```

(2 marks)

Question 9

```
CH3       H
   \     /
    C = C
   /     \
  H       C—OCH3
         //
        O
```

(2 marks)

Question 10

(a) Linear polymers, such as LDPE and HDPE, rarely have chains that are the same length; i.e. the degree of polymerisation varies from chain to chain. Hence when the molar mass of the polymer is calculated it will be an average of the values for the various chains.

(1 mark)

(b) (i) HDPE has a higher melting temperature than LDPE.(1 mark)

(ii) HDPE is harder than LDPE. (1 mark)

(iii) HDPE has fewer branches than LDPE. (1 mark)

(iv) Since the average molar mass is higher HDPE will have longer chains. (1 mark)

(Total = 5 marks)

Answers: Unit 1 Examination

Section A

Question	Answer	Comments
1.	**A.**	The electron attracting ability increases going across a period.
2.	**C.**	79 – 34 = 45 neutrons, 34 + 2 = 36 electrons (negative ion)
3.	**D.**	An unfilled d subshell is characteristic of a transition metal.
4.	**B.**	$m(\text{Cu}) = 6.0 \times 63.54 = 381.2$ g. $n(\text{O}_2) = (4.0 \times 10^{22}) \div (6 \times 10^{23})$; $m(\text{O}_2) = 0.067 \times 32 = 2.13$ g $m(\text{Hg}) = (2.4 \times 10^{23}) \times 200.6 \div (6 \times 10^{23}) = 80$ g
5.	**B.**	Calcium and iodine are metal and non-metal. Other answers are two metals (alloys) or two non-metals (covalent compounds).
6.	**C.**	HCN has a triple bond between C and N.

7.	**A.**	$CHCl_3$ is not symmetrical, other alternatives are symmetrical and thus have no permanent dipole.
8.	**D.**	As the atomic number of the atoms increases, they contain more protons and electrons which increases the magnitude of the intermolecular dispersion forces.
9.	**B.**	The isomers of **A** are $CH_3CH_2CH{=}CH_2$, $CH_3CH{=}CHCH_3$, and $(CH_3)_2C{=}CH_2$. For **C** the isomers are $CH_3CH_2CH_2OH$ and $(CH_3)_2CHOH$ and for **D** they are CH_3COOH and $HCOOCH_3$.
10.	**A.**	Butene has the molecular formula C_4H_8. The other formulas are C_4H_{10}, C_5H_{12} and C_5H_{10}.
11.	**C.**	CH_2O is the simplest whole number ratio of atoms in the molecule.
12.	**B.**	$184.95\ (100 - x) + 186.95x = 186.21 \times 100$ $2x = 18621 - 18495 = 126; x = 63\%$
13.	**D.**	The most reactive metals are the most difficult to extract from their ores.
14.	**B.**	Ethanoic acid has the formula CH_3COOH. Any different molecule that contains the same amount of each atom is a structural isomer.
15.	**C.**	Branching moves polymer chains apart, thus weakening the attraction between the chains.
16.	**A.**	Fe is a metal, KBr is an ionic compound, C_{60} is a molecule and graphite is a giant structure with covalent bonding.
17.	**D.**	Copper is more reactive than silver. Sodium is more reactive than zinc. Zinc is more reactive than iron.
18.	**D.**	Graphite is softer than diamond has a higher melting temperature but a lower density. Graphite is a better conductor than diamond.
19.	**D.**	Mass of In reacting = 2.298 – 1.532 = 0.766 g $n(\text{In})$ = 0.766 ÷ 114.8 = 0.006672 mol Mass of I reacting = 2.54 g $n(\text{I}) = 2.54 \div 126.9 = 0.0200$ mol Ratio I:In = 0.0200: 0.006672 = 3:1
20.	**C.**	The surface layer of iron oxide tends to break off easily allowing further corrosion of the iron.

Section B

Question 1

(a) Sodium is a metal and consists of alternating layers of positive metal ions and delocalised outer-shell electrons. Electrostatic forces of attraction known as metallic bonding exist between the layers and maintain the structure of the metal. Inter particle dispersion forces are also present. Chlorine is a non-metal. The solid consists of diatomic non-polar chlorine molecules in which two chlorine atoms are covalently bonded. The intermolecular bonds are dispersion forces. (2 marks)

(b) Metallic bonding is strong bonding and exists throughout the sodium structure. Dispersion forces are a form of weak bonding between chlorine molecules. When melting occurs the strong metal bonds in sodium must be overcome but the strong bonding within chlorine molecules is unaffected. Only the weak intermolecular dispersion forces are overcome for melting to occur. Hence the melting point of sodium is much higher than that of chlorine. (2 marks)

(c)

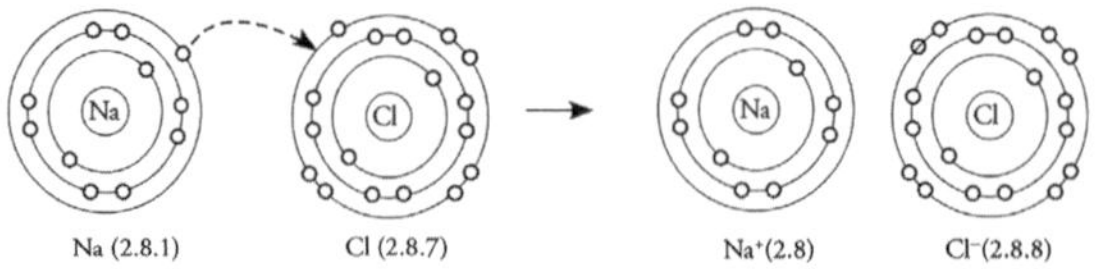

Na (2.8.1) Cl (2.8.7) → Na^+(2.8) Cl^-(2.8.8)

One electron from each sodium atom is transferred to a chlorine atom. The neutral atoms of sodium and chlorine are converted into positive sodium ions and negative chloride ions. (2 marks)

(d) There is very strong attraction between the oppositely charged ions, Na^+ and Cl^-. Also, each ion is surrounded by a number of ions of the opposite charge. This results in a three-dimensional giant structure being formed. There is strong bonding between all of the ions and thus the material has a high melting temperature. (2 marks)

(Total = 8 marks)

Question 2

(a) Li_2O (Or use another metal and non-metal, e.g. LiF, BeO, BeF_2). (1 mark)

(b) (i) CO_2 (Other examples are NO, NO_2, CF_4, B_2O_3, C_2N_2, BF_3). (1 mark)

(ii) >O=C=O< It is non-polar since it is a linear molecule with equal and opposite dipoles in the carbon–oxygen bonds. (2 marks)

(c) (i) A monatomic gas is neon, the diatomic gases are nitrogen, oxygen or fluorine. (2 marks)

(ii) Neon is monatomic as its outer electron shell is full. Nitrogen, oxygen and fluorine need to share 3, 2 and 1 electron pairs respectively to obtain the stability of full outer electron shells and are diatomic gases. (2 marks)

(d) (i) Lithium has the least number of electrons (3). (1 mark)

(ii) Neon atoms have the smallest atomic radius. (1 mark)

(iii) All period two elements have the same number of electron shells. The outer-shell electrons are at approximately the same distance from the nucleus and are attracted by the increasingly positive nuclear charge across the period from left to right. Thus, the diameter of the atoms decreases from left to right. (2 marks)

(Total = 12 marks)

Question 3

(a) But-1-ene and butane have similar molar masses. They are both hydrocarbons so their intermolecular bonding, which has to be overcome on boiling, is dispersion forces of approximately equal strength. Thus, their boiling points are similar. (2 marks)

(b) 1-propanol has a polar –OH group so has intermolecular hydrogen bonding in addition to dispersion forces. Its boiling point is therefore higher as more energy is required to overcome the intermolecular bonding than for butane. (2 marks)

(c) Hydrogen bonding occurs between 1-propanol and water molecules but not between the hydrocarbon and water molecules. Thus 1-propanol is soluble in water, but the hydrocarbons are not soluble. (2 marks)

(Total = 6 marks)

Question 4

(a) Mass C = (4.761 ÷ 44.01) × 12.01 = 1.299 g

% C = (1.299 ÷ 2.167) × 100 = 59.96%

Mass H = (2.605 ÷ 18) × 2 = 0.289 g

% H = (0.289 ÷ 2.167) 100 = 13.36%

% O = 100 – 59.96 – 13.36 = 26.68% (3 marks)

(b)

	C	**H**	**O**
n	= 59.96 ÷ 12.01 = 4.992	= 13.36 ÷ 1.008 = 13.25	26.68 ÷ 16 = 1.668
÷ smallest	4.992 ÷ 1.668 = 2.992	13.25 ÷ 1.668 = 7.944	1.668 ÷ 1.668 = 1.0
whole-number ratio	3	8	1

Empirical formula = C_3H_8O (2 marks)

(c) The molecular formula of a compound is either the same as its empirical formula or a simple multiple of this formula. If C_3H_8O is doubled the formula becomes $C_6H_{16}O_2$. Now there are too many hydrogen atoms to bond to the carbon atoms. The maximum number of hydrogen atoms that can bond to 6 carbon atoms is 14. Hence $C_6H_{16}O_2$ cannot be correct. (1 mark)

(d) Alkanol series (1 mark)

(e)

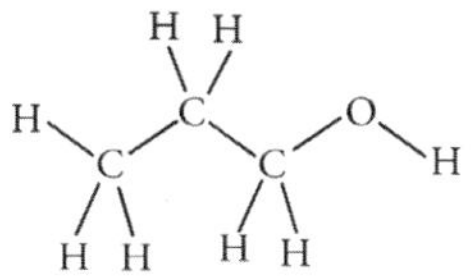

propan-1-ol and propan-2-ol

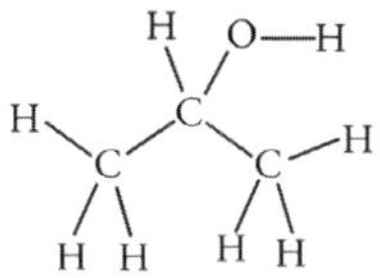

(2 marks)

(Total = 9 marks)

Question 5

Formula of iron(III) sulfate is $Fe_2(SO_4)_3$.

Molar mass = (55.85 × 2) + (32.06 × 3) + (16.00 × 12) = 399.88

% Fe = (111.7 ÷ 399.88) × 100 = 27.93%

% S = (96.18 ÷ 399.88) × 100 = 24.05%

% O = (192 ÷ 399.88) × 100 = 48.01% (3 marks)

Question 6

If the % of ^{24}Mg = x, then % of ^{26}Mg = 90 – x

Hence 24.305 = [23.985x + (10.00 × 24.986) + (90 – x)25.983] ÷100

2430.5 = 23.985x + 249.86 + 2338.47 – 25.983x

2430.5 – 249.86 – 2338.47 = 23.985x – 25.983x

–157.83 = –1.998x

x = 78.99%

Hence % ^{24}Mg = 78.99% and ^{26}Mg = 11.01% (4 marks)

Question 7

I. These properties are characteristic of compounds with ionic bonding, such as NaCl. (1 mark)

II. The first property is characteristic of covalently bonded molecules such as I_2 and CO_2. (1 mark)

III. These properties are those of a covalently network lattice such as diamond or SiO_2. (1 mark)

IV. These properties indicate that the substance is a metal, such as Cu, Zn. (1 mark)

(Total = 4 marks)

Question 8

(a)

```
     H  CH3 H  CH3 H  CH3          H  OH  H  OH  H  OH
      \ /    \ /    \ /             \ /    \ /    \ /
       C      C      C               C      C      C
 \   /   \  /   \  /   \       \   /   \  /   \  /   \
   C       C      C              C       C      C
  / \     / \    / \            / \     / \    / \
 H   H   H   H  H   H          H   H   H   H  H   H
```

(2 marks)

(b) In polypropene the attractive forces between the polymer chains are dispersion forces. However, in polyvinyl alcohol, both dispersion forces between the chains and hydrogen bonding between –OH groups on adjacent chains are possible. Thus, the intermolecular bonding will be stronger in polyvinyl alcohol and the melting temperature will be higher. (2 marks)

(Total = 4 marks)

Question 9

(a)

```
       CH3 CH3  H  H    H  H
          \ /    \ /     \ /
 H         C      C       C       H
   \     /   \  /   \   /   \   /
     C         C      C       C
    / \       / \    / \     / \
   H   H     H  CH3 H   H   H   H
```

(1 mark)

(b)

```
  H  H      H
   \ /     /
 H—C     O     H  H
     \   |     | /
       C       C
 H   /   \   /   \
   C       C       H
  / \     / \
 H   H   H   H
```

(1 mark)

(c)

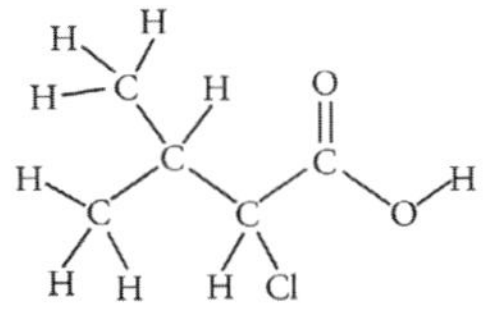

(1 mark)
(Total = 3 marks)

Question 10

(a) 2,5-dimethylheptane (1 mark)
(b) 3,5-dimethyloct-4-ene (1 mark)
(c) 3-methyloct-4-yne (1 mark)
(d) 2-ethyl-2-methylbutanoic acid (1 mark)
(Total = 4 marks)

Answers: Unit 2 Area of Study 1

Multiple choice items

Water as a unique chemical

Question	Answer	Comments
1.	B.	Hydrogen bonds are stronger than dipole-dipole bonding and the dispersion forces in these molecules.
2.	D.	H_2Se and GeH_4 have the same number of electrons and thus the dispersion forces will be similar for these two molecules. GeH_4 is non-polar but H_2Se has a small dipole.
3.	B.	The melting temperatures of these four compounds are in the same order as their boiling temperatures, H_2O is 0°C, H_2S is –86°C, H_2Se is –64°C and H_2Te is –49°C. The dispersion forces increase in the order $H_2Te > H_2Se > H_2S > H_2O$. The melting temperature of H_2O is highest because of hydrogen bonding.
4.	A.	The O–H bond is polar, as oxygen has a higher electronegativity than hydrogen, and the molecule is bent or V shaped and so is asymmetrical.
5.	B.	Ice has intramolecular covalent bonds and intermolecular hydrogen bonds, plus dispersion forces, which are always present between chemical species.
6.	A.	The intermolecular bonding is partially overcome. The intramolecular bonding is unaffected by a change of state.
7.	C.	Dispersion forces occur between all molecules.
8.	B.	When solutes dissolve in water, the freezing point of water decreases, but the boiling point of a solution is higher than that of pure water.

9.	**C.**	Hydrogen bonds in ice, which is a crystalline solid, are fixed in length, strength and direction. In water this is not the case. The molecules have some freedom of movement and are attracted closer together by their polarity.
10.	**A.**	Water transports substances in an organism, is a reactant in biochemical reactions and enables temperature regulation in some living things.
11.	**B.**	Hydrogen bonding is the strongest form of weak bonding and occurs between NH_3 molecules but not between molecules of PH_3, AsH_3 and SbH_3.
12.	**D.**	Latent heat is absorbed when the interparticle bonding is overcome. As this is strong hydrogen bonding in water the latent heat value is high.
13.	**A.**	Energy overcomes the intermolecular bonding at the boiling point of water and does not increase the kinetic energy of the molecules until all have changed state.
14.	**B.**	Ethanol has a lower specific heat and cannot absorb as much energy into its intramolecular bonds as water. The energy increases the kinetic energy of the molecules and hence the temperature rises.
15.	**D.**	Between –10°C and 0°C the heat energy increases the kinetic energy of the molecules. When the temperature reaches 0°C the heat energy is used to break some of the hydrogen bonds (latent heat of fusion).

Acid–base (proton transfer) reactions

Question	Answer	Comments
16.	**A.**	A proton is transferred from HCN (the acid) to H_2O (the base) in a Brønsted–Lowry acid–base reaction.
17.	**C.**	The two chemical species in a conjugate acid–base pair differ by one proton.
18.	**B.**	Hydrogen cyanide is a weak acid. The reversible arrow is used to indicate that for weak acids and bases the ionisation reaction with water is incomplete.
19.	**D.**	Vinegar solutions have a pH of ~2.9, lemon juice has a pH of ~2.0 and soda water a pH between 3.0 and 4.0. Indigestion tablets have anti-acid properties. Baking powder contains sodium hydrogen carbonate, a weak base, and tartaric acid, a weak acid. The approximate pH of the other substances are laundry detergent ~11, oven cleaner ~14, coffee ~5.0, sea water ~ 8.0, wine ~3.5. Deionised water and oil are neutral.
20.	**A.**	A ‘soapy’ feel on skin is typical of bases, which react with fatty acids in the body to produce soaps.

21. **B.** Sodium chloride exists as ions in solution. The partial self-ionisation of water produces equal numbers of hydronium and hydroxide ions. $2H_2O(l) \rightarrow H_3O^+(aq) + OH^-(aq)$

22. **A.** In 1776, Lavoisier suggested that acids contained oxygen. In the early 1800s, Davy suggested that acids contained hydrogen. In 1884, Arrhenius suggested that acids produce H^+ ions in solution. Brønsted and Lowry suggested their theory of acids and bases in 1923.

23. **D.** Sulfur trioxide has one more oxygen atom than sulfur dioxide so the synthesis reactions with water produce respectively sulfuric and sulfurous acids.

24. **C.** An amphiprotic substance can either gain or lose a proton. $H_2PO_4^-(aq) + H^+(aq) \rightarrow H_3PO_4\,(aq)$ or $H_2PO_4^{\ -}(aq) \rightarrow HPO^{2-}(aq) + H^+(aq)$

25. **D.** In ethanoic acid the hydrogen atoms of the methyl group ($-CH_3$) are unreactive. Ammonia and aluminium hydroxide are bases, but hydroboric acid has three reactive hydrogen atoms.

26. **D.** An amphiprotic substance can either gain or lose a proton. H_3PO_4 can only lose protons and PO_4^{3-} can only gain protons.

27. **C.** When acting as an acid H_2O donates H^+. This occurs in III and IV.

28. **B.** Acid-base reactions involve the transfer of H^+ from one substance to another.

29. **A.** **B** and **C** both involve monoprotic acids and **D** involves a triprotic acid.

30. **B.** Some indicators are red at low pH. Others such as phenolphthalein, which is colourless, are not.

31. **C.** $[H_3O^+] = 3 \times 0.05$ M , = 0.15 M, pH = $-\log(0.15) = 0.82$

32. **A.** Formula of barium hydroxide is $Ba(OH)_2$. Hence $[OH^-]$ is 0.0002 and $[H^+] = 10^{-14} \div 0.0002 = 5 \times 10^{-11}$. pH $= -\log(5 \times 10^{-11}) = 10.3$

33. **C.** When the pH $= x$ then $[H_3O^+] = 10^{-x}$ mol L^{-1}. $[H_3O^+][OH^-] = 10^{-14}$.

34. **A.** At this pH the indicators will have the following colours: congo red – red; phenol red – yellow; methyl red – yellow; phenolphthalein – colourless; bromothymol blue – green.

35. **C.** When the pH of a solution changes by 1 unit, $[H^+]$ has changed by a factor of 10. Also, when the pH increases the concentration of hydrogen ions falls. Thus, when the pH changes from 9 to 13 $[H^+]$ has fallen by 10 000.

36. **C.** NaOH is a base and all of its solutions will have a pH greater than 7. KCl and $NaNO_3$ are neutral salts and their solutions will have pH = 7.0. NH_4^+ ions are weakly acidic and react with H_2O to produce a small amount of H^+.

37.	A.	When carbonates react with an acid, two of the products are CO_2 and H_2O.
38.	C.	Metal hydroxides do not release a gas when reacted with an acid. Hydrogen carbonates and carbonates give CO_2.
39.	D.	Metal hydroxides do not release a gas when reacted with an acid. Hydrogen carbonates and carbonates give CO_2. Metals such as zinc produce H_2 gas with acids.
40.	C	Sodium hydrogen carbonate, $NaHCO_3$, is a weak base. It reacts with acids to release carbon dioxide. When the fizzing stops, the acid has been neutralised and the residue can be safely removed.
41.	D.	CO has no acid-base properties.

Redox (electron transfer) reactions

Question	Answer	Comments
42.	C.	Magnesium is a stronger reductant than gold, therefore magnesium reduces gold ions to gold atoms by donating electrons. The gold ions are reduced.
43.	A.	The conventional electrochemical series is written as reduction half-reactions in order of decreasing oxidant strength. Thus, the strongest oxidant is at the top and on the left of the equation.
44.	A.	Mg has been oxidised from 0 to +2 and H has reduced from +1 to 0.
45.	C.	The two parts of a conjugate redox pair only differ by 1, 2, 3 etc. electrons.
46.	A.	In a reduction reaction, a species gains electrons.
47.	A.	The Fe in the steel will react with those cations that are lower in the reactivity series; i.e. Pb^{2+}, Ag^+ and Cu^{2+}.
48.	D.	From the information, H_2 is more reactive than R; S is more reactive than H_2 and also R. T is more reactive than H_2 but less reactive than S.
49.	D.	From the first experiment, *R* is more reactive than *Q*. From the last two experiments, *T* is more reactive than *R* and *Q* since *T* is not displaced from the solution.
50.	C.	K is the most reactive metal of those in the question and will donate its electrons most easily.
51.	B.	Iron forms a crumbly hydrated oxide, sodium oxidises rapidly and completely, gold is unreactive in air, aluminium forms a strongly bonded surface layer of oxide which protects the metal from further oxidation. To some extent these reactions are consistent with the position of the metals in the electrochemical series.

Extended response questions

Water as a unique chemical

Question 1

All four molecules are V-shaped and are polar. The difference in electronegativity between the group 16 element and hydrogen is largest for H_2O. Water has the largest dipole and thus the dipole-dipole bonding (hydrogen bonding) is greatest for water. This hydrogen bonding results in a much higher boiling temperature for water, compared to the other three substances. The dipoles for the other molecules are much smaller. The intermolecular bonding of H_2S, H_2Se and H_2Te, is dominated by dispersion forces. These forces increase with increasing number of electrons and thus are greatest for H_2Te and smallest for H_2S.

(4 marks)

Question 2

	(a) Explanation	**(b) Importance to life**
Property 1	The number of hydrogen bonds between the water molecules is at a maximum in ice. For this to occur these bonds are longer than the hydrogen bonds in water, thus the density decreases.	Ice provides a hard surface for animals to move on. The water underneath the ice provides a safer, warmer aquatic environment.
Property 2	Water has a high capacity to store heat energy in hydrogen bonds.	This high value helps to stabilise Earth's temperature.
Property 3	Polar water molecules attract ionic substances, which dissociate as they dissolve. Water reacts with some non-polar molecules that ionise and dissolve. It will also dissolve those substances that can form hydrogen bonds with water.	Water provides transport and cooling systems in living things. Water acts as a solvent for inorganic substances.

(Total = 2 + 2 + 2 = 6 marks)

Question 3

(a) The high specific heat of water means that the absorption of a large quantity of heat produces a smaller temperature increase than would be the case with liquids having a lower specific heat. Thus, it is an efficient coolant. (2 marks)

(b) The dissolved salts in natural water together with its motion mean that ice is less likely to form. Water also maintains a steady temperature more effectively than air because of its high specific heat value. When ice does form it is at the surface because of its open crystal structure and lower density so fish continue to live beneath the ice. (2 marks)

(c) Water is a good solvent and readily dissolves salt. Salinity of water where crops are grown leads to poor plant growth as water may be leached out of plants by osmosis from plant roots, instead of entering the plant through its roots. (2 marks)

(Total = 6 marks)

Question 4

(a) From 0.5 to 4.5 minutes. (1 mark)

(b) Energy = (18.0 × 4.18 × 100) J = 7524 J or 7.52 kJ (2 marks)

(c) Time to heat water from 0 to 100°C = 9.5 – 4.5 = 5.0 minutes.
Energy delivered per minute = 7.524/5.0 = 1.51 kJ min^{-1} (1 mark)

(d) $n(H_2O)$ = 18.0/18.0 = 1.0 mol

(i) Time to melt ice = 4.0 minutes
Energy delivered = 1.505 kJ per minute
Energy absorbed to melt 1 mol of ice = (1.505 × 4.0) kJ = 6.02 kJ mol^{-1}
Heat of fusion of water = 6.02 kJ mol^{-1}

(ii) Time to boil water = 29.33 min
Energy delivered = 1.505 kJ per minute
Energy absorbed to vaporise 1 mol of water = (1.505 × 29.33) = 44.1 kJ mol^{-1}

(iii) Heat of vaporisation of water = 44.1 kJ mol^{-1}
Energy to warm ice from –20 to 0°C = 1.505 × 0.5 = 0.7525 kJ
Heat capacity of ice = 0.7525/(20 × 18) = 2.09 J g^{-1} K^{-1}

(2 + 2 + 2 = 6 marks)
(Total = 10 marks)

Question 5

(a) The heat of vaporisation is the energy required to overcome all of the bonding between 1 mole of water molecules. It represents the amount by which the kinetic energy of the molecules must be increased to overcome the intermolecular attractive forces. The heat of vapourisation will be less at 100°C since some energy has already been supplied to raise the temperature (the average kinetic energy) of the molecules. (2 marks)

(b) The specific heat capacity is the energy required to raise the temperature of 1 g of water by 1°C; i.e. to increase the average kinetic energy of the molecules. This value is large for water since the hydrogen bonding between the molecules tends to prevent them moving. In steam all of the intermolecular forces have been overcome, hence less energy is needed to increase the average kinetic energy of the molecules. (2 marks)

(Total = 4 marks)

Question 6

(a) polar molecule: H_2O, $CHCl_3$
non-polar molecules: C_4H_{10} (3 marks)

(b) Intermolecular bonding is stronger between polar water molecules as it is hydrogen bonding (and weak dispersion forces). Between trichloromethane molecules there are dispersion forces and also dipole-dipole attractions. However, these dipole-dipole attractions are much weaker than the hydrogen bonds between water molecules. Butane molecules are non-polar and the only intermolecular bonding is relatively weak dispersion forces. More energy is needed to overcome the stronger bonding between water molecules. (3 marks)

(Total = 6 marks)

Acid–base (proton transfer) reactions

Question 7

(a) $HSO_4^-(aq) + H_2O(l) \rightarrow SO^{2-}(aq) + H_3O^+(aq)$ (1 mark)

$HCO_3^-(aq) + H_2O(l) \rightarrow H_2CO_3(aq) + OH^-(aq)$ (1 mark)

(b) Conjugate acids are H_3O^+ and H_2CO_3

Conjugate bases are SO_4^{2-} and OH^- (2 marks)

(c) $HX(aq) + HSO_4^-(aq) \rightarrow X^-(aq) + H_2SO_4(l)$ (2 marks)

(d) $ZOH(aq) + HCO_3^-(aq) \rightarrow H_2O(l) + CO_3^{2-}(aq) + Z^+(aq)$ (2 marks)

(Total = 8 marks)

Question 8

(a) $Cl_2(aq) + H_2O(l) \rightleftharpoons HOCl(aq) + HCl(aq)$

$OCl^-(aq) + H_2O(l) \rightleftharpoons HOCl(aq) + OH^-(aq)$ (2 marks)

(b) From the equations in part (a), addition of Cl_2 will lower the pH of the pool since HOCl and HCl are acids. While addition of NaOCl to a swimming pool will raise the pH of the water since OH^- is produced. (2 marks)

(Total = 4 marks)

Question 9

Substances that are amphiprotic can behave as both an acid and as a base.

As an acid: $H_2PO_4^-(aq) + H_2O(l) \rightarrow HPO_4^{2-}(aq) + H_3O^+(aq)$

As a base: $H_2PO_4^-(aq) + H_2O(l) \rightarrow H_3PO_4(aq) + OH^-(aq)$

(Total = 3 marks)

Question 10

(a) pH = 4.7

$[H_3O^+] = 10^{-4.7}\ M = 2 \times 10^{-5}M$ (1 mark)

$[OH^-] = 10^{-14}/10^{-4.7} = 10^{-9.3}\ M = 5.01 \times 10^{-10}\ M$ (1 mark)

(b) pH = 2.0

$[H_3O^+] = 10^{-2}\ M$ (1 mark)

Although the two acids are of equal concentration, acid B has a lower pH and a higher $[H_3O^+]$, therefore acid B must be a stronger acid and has a higher degree of ionisation in water. (1 mark)

(Total = 4 marks)

Question 11

(a) $HOOCCH_2COOH(aq) + H_2O(l) \rightarrow HOOCCH_2COO^-(aq) + H_3O^+(aq)$

$HNO_3(aq) + H_2O(l) \rightarrow NO_3^-(aq) + H_3O^+(aq)$ (2 marks)

(b) HNO_3 is a strong acid and is almost completely ionised in water. Malonic acid is a weak acid and is only partially ionised. Since the two solutions have the same concentration, there will be more ions present in the solution of HNO_3 and thus this solution will have a higher conductivity. (2 marks)

(c) (i) Malonic acid is a diprotic acid (there are two –COOH groups).
Nitric acid is a monoprotic acid. (2 marks)
(ii) In malonic acid, two of the H atoms are attached to a C atom and are not ionised.
In nitric acid, the single H atom is easily ionised. (2 marks)
(Total = 8 marks)

Redox (electron transfer) reactions

Question 12

(a) (i) Copper; it is the only metal that is a weaker reductant than nickel. (1 mark)
(ii) $Ni(s) + Cu(NO_3)_2(aq) \rightarrow Ni(NO_3)_2(aq) + Cu(s)$ (1 mark)
(iii) Oxidant: Cu^{2+}. reductant: Ni (1 mark)

(b) Fe^{2+} ions are responsible for the green colour of the solution. On exposure to the air the Fe^{2+} ions are oxidised by atmospheric oxygen to Fe^{3+} ions, which cause the red-brown colour. Hydroxide ions are also formed. If the solution is sufficiently concentrated, a red-brown precipitate of iron(III) hydroxide is seen.
$Fe^{2+}(aq) \rightarrow Fe^{3+}(aq) + e^- \times 4$; i.e. $4Fe^{2+}(aq) \rightarrow 4Fe^{3+}(aq) + 4e^-$
$O_2(aq) + 2H_2O(l) + 4e^- \rightarrow 4OH^-(aq)$
$4Fe^{2+}(aq) + O_2(aq) + 2H_2O(l) \rightarrow 4Fe^{3+}(aq) + 4OH^-(aq)$ (2 marks)

(c) Reasons why a predicted reaction may not occur:
- The metal may be covered by a thin impervious layer of oxide preventing the metal from reacting. (1 mark)
- The rate of the reaction may be very slow, so the predicted reaction does not occur. (1 mark)

(Total = 7 marks)

Question 13

(a) Oxidation half-equation: $Fe^{2+} \rightarrow Fe^{3+} + e^-$ (1 mark)
Reduction half-equation $MnO_2 + 4H^+ + 2e^- \rightarrow Mn^{2+} + 2H_2O$ (2 marks)

(b) Oxidant is MnO_2 and the reductant is Fe^{2+}. (1 mark)
A conjugate redox pair is Fe^{2+}/Fe^{3+} (1 mark)

(c) Multiply the oxidation half-equation by 2 to balance electrons:
$2Fe^{2+} \rightarrow 2Fe^{3+} + 2e^-$
Add this equation to the reduction half-equation, eliminating electrons:
$2Fe^{2+} + MnO_2 + 4H^+ \rightarrow 2Fe^{3+} + Mn^{2+} + 2H_2O$ (2 marks)
(Total = 7 marks)

Question 14

(a) $2Al(s) + 3Pb^{2+}(aq) \rightarrow 2Al^{3+}(aq) + 3Pb(s)$
Oxidant is Pb^{2+}; reductant is Al;
Conjugate redox pairs are Al/Al^{3+} and Pb/Pb^{2+} (3 marks)

(b) $2Fe^{3+}(aq) + 2I^-(aq) \rightarrow 2Fe^{2+}(aq) + I_2(aq)$
Oxidant is Fe^{3+}; reductant is I^-;
Conjugate redox pairs are Fe^{3+}/Fe^{2+} and I_2/I^- (3 marks)
(Total = 6 marks)

Question 15

(a) Sodium is a main group metal (group I) and zinc is a transition metal. Main group metals are generally more reactive (higher in the activity series) than transition metals. The outer-shell electron configuration of sodium is s^1 and that of zinc is $d^{10}s^2$. This means that sodium can react with water even when the water is cold but zinc requires the water to be hot. (2 marks)

(b) Magnesium is a main group metal (group II) and copper is a transition metal. Main group metals are generally more reactive (higher in the activity series) than transition metals. The outer-shell electron configuration of magnesium is s^2 and that of copper is $d^{10}s^1$. Magnesium can therefore react with the acid, while copper cannot (when it is dilute). (2 marks)

(c) Gold, silver and copper are all low in the activity series and are all transition metals, whereas aluminium and potassium are main group metals. Therefore, the gold, silver and copper are more likely to be found in their pure form in nature as they likely have not encountered conditions that would make them react to form compounds. (2 marks)

(Total = 6 marks)

Question 16

(a) (i) Reduced as it gains two electrons per Sn^{2+} ion.

(ii) The oxidant as it acquires electrons from the reductant which donates them and is oxidised.

(iii)Two electrons per tin ion as each ion has two positive charges.

(1 + 1 + 1 = 3 marks)

(b) (i) Oxide ions: $6O^{2-}$(cryolite) $\rightarrow$ $3O_2$(g) + $12e^-$

(ii) Aluminium ions: Al^{3+}(cryolite) + $3e^-$ $\rightarrow$ Al(l)

(iii) $12e^-$ (1 + 1 + 1 = 3 marks)

(Total = 6 marks)

Question 17

(a) X(s) + Z^{2+}(aq) $\rightarrow$ X^{2+}(aq) + Z(s) (1 mark)

(b) X is the reductant and Z^{2+} is the oxidant. (1 mark)

(c) X is higher in the activity series of metals since it displaces Z from the solution.

(2 marks)

(Total = 4 marks)

Answers: Unit 2 Area of Study 1 test

Multiple choice items

Acid–base (proton transfer) reactions

Question	Answer	Comments
1.	**B.**	Only species which participate in the reaction and undergo a specific change are included in the ionic equation. Na^+ ions are spectator ions and so should not be included. $HClO_2$ is a weak acid so very little ClO_2^- is present initially.
2.	**C.**	$[OH^-] = 10^{-14} \div 10^{-3.2} = 10^{-10.8}$ mol L^{-1}
3.	**C.**	This anion can donate two protons and can also accept one proton. **A** and **D** can both donate two protons but not accept any. **B** can only accept a proton.
4.	**A.**	K_w varies with temperature. Values of K_w are valid for any aqueous solution at that temperature.
5.	**D.**	Ethanoic acid is a weak acid and a 10^{-3} mol L^{-1} solution is considered to be dilute.
6.	**B.**	HNO_3 is a strong acid and is fully ionised in aqueous solution. Ethanoic acid is a weak acid and is only partially ionised in water. The solution of the HNO_3 is more dilute than that of the ethanoic acid.
7.	**A.**	Sulfuric acid is a strong diprotic acid $[H_3O^+] = 2[H_2SO_4]$, HCl is a strong monoprotic acid $[H_3O^+] = [HCl]$, ethanoic acid is a weak acid and lithium hydroxide is basic.
8.	**C.**	The weakest acid produces the smallest amount of H^+ compared to its concentration.
9.	**B.**	For a strong monoprotic acid (e.g. HCl) $[HCl] = [H^+]$ since it is fully ionised. Acid II produces more H^+ than this $[H^+] > [acid]$. This can only occur if there is more than one H atom per molecule that can be ionised.
10.	**C.**	HCl is a strong acid and will have the lowest pH. NaOH is a strong base and will have the highest pH. Solutions of NaCl will be neutral and have pH = 7.
11.	**B.**	Dilute solutions have small amounts of solute compared with the amount of solvent. The acid will only be completely ionised if it is a strong acid.
12.	**B.**	Solutions of acids have pH of less than 7.
13.	**A.**	Hydrogen chloride is fully ionised in aqueous solution and reacts with water to form hydronium ions and chloride ions.
14.	**B.**	Chloride ions, $Cl^-(aq)$ are the only spectator ions in this reaction.

Redox (electron transfer) reactions

Question	Answer	Comments
15.	C.	Pb is oxidised and PbO_2 is reduced. H_2SO_4 is consumed by this reaction, hence $[H^+]$ falls and the pH rises. The half-equation for the reduction of is PbO_2 $PbO_2(s) + 4H^+(aq) + 2e^- \rightarrow PbSO_4(s) + 2H_2O(l)$ The reaction both acid-base and redox.
16.	C.	**A** is a precipitation reaction. **B** and **D** are acid-base reactions. In **C**, Cu^{2+} is reduced to Cu^+ and I^- is oxidised to I_2.
17.	D.	Ag^+ is reduced by Cu and Fe^{3+} is reduced by I^-.
18.	A.	Magnesium is a stronger reductant than nickel. Nickel ions are a stronger oxidant than magnesium ions; i.e. nickel ions and magnesium are diagonally opposed in the series with nickel ions, the oxidant, higher on the left.
19.	C.	Tin is a weaker reductant than iron and would act as the cathode. Zinc, magnesium and chromium are all stronger reductants than iron and would therefore act as the anode.
20.	C.	Pb will only reduce those cations that are lower in the reactivity series; i.e. Ag^+ and Cu^{2+}.
21.	C.	Metals displace from solution ions of metals which are weaker reductants than they are themselves; i.e. metals which are lower on the activity series. Lead and silver are lower than nickel, but aluminium and zinc are higher, thus **C** is the correct answer.

Extended response questions

Acid–base (proton transfer) reactions

Question 1

(a) Hydrochloric acid is a strong acid. Hence $[HCl] = [H^+] = 10^{-3}$ mol L^{-1}. Ethanoic acid is a weak acid and is only partially ionised in solution. Hence $[CH_3COOH] > [H^+]$. To achieve a pH = 3.0, the concentration of ethanoic acid must be greater than 10^{-3} mol L^{-1}. (3 marks)

(b) $[H^+][OH^-] = 10^{-14}$; if $[H^+] = 10^{-3}$ then $[OH^-] = 10^{-11}$. (1 mark)

(Total = 4 marks)

Question 2

(a) $2Al(s) + 6HCl(aq) \rightarrow 2AlCl_3(aq) + 3H_2(g)$ (1 mark)
$2Al(s) + 6H^+(aq) \rightarrow 2Al^{3+}(aq) + 3H_2(g)$ (1 mark)

(b) $NaOH(aq) + H_3PO_4(aq) \rightarrow Na_3PO_4(aq) + 3H_2O(l)$ (1 mark)
$OH^-(aq) + H^+(aq) \rightarrow H_2O(l)$ (1 mark)

(c) $2HCl(aq) + K_2CO_3(aq) \rightarrow 2KCl(aq) + CO_2(g) + H_2O(l)$ (1 mark)
$2H^+(aq) + CO_3^{2-}(aq) \rightarrow CO_2(g) + H_2O(l)$ (1 mark)

(d) $2NaHCO_3(aq) + H_2SO_4(aq) \rightarrow Na_2SO_4(aq) + 2CO_2(g) + 2H_2O(l)$ (1 mark)
$HCO_3^-(aq) + H^+(aq) \rightarrow CO_2(g) + H_2O(l)$ (1 mark)
(e) $CuO(s) + H_2SO_4(aq) \rightarrow CuSO_4(aq) + H_2O(l)$ (1 mark)
$CuO(s) + 2H^+(aq) \rightarrow Cu^{2+}(aq) + H_2O(l)$ (1 mark)
(Total = 10 marks)

Question 3

Methanoic acid is a weak acid. In an aqueous solution the concentration of methanoic acid is much larger than the concentration of H_3O^+. HCl is a strong acid almost all of the HCl molecules are ionised to form H_3O^+. To produce the same pH the amount of HCl required will be much less than the amount of HCOOH.

(Total = 3 marks)

Question 4

$H_3AsO_4(aq) + H_2O(l) \rightleftharpoons H_2AsO_4^-(aq) + H_3O^+(aq)$
$H_2AsO_4^-(aq) + H_2O(l) \rightleftharpoons HAsO_4^{2-}(aq) + H_3O^+(aq)$
$HAsO_4^{2-}(aq) + H_2O(l) \rightleftharpoons AsO_4^{3-}(aq) + H_3O^+(aq)$

(Total = 3 marks)

Question 5

(a) $2NaHCO_3(s) \rightarrow Na_2CO_3(s) + H_2O(g) + CO_2(g)$ (1 mark)
(b) $Fe(s) + H_2SO_4(aq) \rightarrow FeSO_4(aq) + H_2(g)$
$Fe(s) + 2H^+(aq) \rightarrow Fe^{2+}(aq) + H_2(g)$ (2 marks)
(c) $Mg(OH)_2(s) + 2HCl(aq) \rightarrow MgCl_2(aq) + 2H_2O(l)$
$Mg(OH)_2(s) + 2H^+(aq) \rightarrow Mg^{2+}(aq) + 2H_2O(l)$ (2 marks)
(d) $CaCO_3(s) + 2HNO_3(aq) \rightarrow Ca(NO_3)_2(aq) + H_2O(l) + CO_2(g)$
$CaCO_3(s) + 2H^+(aq) \rightarrow Ca^{2+}(aq) + H_2O(l) + CO_2(g)$ (2 marks)
(Total = 7 marks)

Question 6

(a) $CuCO_3(s) + 2HCl(aq) \rightarrow CuCl_2(aq) + H_2O(l) + CO_2(g)$ (1 mark)
(b) $Zn(s) + 2HCl(aq) \rightarrow ZnCl_2(aq) + H_2(g)$ (1 mark)
(c) $MgSO_3(s) + 2HCl(aq) \rightarrow MgCl_2(aq) + H_2O(l) + SO_2(g)$ (1 mark)
(d) $CaS(s) + 2HCl(aq) \rightarrow CaCl_2(aq) + H_2S(g)$ (1 mark)
(Total = 4 marks)

Redox (electron transfer) reactions

Question 7

(a) precipitation (b) redox (c) dissociation
(d) precipitation (e) ionisation (f) acid-base
(g) redox (reduction)

(Total = 7 × 1 = 7 marks)

Question 8

(a) Strontium. Strontium is in group II and cobalt is a transition metal. Main group metals are more reactive than transition metals. (2 marks)

(b) From experiment 1, V is higher in the activity series than Zn. Experiment 3 shows that Zn is higher in the series than Ni and experiment 4 shows that Ni is higher in the series than Sn.
V > Zn > Ni > Sn. (3 marks)

(Total = 5 marks)

Question 9

(a) Magnesium is a stronger reductant than nickel and will displace nickel from a solution of nickel chloride. Aqueous nickel ions are green. As the reaction proceeds, the concentration of $Ni^{2+}(aq)$ falls and the solution becomes a lighter green. When nickel ions are reduced nickel metal is formed, which accounts for the silvery grey solid. Magnesium will also react slowly with water and form small amount of hydrogen. (3 marks)

(b) $Ni^{2+}(aq) + Mg(s) \rightarrow Ni(s) + Mg^{2+}(aq)$ (1 mark)

(c) Reaction of magnesium with water will produce hydrogen gas.
$Mg(s) + 2H_2O(l) \rightarrow Mg(OH)_2(aq) + H_2(g)$ (2 marks)

(d) From the equation in part (b): $n(Ni)$ formed = $n(Mg)$ reacted.
$n(Ni) = 0.880 \div 58.69 = 1.499 \times 10^{-2}$ mol
mass of Mg reacting = $1.499 \times 10^{-2} \times 24.31 = 0.3645$ g (2 marks)

(e) Some of the Mg has reacted with the water, increasing the mass loss of the Mg. (1 mark)

(Total = 9 marks)

Answers: Unit 2 Area of Study 2

Multiple choice items

Measuring solubility and concentration

Question	Answer	Comments
1.	**B.**	Solubility in g/100 g = (0.30 × 100)/15 = 2.0 g/100 g
2.	**D.**	Mass of KBr = 39.1 + 79.9 = 119 g. Mass of water required is (119 × 100) ÷ 68 = 175 g
3.	**B.**	The molarities (in mol L^{-1}) are **A** = 307/74.6 = 4.11; **B** = 319/101.1 = 3.16; **C** = 583/102.9 = 5.66; **D** = 317/58.4 = 5.42.
4.	**B.**	Solubility decreases with decreasing temperature, making crystallisation more likely. Adding water will decrease the concentration of the solution, making crystallisation less likely.
5.	**C.**	The solubility of gases decreases with increasing temperature at constant pressure. The solubility of most salts increases with increasing temperature.

6. **C.** Mass of $NaNO_3$ dissolved at 60°C = 124 × 1.5 = 186 g.
Mass of $NaNO_3$ dissolved at 20°C = 88.1 × 1.5 = 132.2 g.
Mass precipitated = 186 – 132.2 = 53.8 g.

7. **B.** $n = cV$, n(KNO_3) = 2.2 × 0.75 = 1.65 mol. m(KNO_3) = $n \times M$,
= 1.65 × 101.1 = 166.8 g.

8. **A.** $c_1V_1 = c_2V_2$ and 35 × 0.200 = 5 × V_2 Hence V_2 = 1.400 L or 1400 mL. Volume of water to be added is (1400 – 200) = 1200 mL or 1.2 L:

9. **C.** Dilution only involves adding water, the number of moles of solute is unchanged.

10. **B.** Mass NH_3 = $3.70 \times 10^{-4} \times 17 = 6.29 \times 10^{-3}$ g. Mass NH_3 in 1.0 L = 6.29×10^{-2} g L^{-1}

11. **C.** n($AgNO_3$) = 2/169.9 mol = 0.0118 mol,
c($AgNO_3$) = 0.0118/0.3 mol L^{-1} = 0.0392 mol L^{-1}

12. **C.** n($CuCl_2$) = 5.7/134.4 mol = 0.0424 mol. n(Cl^-) = 2 × 0.0424 = 0.0848 mol;
Mass Cl^- = 0.0848 × 35.5 = 3.01 g. c(Cl^-) = 3.01/0.75 = 4.01 g L^{-1}.

13. **B.** mol ratio $AlCl_3$: Cl^- = 1 : 3, c(Cl^-) = 3 × 1.2 = 3.6 M

14. **B.** $c_1V_1 = c_2V_2$, 2.0 × 0.20 = 0.50 × c_2, c_2 = 0.80 M

15. **D.** c($PbCl_2$) = (1.08/278.1) ÷ 0.1 = 0.0388 mol L^{-1}.
c($PbCl_2$) = 1.08/0.1 = 10.8 g L^{-1}or 10800 mg L^{-1} (× ppm).

16. **D.** n(NaCl) = (0.25 × 1000 ÷ 58.45) × 0.4 = 1.7 mol. Other answers are **A** = 1.2 mol, **B** = 0.205 mol, **C** = 0.12 mol.

17. **D.** For **D**, n(NO^-) = 0.25 × 0.25 × 4 = 0.25 mol. Other three answers are **A** = 0.27 mol, **B** = 0.30 mol and **C** = 0.27 mol.

18. **C.** The concentration is 0.75 mole in 1.0 L of *solution*. 0.75 mol of $CaBr_2$ is 0.75 × 200 = 150 g L^{-1} or 0.15 g mL^{-1}.

19. **A.** In **A**: n(Cl^-) = 0.05 and [Cl^-] = 0.05 ÷ 0.10 = 0.50 M.
In **B**: n(Cl^-) = 0.03 × 2 and [Cl^-] = 0.06 ÷ 0.10 = 0.60 M.
In **C**: n(Cl^-) = 0.04 × 3 and [Cl^-] = 0.12 ÷ 0.10 = 1.2 M.
In **D**: n(Cl^-) = 0.02 × 4 and [Cl^-] = 0.08 ÷ 0.10 = 0.8 M.

20. **B.** n(SO_4^{2-}) from K_2SO_4 = 0.26 × 0.50 = 0.13 mol
n(SO_4^{2-}) from $Al_2(SO_4)_3$ = 3 × 0.43 × 1.7 = 2.19 mol
total n(SO_4^{2-}) = 0.13 + 2.19 = 2.32
[(SO_4^{2-})] = 2.32 ÷ (0.26 + 0.43) = 3.37 mol L^{-1}

21. **A.** c(m/m) is 40.0 g in 100 g of solution.
Volume of solution = 100/0.932 = 107.3 mL
c(m/v) = (40.0/107.3) × 100 = 37.3

Analysis for acids and bases

Question	Answer	Comments
22.	C.	The equation for the reaction is $2H^+ (aq) + CO_3^{2-}(aq) \rightarrow H_2O + CO_2(g)$ Hence the equivalence point is reached when the number of H^+ ions is just twice the number of $CO_3^{2-}(aq)$. The amount of H^+ will need to be just greater than this to change the colour of the indicator.
23.	B.	Washing the pipette with water will mean that less base will be taken. Hence less acid would be needed. Subsequent titrations would not be affected since the pipette would now be wet with base. Answers A and C would mean that more acid would have been used. D is correct analysis procedure and should produce consistent results.
24.	B.	$n(Na_2CO_3) = 0.25 \times 0.065 = 0.01625$ mol $Mass(Na_2CO_3) = 0.01625 \times 106 = 1.722$ g
25.	D.	$n(HCl) = 0.02 \times 0.100 = 2 \times 10^{-3} = n(H^+)$ $CO_3^{2-} + 2H^+ \rightarrow CO_2 + H_2O$ $n(CO_3^{2-}) = 2 \times 10^{-3} \div 2 = 1 \times 10^{-3} = n(M_xCO_3)$, where M is metal and x is 1 or 2. Molar mass of $M_xCO_3 = 0.148 \div (1 \times 10^{-3}) = 148$ Molar of $M_x = 148 - 60 = 88$, M = Sr and $x = 1$
26.	C.	$n(NaOH) = 0.136 \times 0.02062 = 2.804 \times 10^{-3}$ mol Since the ratio n(base):n(acid) is 2:1 then $n(\text{acid}) = 1.402 \times 10^{-3}$ mol Molar mass acid = $0.1851/(1.402 \times 10^{-3}) = 132.0$ g mol^{-1}
27.	B.	$n(HCl) = (0.20 \times 0.10) + (0.20 \times 0.20) + (0.10 \times 0.40)$ $= 0.10$ mol; $c(HCl) = 0.10 \div 0.50 = 0.20$ mol L^{-1}
28.	C.	$n(\text{nitric acid}) = 0.1 \times 2.00 = 0.200$ mol. Final volume = $0.200 \div 0.100 = 2.0$ L Volume H_2O to be added = $2.00 - 0.10 = 1.90$ L

Measuring gases

Question	Answer	Comments
29.	C.	Not all neon atoms in the sample will have the same kinetic energy at a certain temperature but their average kinetic energy is proportional to the temperature.
30.	D.	If the gas samples are at the same temperature their average kinetic energy will be the same. Since p, V and T are the same for both gases, the samples will contain the same number of moles but not the same mass.

31.	**B.**	The volume of a gas at fixed temperature and pressure conditions depends on the number of particles, and whether the gas behaves as an ideal gas with no attractive forces between particles. Thus **B**, which compares the volumes of 1 mole of each of two monatomic inert gases, is the only correct answer.
32.	**B.**	At room temperature, the volume of water will be negligible. Mol ratio ethane : oxygen = 2 : 7 Hence, volume of oxygen reacting = s = 350 mL $V(O_2)$ remaining = 500 – 350 mL = 150 mL Mol ratio $C_2H_6 : CO_2 = 2 : 4$, hence $V(CO_2)$ = 200 mL Total volume of gas = 150 + 200 = 350 mL
33.	**D.**	$n(H_2S) = 3 \times 0.200 = 0.600$ mol; $V(H_2S) = 0.600 \times 24.8$ L
34.	**C.**	$p = \frac{nRT}{V} = \frac{2.80 \times 8.314 \times 333}{44 \times 0.300} = 587$ kPa
35.	**A.**	$n(O_2) = \frac{76.0 \times 1.60}{8.31 \times 292} = 0.0501$ mol; $n(NaClO_3) = \frac{2 \times 0.0501}{3}$ Mass $NaClO_3 = 0.0334 \times 106.5 = 3.56$ g
36.	**D.**	$n(CO_2) = \frac{5.68}{44} = 0.129$ mol; $n(C_2H_5OH) = n(CO_2)$ since in the equation the ratio is 2 : 2. Mass $C_2H_5OH = 0.129 \times 46 = 5.93$ g

Analysis for salts

Question	Answer	Comments
37.	**C.**	$n(BaCl_2.2H_2O) = 7.329 \div 244.3 = 0.0300$ mol $c(BaCl_2.2H_2O) = 0.0300 \div 0.600 = 0.0500$ M Mole ratio $Cl^- : BaCl_2.2H_2O$ = 2:1; $c(Cl^-) = 2 \times 0.050$ M
38.	**B.**	A solution of methanol contains no charged particles (ions or electrons) that are free to move.
39.	**B.**	The most appropriate wavelength will be where the yellow and blue dyes have zero absorbance and the red dye has a large absorbance, but not necessarily its maximum.
40.	**B.**	$n(Na_2CO_3) = 0.15 \times 0.020 = 0.0030$ mol $n(AgNO_3) = 0.25 \times 0.030 = 0.0075$ mol Since the molar ratio is 1:2 0.0030 mol of Na_2CO_3 reacts with 0.0060 mol of $AgNO_3$; i.e. $AgNO_3$ is in excess. $n(Ag_2CO_3) = n(Na_2CO_3) = 0.0030$ mol Mass $(Ag_2CO_3) = 0.0030 \times 275.8 = 0.827$ g
41.	**D.**	$n(KI) = 7.70 \div (39.1 + 126.9) = 0.04639$ mol The equation for reaction is $2KI(aq) + Pb(NO_3)_2(aq) \rightarrow PbI_2(s) + 2KNO_3(aq)$

$n(Pb(NO_3)_2) = 0.04639 \div 2 = 0.02319 = \text{volume(L)} \equiv 2.0$
Volume (mL) = $23.19 \div 2 = 11.6$ mL

42. **A.** The spectrum is a result of electrons moving from a lower to a higher energy level. 400 nm could also be used to determine the concentration of solutions of this compound.

43. **A.** $n(CH_4) = 3.2/16 = 0.20$ mol; $n(O_2) = 3.2/32 = 0.10$ mol.
Since molar ratio is 1:2 then 0.10 mol of O_2 reacts with 0.050 mol of CH_4; i.e.CH_4 is in excess. $n(CH_4) = n(CO_2)$.
Mass $CO_2 = 0.050 \times 44 = 2.2$ g

44. **B.** $n(Cl^-) = n(AgCl) = \dfrac{0.177}{143.32} = 1.235 \times 10^{-3}$ mol
Mass Cl = $1.235 \times 10^{-3} \times 35.45 = 0.04378$ g
$\%Cl = \dfrac{0.04378 \times 100}{1.75} = 2.50$

45. **C.** $n(UF_6) = \dfrac{5.84}{352}$; $n(F) = \dfrac{6 \times 5.84}{352} = 0.0995$

Extended response questions

Measuring solubility and concentration

Question 1

(a) Mass of sodium nitrate dissolving at 70°C is $40/100 \times 135 = 54$ g (1 mark)
(b) Mass of sodium nitrate precipitating = $54 - 35.2 = 18.8$ g (2 marks)
(c) Mass of water needed to dissolve 18.8 g $NaNO_3 = 18.8/88 \times 100 = 21.4$ g (2 marks)
(Total = 5 marks)

Question 2

(a) B is a gas as its solubility decreases as the temperature increases. (2 marks)
(b) 65 g/ 100 g H_2O (1 mark)
(c) Solubility of A = 54.5 g /100 g at 60°C
Volume of water needed for saturated solution = $50/54.5 \times 100 = 91.7$ mL (Assumes the density of water to be 1 g mL^{-1}.) (2 marks)
(d) Solubility of C at 40°C = 58 g /100 g
Mass of C dissolving in 60 g water = $58 \times 60/100 = 34.8$ g
Mass of C undissolved = $80 - 34.8 = 45.2$ g (3 marks)
(Total = 8 marks)

Question 3

(a) v(ethanol) = $15.3 \div 0.785 = 19.5$ mL (1 mark)
(b) expected volume of solution = $120 + 19.5 = 139.5$ mL (1 mark)
(c) There is a contraction in volume caused by hydrogen bonding between the ethanol and water molecules. Each water molecule can hydrogen bond to two ethanol molecules.
(1 mark)

(d) (i) n(ethanol) = 15.3 ÷ 46 = 0.333 mol
c(ethanol) = 0.333 ÷ 0.135 = 2.46 M (1 mark)
(ii) 15.3 g per 0.135 L = (1 ÷ 0.135) × 15.3 g L^{-1} = 113.3 g L^{-1} (1 mark)
(iii) Assume density of ethanol solution = 1 g mL^{-1}
% m/m(ethanol solution) = 15.3/135 × 100 = 11.3% m/m (1 mark)
(Total = 5 marks)

Analysis for acids and bases

Question 4

(a) (i) $H_2SO_4(aq) + 2NaOH(aq) \rightarrow Na_2SO_4(aq) + 2H_2O(l)$ (1 mark)
(ii) n(NaOH) = 0.100 × 0.02260 = 0.00226 mol (1 mark)
mol ratio NaOH : H_2SO_4 = 2 : 1
n(H_2SO_4) = 0.5 × 0.00226 = 0.00113 mol in 20 mL (1 mark)
n(H_2SO_4) in 250 mL = 0.00113 × 250/20 = 0.0283 mol (1 mark)
This is n(H_2SO_4) in 50.0 mL undiluted acid.
c(H_2SO_4) undiluted acid = 0.0283/0.050 = 0.565 M (1 mark)

(b) (i) $H_2SO_4(aq) + BaCl_2(aq) \rightarrow 2HCl(aq) + BaSO_4(s)$ (1 mark)
(ii) n($BaSO_4$) = 7.96/233.34 = 0.0341 mol (1 mark)
mol ratio $BaSO_4$: H_2SO_4 = 1 : 1, (1 mark)
hence n(H_2SO_4) = 0.0341 (1 mark)
c(H_2SO_4) = 0.0341/0.05 = 0.682 M (1 mark)

(c) Possible errors in volumetric analysis:
- inaccurate observation of end point
- inaccurate filling of pipette or volumetric flask
- inaccurate reading of burette
- failure to shake flask so that the diluted solution is homogeneous. (1 mark)

Possible errors in precipitation experiment:
- no excess of barium chloride solution so incomplete precipitation
- failure to dry precipitate to constant mass
- inaccurate weighing
- a non-acidic impurity precipitates along with $BaSO_4$
- failure to completely filter and transfer precipitate. (1 mark)

(Total = 12 marks)

Question 5

(a) $CuCO_3(s) + H_2SO_4(aq) \rightarrow CuSO_4(aq) + H_2O(l) + CO_2(g)$ (2 marks)
(b) n($CuCO_3$) = n(H_2SO_4) = 0.2516 × 0.02350 = 5.913 × 10^{-3} mol
Mass $CuCO_3$ = 5.913 × 10^{-3} × 123.5 = 0.7302 g (2 marks)
(c) % $CuCO_3$ = (0.7302 ÷ 1.052) × 100 = 69.41% (1 mark)
(d) Molar ratio H_2SO_4 : H_2O = 1 : 1; n(H_2O) = 5.913 × 10^{-3} mol (1 mark)
Mass(H_2O) = 5.913 × 10^{-3} × 18 = 0.1064 g (1 mark)
(Total = 7 marks)

Question 6

(a) $n(Na_2CO_3) = 0.0200 \times 0.168 = 3.36 \times 10^{-3}$ mol (1 mark)

(b) Ratio $n(HCl):n(Na_2CO_3) = 2:1$

Hence $n(HCl) = 2 \times 3.36 \times 10^{-3} = 6.72 \times 10^{-3}$ mol (1 mark)

(c) 18.39 mL of acid contains 6.72×10^{-3} mol

Hence $n(HCl)$ in 250 mL $= \frac{250}{18.39} \times 6.72 \times 10^{-3} = 0.0914$ mol (1 mark)

(d) Mass of HCl in volumetric flask = 0.0914 × 36.45 = 3.33 g (1 mark)

(e) 3.33 g of acid is present in 10.00 mL of concentrated acid.

Hence in 1 L of concentrated acid, there are $\frac{3.33 \times 1000}{10.00} = 333$ g

Concentration of undiluted acid = 333 g L^{-1} (1 mark)

(f) *Either:* It is a corrosive substance and could damage skin or eyes if it comes into contact. Should not be ingested. (1 mark)

Or: Avoid contact with skin or eyes – wash well with large amounts of water if this occurs or neutralise with a dilute base, such as baking powder (sodium hydrogen carbonate) in water. Protective clothing, such as rubber gloves, should be worn. (1 mark)

(Total = 6 marks)

Question 7

(a) $2NaOH(aq) + H_2SO_4(aq) \rightarrow Na_2SO_4(aq) + 2H_2O(l)$ (1 mark)

(b) Any two of: wearing a laboratory coat; wearing safety glasses; wearing gloves; use an automatic pipette filler. (2 marks)

(c) (i) $n(H_2SO_4) = 0.05134 \times 0.02028 = 1.041 \times 10^{-3}$ mol (1 mark)

(ii) $n(NaOH):n(H_2SO_4) = 2:1$, and hence $n(NaOH) = 2 \times n(H_2SO_4)$ $n(NaOH)$ in 20.00 mL $= 2 \times 1.041 \times 10^{-3} = 2.082 \times 10^{-3}$ mol (1 mark)

(iii) $n(NaOH)$ in 250.0 mL of diluted solution $= \frac{250 \times 2.082 \times 10^{-3}}{20}$ mol = 0.02603 mol

Mass of NaOH = 0.02603 × 40.0 = 1.041 g (2 marks)

(iv) % NaOH in oven cleaner $= \frac{1.041 \times 100}{23.74} = 4.39\%$ (1 mark)

(Total = 8 marks)

Measuring gases

Question 8

Complete the following unit conversions.

(a) $200 \times 103 = 2.00 \times 10^5$ mL (3 significant figures) (1 mark)

(b) 4.62 × 101.35 = 468 kPa (3 significant figures) (1 mark)

(c) 25 + 273 = 298 K (3 significant figures) (1 mark)

(d) $9.62 \times 10^6 \div 10^3 = 9.62 \times 10^3$ kPa (3 significant figures) (1 mark)

(Total = 4 marks)

Question 9

(a) $n(N_2) = \frac{PV}{RT} = \frac{100 \times 5.00}{8.31 \times 315} = 0.191$ mol (3 significant figures) (1 mark)

(b) $n(H_2) = \frac{m}{M} = \frac{5.0}{2.0} = 2.5$ mol

$V = n \times V_m = 2.5 \times 24.5 = 61.25 = 61$ L (2 significant figures) (2 marks)

(c) $T = \frac{PV}{nR} = \frac{200 \times 1.5}{2.00 \times 8.31} = 18.05 = 18$ K (2 significant figures) (1 mark)

(Total = 4 marks)

Question 10

(a) $V(CO_2) = \frac{3}{1} \times V(C_3H_8) = 3 \times 20 = 60$ mL

$V(H_2O) = \frac{4}{1} \times V(C_3H_8) = 4 \times 20 = 80$ mL

Total volume of products = $V(CO_2) + V(H_2O) = 60 + 80 = 140$ mL (3 marks)

(b) One mark for each of:

- CO_2 would contribute to the enhanced greenhouse effect while H_2O would not.
- The CO_2 produce would contribute to a higher concentration of CO_2 in the atmosphere, particularly if the propane was originally sourced from crude oil (fossil fuel). The H_2O is a greenhouse gas but it will quickly enter the water cycle, liquefying and being removed, not increasing the actual concentration of gaseous water in the atmosphere and thus not contributing to a real increase in the greenhouse effect. (2 marks)

(Total = 5 marks)

Question 11

(a) 6.0 mL × 60 × 24 = 8640 mL = 8.64 L (in a day)

$n(O_2) = \frac{PV}{RT} = \frac{100 \times 8.6}{8.31 \times (28 + 273)} = 0.345$ mol

$n(Fe_2O_3) = n(O_2) \times \frac{2}{3} = 0.345 \times \frac{2}{3} = 0.230$ mol

$m(Fe_2O_3) = n \times M = 0.230 \times 159.6 = 36.7 = 37$ g (2 significant figures) (4 marks)

(b) $V = \frac{nRT}{P} = \frac{1.00 \times 8.31 \times (28 + 273)}{100} = 25$ L for one mole of gas, therefore the molar volume is 25 L mol^{-1}. (2 marks)

(Total = 6 marks

Analysis for salts

Question 12

(a) $Ba(OH)_2(aq) + H_2SO_4(aq) \rightarrow BaSO_4(s) + 2H_2O(l)$ (2 marks)

(b) Initially the beaker contains a solution in which $Ba^{2+}(aq)$ and $OH^-(aq)$ ions are present. The presence of these ions means that initially the conductivity of the solution is high. When sulfuric acid is added these ions are gradually removed from solution, either precipitated as $BaSO_4$ or reacted with $H^+(aq)$. Hence the conductivity of the solution falls. This continues until all of the $Ba(OH)_2$ has reacted. After this point the conductivity rises again due the presence of the ions from excess sulfuric acid, $H^+(aq)$ and $SO_4^{2-}(aq)$. (3 marks)

(c) The equivalence point of the reaction occurred at 18.00 mL of sulfuric acid.
$n(H_2SO_4) = n(Ba(OH)_2) = 0.0200 \times 0.105 = 2.100 \times 10^{-3}$ mol
$c(H_2SO_4) = (2.100 \times 10^{-3}) \div 0.01800 = 0.117$ mol L^{-1}. (2 marks)
(Total = 7 marks)

Question 13

(a) $ZnCl_2(aq) + K_2CO_3(aq) \rightarrow 2KCl(aq) + ZnCO_3(s)$ (1 mark)
(b) mol ratio $ZnCl_2 : K_2CO_3 = 1 : 1$
$n(ZnCl_2) = n(K_2CO_3)$. $n(ZnCl_2) = (0.250 \times 0.050)$ mol $= 0.0125$ mol
$n(K_2CO_3) = (0.500 \times 0.050) = 0.025$ mol, K_2CO_3 is in excess.
$n(ZnCO_3) = n(ZnCl_2) = 0.0125$ mol
mass $(ZnCO_3) = n \times M_r = (0.0125 \times 125.38)$ g $= 1.57$ g (mass of precipitate) (2 marks)
(c) The potassium ions are spectator ions and all of them remain in the solution.
$n(K^+)$ added $= 2 \times 0.05 \times 0.500 = 0.0500$ mol
Volume of final solution = 50 + 50 = 100 mL
$c(K^+) = n/V = 0.0500/0.100 = 0.500$ mol L^{-1} (2 marks)
(Total = 5 marks)

Question 14

(a) $Fe_2(SO_4)_3(aq) + 6NaOH(aq) \rightarrow 3Na_2SO_4(aq) + 2Fe(OH)_3(s)$ (1 mark)
(b) Molar ratio: $Fe_2(SO_4)_3 : NaOH = 1 : 6$
$n(Fe_2(SO_4)_3) = 3.00 \times 0.200$ mol $= 0.600$ mol
$n(NaOH) = 5.00 \times 0.120 = 0.600$ mol
NaOH is the limiting reactant since 0.600 mol $Fe_2(SO_4)_3$ requires 6×0.6 mol NaOH for complete reaction and only 0.600 mol is present.
$Fe_2(SO_4)_3$ is in excess since 0.60 mol NaOH requires only $0.60/6 = 0.1$ mol $Fe_2(SO_4)_3$ for complete reaction. (3 marks)
(c) $n(Fe_2(SO_4)_3)$ unreacted $= 0.600 - 0.100$ mol $= 0.500$ mol
$c(Fe_2(SO_4)_3)$ remaining $= 0.500/(0.200 + 0.120) = 1.56$ mol L^{-1} (2 marks)
(d) Molar ratio $NaOH : Fe(OH)_3 = 6 : 2$; i.e. 3 : 1
0.600 mol NaOH reacts to form $0.600/3 = 0.200$ mol $Fe(OH)_3$
Mass $Fe(OH)_3 = 0.200 \times (55.85 + 48 + 3.03) = 21.4$ g (2 marks)
(Total = 8 marks)

Question 15

(a) $AgNO_3(aq) + KCl(aq) \rightarrow KNO_3(aq) + AgCl(s)$ (1 mark)
(b) Molar ratio $AgNO_3 : KCl = 1 : 1$
$n(AgNO_3) = (1.20 \times 0.0500)$ mol $= 0.0600$ mol
$n(KCl) = (0.800 \times 0.0750)$ mol $= 0.0600$ mol
Since the number of mole of the reactants are the same and the mol ratio is 1:1, neither reactant is in excess. (2 marks)
(c) Silver chloride is the insoluble product. $n(AgCl) = n(AgNO_3)$
Mass AgCl = $(0.06 \times (107.87 + 35.45)) = 8.60$ g (2 marks)
(d) Ionic equation: $Ag^+(aq) + Cl^-(aq) \rightarrow AgCl(s)$
Spectator ions: $K^+(aq)$ and $NO_3^-(aq)$ (2 marks)
(Total = 7 marks)

Question 16

(a) Solutions of potassium permanganate absorb the green and yellow frequencies but not the red and blue ones. (1 mark)

(b)

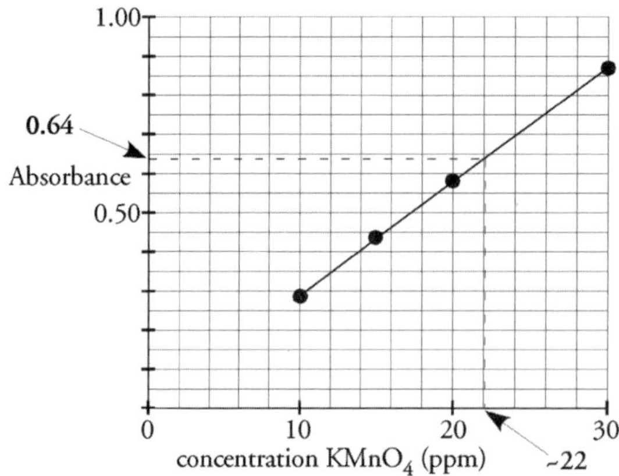

The concentration of KMnO4 in the sample of treated water is 22 ppm. (2 marks)

(c) The concentration of $KMnO_4$ is 22 ppm, which is 22 mg L^{-1}. A person drinking 500 mL of this water would ingest $0.5 \times 22 = 11$ mg of $KMnO_4$. (2 marks)

(Total = 5 marks)

Question 17

(a)

Stream	**Measured absorbances**	**Average absorbance**	**Average phosphate concentration (mg L^{-1})**
A	0.15, 0.18, 0.12	0.15	0.040
B	0.22, 0.26, 0.30	0.26	0.071
C	0.45, 0.52, 0.51	0.50	0.137

(3 marks)

(b) Stream C (1 mark)

(c)
- Run-off from farmland
- Contamination of the stream by domestic wastewater
- Industrial wastewater. (1 mark)

(Total = 5 marks)

Answers: Unit 2 Area of Study 2 test

Multiple choice items

Analysis of substances in water

Question	Answer	Comments
1.	**D.**	The solubility of gases decreases with increasing temperature. In aqueous solution carbon dioxide reacts with water forming H_3O^+, HCO_3^-, and CO_3^{2-} ions. The lower the concentration of H_3O^+ ions, the higher the pH.
2.	**D.**	$M_r(NiSO_4.6H_2O) = \{58.69 + 32.06 + 64 + (6 \times 16.02)\} = 262.9$ 262.9 g $NiSO_4.6H_2O$ contains 58.69 g Ni 1×10^6 g $NiSO_4.6H_2O$ contains $1 \times 10^6 \times 58.69/262.9$ $= 2.23 \times 10^5$ g Ni Therefore ppm (Ni) = 2.23×10^5.
3.	**A.**	$CuCO_3(s) + 2HCl(aq) \rightarrow CuCl_2(aq) + H_2O(l) + CO_2(g)$ $n(CO_2) =$ $1.23/44 = 0.0280$ mol mol ratio $CO_2 : CuCO_3 = 1 : 1$, $n(CuCO_3) = 0.028$ mol, $m(CuCO_3) =$ $0.028 \times 123.55 = 3.454$ g, m(impurity) = (4.12 – 3.454) = 0.666 g.
4.	**A.**	Mass NH_4Cl dissolved = $39.0 \times 250 \div 100 = 97.5$ g Mass NH_4Cl undissolved = 150 – 97.5 = 52.5 g
5.	**D.**	$2NaOH(aq) + H_2SO_4(aq) \rightarrow Na_2SO_4(aq) + 2H_2O(l)$ $n(H_2SO_4) =$ $0.0496 \times 0.02256 = 1.119 \times 10^{-3}$ mol $n(NaOH) = 2 \times 1.119 \times 10^{-3} = 2.238 \times 10^{-3}$ mol $c(NaOH) = 2.238 \times 10^{-3} \div 0.02000 = 0.112$ mol L^{-1}.
6.	**C.**	$n(CO) = 40/28 = 1.429$ mol; $n(O_2) = 20/32 = 0.625$ mol Molar ratio $CO:O_2 = 2:1$, hence CO is in excess. $n(CO_2) = 0.625 \times 2 = 1.25$ mol Mass $CO_2 = 1.25 \times 44 = 55.0$ g
7.	**A.**	Mass $Pb(NO_3)_2$ dissolved at 60°C = $88.0 \times 50 \div 100 = 44.0$ g Mass $Pb(NO_3)_2$ dissolved at 20°C = $52.3 \times 50 \div 100 = 26.15$ g Mass $Pb(NO_3)_2$ precipitated = 44.0 –26.15 = 17.85 g

Extended response questions

Question 1

(a) $Ag_2O(s) + 2HNO_3(aq) \rightarrow 2AgNO_3(aq) + H_2O(l)$
$AgNO_3(aq) + NaCl(aq) \rightarrow AgCl(s) + NaNO_3(aq)$ (2 marks)

(b) To remove any water-soluble salts, such as $NaNO_3$, that might remain on the solid. (1 mark)

(c) $n(AgNO_3) = n(AgCl) = 1.717/143.3 = 0.01198$ mol
$n(Ag_2O) = \frac{1}{2}\, n(AgNO_3) = 0.1198 \div 2 = 0.005991$ mol
Mass $Ag_2O = 0.005991 \times 231.7 = 1.388$ g
% $Ag_2O = (1.388 \div 1.634) \times 100 = 84.95\%$ (3 marks)
(Total = 6 marks)

Question 2

(a) $n(Ca(OH)_2 = 4.5/(40.08 + 32 + 2.02) = 0.06$ mol
$n(OH^-) = 2 \times 0.06 = 0.12$ mol
$c(OH^-) = 0.12/0.500 = 0.24$ mol L^{-1}. (3 marks)

(b) $2HCl + Ca(OH)_2 \rightarrow CaCl_2 + 2H_2O$; $n(HCl) = 0.100 \times 0.10 = 0.010$ mol
mol ratio $HCl : Ca(OH)_2 = 2 : 1$, $n(Ca(OH)_2) = 0.010/2 = 0.0050$ mol, volume $Ca(OH)_2$ $= 0.0050/0.12 = 0.042$ L or 42 mL. (3 marks)

(c) (i) $2H_3PO_4(aq) + 3Ca(OH)_2(aq) \rightarrow Ca_3(PO_4)_2(s) + 6H_2O(l)$ (1 mark)
(ii) $n(H_3PO_4) = 0.010$ mol and $n(Ca(OH)_2) = 0.015$ mol
Hence volume ratio = 1 : 3 (1 mark)
(iii) Calcium chloride is soluble, but calcium phosphate is insoluble so precipitation of this salt would be seen. (1 mark)
(Total = 9 marks)

Question 3

(a) $Fe_2(SO_4)_3(aq) + 6NaOH(aq) \rightarrow 2Fe(OH)_3(s) + 3Na_2SO_4(aq)$ (1 mark)

(b) $n(Fe_2(SO_4)_3) = 1.5 \times 0.10 = 0.150$ mol
$n(NaOH) = 2.50 \times 0.060 = 0.150$ mol
mol ratio $Fe_2(SO_4)_3 : NaOH = 1 : 6$
0.15 mol of iron(III) sulfate requires $6 \times 0.15 = 0.90$ mol NaOH for complete reaction, only 0.150 mol of NaOH are present so the iron(III) sulfate cannot react completely and is the excess reactant. (3 marks)

(c) Iron(III) sulfate is in excess by $0.150 - 0.025 = 0.125$ mol
$c(Fe_2(SO_4)_3) = 0.125/(0.100 + 0.060) = 0.781$ M (2 marks)

(d) 0.15 mol of sodium hydroxide requires only $0.150/6 = 0.025$ mol iron(III) sulfate for complete reaction, so is the limiting reactant.
Mol ratio $NaOH : Fe(OH)_3 = 6 : 2$, i.e. 3 : 1
$n(Fe(OH)_3) = 1/3 \times 0.15 = 0.050$ mol
$m(Fe(OH)_3) = 0.050 \times 55.85 = 2.8$ g (2 marks)
(Total = 8 marks)

Question 4

$n(NaNO_3) = 34.0 / 85.0 = 0.400$ mol; $n(KI) = 66.4/166.0 = 0.400$ mol.

In the mixed solution, the following amounts of the ions are present:

$n(Na^+) = 0.400$ mol, $n(NO_3^-) = 0.400$ mol, $n(K^+) = 0.400$ mol, $n(I^-) = 0.400$ mol.

Since the mass of water has doubled (to 100 g) both $NaNO_3$ and KI will remain dissolved.

Mass NaI present = $0.400 \times 149.9 = 60.0$ g. Since the solubility of NaI is 179.0 g in 100 g of water, then NaI will remain in solution.

Mass KNO_3 present = $0.400 \times 101.1 = 40.4$ g. The solubility of KNO_3 is only 31.6 g in 100 g of water.

Mass KNO_3 that precipitates = $40.4 - 31.6 = 8.8$ g.

(Total = 3 marks)

Answers: Unit 2 Examination

Section A

Question	Answer	Comments
1.	**A.**	A base accepts a proton. When an acid donates a proton, what remains is a conjugate base.
2.	**A.**	$[H_3O^+] = 10^{-14}$ and $[OH^-] = 1.0 \times 10^{-3}$ mol L^{-1}. $[Ba(OH)_2] = 1.0 \times 10^{-3} \div 2$ mol L^{-1}.
3.	**B.**	Since HNO_3 is a strong acid it will be fully ionised and $[H^+] = 0.15$ mol L^{-1}. HNO_2 is a weak acid and only partially ionised. In this case $[H^+] < 0.25$ mol L^{-1}.
4.	**C.**	The excellent solvent properties of water result in many natural substances, such as atmospheric gases and soluble minerals, dissolving in rainwater, runoff water etc.
5.	**B.**	H_2O_2 has two –OH groups that can form hydrogen bonds to other molecules. CH_3OH has only one –OH group. N_2H_4 has two $-NH_2$ groups but generally –OH groups form stronger hydrogen bonds than $-NH_2$ groups. The boiling temperatures (in °C) are C_2H_6 –89; CH_3OH 65; H_2O_2 150; N_2H_4 114.
6.	**B.**	$n(KI) = 1.50 \times 0.2$ mol = 0.3 mol, $n(Pb(NO_3)_2) = 0.5 \times 0.15$ mol = 0.075 mol $2KI + Pb(NO_3)_2 \rightarrow 2KNO_3 + PbI_2$ mol ratio KI: $Pb(NO_3)_2$ = 2:1 0.3 mol KI requires 0.15 mol $Pb(NO_3)_2$; $Pb(NO_3)_2$ is in excess mol ratio $Pb(NO_3)_2:PbI_2$ = 1:1, $n(PbI_2) = 0.075$ mol $m(PbI_2) = 0.075 \times (207.2 + (2 \times 126.9)) = 34.6$ g

7. **A.** The polar –OH group in ethanoic acid will form hydrogen bonds with water molecules. CCl_4 and C_8H_{18} are non-polar and the non-polar hydrocarbon section of $C_7H_{15}OH$ will prevent solubility even though there is an –OH group.

8. **B.** $H_2PO_4^-$ ions both gain and lose a proton in the reaction.

9. **D.** $n(HNO_3) = 0.300 \times 0.200 = 0.0600$ mol
$n(Ba(OH)_2) = 0.500 \times 0.100 = 0.0500$ mol $2HNO_3 + Ba(OH)_2 \rightarrow Ba(NO_3)_2 + 2H_2O$
mol ratio $HNO_3{:}Ba(OH)_2 = 2{:}1 = 0.0600 : 0.0300$
$Ba(OH)_2$ is in excess by $0.0500 - 0.0300 = 0.0200$ mol

10. **A** $C_1V_1 = C_2V_2$, $9 \times 0.02 = 1.5 \times V_2$, $V_2 = 0.12$ L or 120 mL.
Thus, 100 mL must be added.

11. **D.** NaCl is a neutral salt and its solutions will have a pH of 7.0. CO_2 solutions are weakly acidic. A pH of 2.0 for a 0.01 mol L^{-1} solution is only correct for a strong acid. NaOH is a strong base, whereas NH_3 is a weak base.

12. **B.** $n(KOH) = 0.2 \times 0.6 = 0.12$ mol, $n(HCl) = 0.2 \times 1.0 = 0.2$ mol
Mol ratio KOH : HCl = 1:1, HCl is in excess by 0.08 mol $[H_3O^+] = 0.08/0.4 = 0.2$ M, pH = –log 0.2 = 0.7

13. **A.** Reaction of ammonia molecules with water produces ions from reactant molecules, thus this is ionisation.

14. **C.** $n(SO_2) = 10/64 = 0.156$ mol and $n(O_2) = 10/32 = 0.312$ mol.
From the mol ratio in the equation O_2 is in excess. $n(SO_3)$ formed = 0.156 mol and mass = $0.156 \times 80 = 12.5$ g.

15. **D.** Aluminium oxide is a coherent oxide which coats the surface of aluminium and remains bonded to it, thus protecting the metal from further reaction with air.

16. **C.** Zinc, iron and magnesium are all stronger reductants than nickel (i.e. are higher in the reactivity series of metals). Tin is a weaker reductant than nickel so would not be preferentially oxidised.

17. **B.** In normal phase HPLC the stationary phase is polar, and the mobile phase is non-polar. The polarities of the phases are reversed in reverse phase HPLC. Hence now the mobile phase should be polar.

18. **C.** The N^{3-} ion has accepted protons to form a NH_2^- ion. Two atoms of hydrogen have lost an electron to form H^+ to donate to N^{3-}, while the other two atoms have gained an electron to form H^- ions.

19. **C.** $V(O_2)_r = 2 \times V(CH_4) = 2 \times 200 = 400$ mL
$V(O_2)_e = V_i - V_r = 600 - 400 = 200$ mL
$V(CO_2) = V(CH_4) = 200$ mL
Total volume = $V(CO_2) + V(O_2)_e = 200$ mL + 200 mL = 400 mL

20. **D.** Using $PV = nRT$, given that the temperature and pressure are constant, the moles of gas is proportional to its volume. The volume of oxygen is double that of hydrogen and therefore contains double the number of moles.

Section B

Question 1

(a) Reaction (i) indicates that X is a stronger reductant than Y. Reaction (ii) indicates that X is a stronger reductant than Z. Reaction (iii) indicates that Z is a stronger reductant than Y.
The order of increasing reactivity is Y, Z & X (2 marks)

(b) **$AuNO_x$**
Gold(I) nitrate is a colourless solution. A yellow deposit of gold would appear on the tin rod as $Au^{2+}$is reduced to Au by the stronger reductant, tin.
$2AuNO_3(aq) + Sn(s) \rightarrow Sn(NO_3)_2(aq) + 2Au(s)$ (1 mark)
$CuSO_4$
Copper sulfate is a blue solution. A brown deposit of copper would appear on the tin rod as $Cu^{2+}$is reduced to Cu by the stronger reductant, tin. The solution would slowly decolourise.
$CuSO_4(aq) + Sn(s) \rightarrow SnSO_4(aq) + Cu(s)$ (1 mark)
$FeSO_4$ No reaction as tin is a weaker reductant than iron. (1 mark)
$ZnCl_2$ No reaction as tin is a weaker reductant than zinc. (1 mark)

(c) e.g. $Zn(s) + SnCl_2(aq) \rightarrow ZnCl_2(aq) + Sn(s)$ (1 mark)
Or any suitably reactive metal, which is a stronger reductant than tin.
(Total = 7 marks)

Question 2

(a) Group 15. The electronegativities of the elements in these two groups differ from that of hydrogen. Hence the bonds in all eight molecules will be polar. In the hydrides of group 14 the bond dipoles cancel out because of the tetrahedral symmetry of the molecules. These molecules are non-polar. In the group 15 hydrides the bond dipoles do not cancel and the central atom also has a lone pair of electrons. All the group 15 molecules have a dipole. (3 marks)

(b) SbH_3 and SnH_4 have the same number of electrons and similar molar masses, hence the dispersion forces between the molecules should be similar. However, SbH_3 has a small molecular dipole whereas SnH_4 is non-polar which results in greater intermolecular attractive forces for SbH_3 and an increased boiling temperature. (2 marks)

(c) Nitrogen has a greater electronegativity than the other elements and NH_3 has a larger bond dipole and a larger molecular dipole than any of the other molecules. The intermolecular bonding (hydrogen bonding) between NH_3 molecules is thus larger leading to a higher boiling temperature.

hydrogen bond

(2 marks)

(d) All four molecules are non-polar. The only attractive forces between the molecules are dispersion forces. These increase as the number of electrons and molar mass increases.

(1 mark)

(Total = 8 marks)

Question 3

(a) $N_2H_4 \rightarrow N_2 + 4e^- + 4H^+$

Nitrogen is oxidised from oxidation state –2 to oxidation state 0. (1 mark)

(b) $2H_2O_2 + 4e^- + 4H^+ \rightarrow 4H_2O$

Oxygen is reduced from oxidation state –1 to oxidation state –2. (1 mark)

(c) $n(N_2H_4) = 500 \times 10^3/32 = 15625$ mol $n(H_2O_2) = 500 \times 10^3/34 = 14\ 706$ mol

Since the molar ratio $n(N_2H_4) : n(H_2O_2)$ is 1 : 2 the N_2H_4 is in excess.

$n(H_2O) = 2 \times n(H_2O_2) = 2 \times 14\ 706 = 29\ 412$ mol

mass $(H_2O) = 29\ 412 \times 18 = 529\ 412 = 5.29 \times 10^2$ kg (3 marks)

(Total = 5 marks)

Question 4

(a) Magnesium and copper sulfate. Magnesium is a more reactive metal than copper.

(2 marks)

(b) $Mg(s) + Cu^{2+}(aq) \rightarrow Mg^{2+}(aq) + Cu(s)$ (1 mark)

(c) Mg/Mg^{2+} and Cu/Cu^{2+} (1 mark)

(Total = 4 marks)

Question 5

(a) $3Ca(NO_3)_2(aq) + 2Na_3PO_4(aq) \rightarrow Ca_3(PO_4)_2(s) + 6NaNO_3(aq)$

$3Ca^{2+}(aq) + 2PO_4^{3-}(aq) \rightarrow Ca_3(PO_4)_2(s)$ (2 marks)

(b) $2KHCO_3(aq) + H_2SO_4(aq) \rightarrow K_2SO_4(aq) + 2CO_2(g) + 2H_2O(l)$

$2HCO_3^-(aq) + H_2SO_4(aq) \rightarrow SO_4^{2-}(aq) + 2CO_2(g) + 2H_2O(l)$ (2 marks)

(Total = 4 marks)

Question 6

(a) Energy (J) = mass × specific heat × temperature change

Energy = $10.0 \times 10^3 \times 4.18 \times (29 - 18)$ J = 459 800 J (2 marks)

(b) Temperature change = Energy/(mass × specific heat)

Temperature change = 459 800/(10 000 × 0.46) = 99.96°C (2 marks)

(c) The specific heat of water is higher than steel because the hydrogen bonds between water molecules can absorb large amounts of energy. (2 marks)

(Total = 6 marks)

Question 7

(a) $HClO_4(aq) + H_2O(l) \rightarrow ClO_4^-(aq) + H_3O^+(aq)$

$CH_3COOH(aq) + H_2O(l) \rightleftharpoons CH_3COO^-(aq) + H_3O^+(aq)$ (2 marks)

(b) 0.10 M perchloric acid is a dilute acid as its molarity is low but is a strong acid as it is fully ionised in water.

5.0 M perchloric acid is a concentrated acid as its molarity is high and is a strong acid as it is fully ionised in water.

0.10 M propanoic acid is a dilute acid as its molarity is low and is a weak acid as it is not fully ionised in water.

5.0 M propanoic acid is a concentrated acid as its molarity is high and is a weak acid as it is not fully ionised in water. (4 marks)

(c) $n(HClO_4) = 0.25 \times 0.500 = 0.125$ mol and

$n(KOH) = 0.300 \times 0.200 = 0.060$ mol

$HClO_4(aq) + KOH(aq) \rightarrow KClO_4(aq) + H_2O(l)$

Mol ratio $HClO_4$: KOH = 1:1

0.060 mol KOH requires 0.060 mol $HClO_4$ for complete reaction, thus $HClO_4$ is in excess by 0.125 – 0.060 = 0.065 mol

$[H_3O^+] = 0.065/(0.300+0.200) = 0.13$ M; pH = –log (0.13) = 0.9 (3 marks)

(Total = 9 marks)

Question 8

(a) $n(NaOH) = 0.0200 \times 0.1056 = 2.112 \times 10^{-3}$ mol (1 mark)

(b) $n(CH_3COOH)$ in average titre = 2.112×10^{-3} mol

$n(CH_3COOH)$ in 250 mL = $(2.112 \times 10^{-3} \times 250) \div 18.62 = 0.02836$ mol (1 mark)

(c) Mass ethanoic acid in 250 mL = $0.02836 \times 60.1 = 1.704$ g (1 mark)

(d) Volume of vinegar = mass vinegar/density = 39.62/1.01 = 39.23 mL (1 mark)

(e) %(m/v) = $(1.704 \times 100) \div 39.23 = 4.34\%$ (1 mark)

(f) (i) The diluted vinegar solution

(ii) Water

(iii) The sodium hydroxide solution (3 marks)

(Total = 8 marks)

Question 9

Energy needed to heat water = $4.18 \times 100 \times 80 = 33440$ J or 33.44 kJ

$n(H_2O) = 100/18 = 5.556$ mol

Energy needed to vaporise the water = $40.0 \times 5.556 = 222.2$ kJ

Total energy needed = 33.44 + 222.2 = 255.7 or 256 kJ.

(Total = 3 marks)

Question 10

(a) Curve I (the solubility of gases decreases with increasing temperature) (1 mark)

(b) Substance V. Lead chloride has very low solubility in water. (1 mark)

(c) 30.0 g of substance III dissolves in 100 g of water at 70°C.
75 g of water will dissolve $(30.0 \times 75) \div 100 = 22.5$ g (1 mark)

(d) Solubility of $NH_4Cl = (24.0 \times 100) \div 60 = 40$ g /100 g H_2O; i.e. substance II. (1 mark)

(e) Substances III and IV at ~43°C. (1 mark)

(f) 45 g in 250 g of water corresponds to a solubility of 18 g / 100 g H_2O. Substances I and II have a greater solubility than this at 30°C and will be completely dissolved.
Substances III, IV and V will not dissolve completely in this amount of water. (2 marks)

(Total = 7 marks)